YES
YOU CAN!

A Guide for Parents
of Children with Disabilities

Mark Nagler, Ph.D.
with Adam Nagler

Stoddart

TORONTO · BUFFALO

Published in 1997 by
Stoddart Publishing Co. Limited

Distributed in Canada by
General Distribution Services Inc.
30 Lesmill Road
Toronto, Canada M3B 2T6
Tel. (416) 445-3333
Fax (416) 445-5967
e-mail Customer.Service@ccmailgw.genpub.com

Distributed in the United States by
General Distribution Services Inc.
85 River Rock Drive, Suite 202
Buffalo, New York 14207
Toll-free tel. 1-800-805-1083
Toll-free fax 1-800-481-6207
e-mail gdsinc@genpub.com

01   00   99   98   97   1   2   3   4   5

Cataloging in Publication Data

Nagler, Mark
Yes you can!: a guide for parents of children with disabilities

ISBN 0-7737-5866-6

1. Handicapped children — Home care. 2. Parents of handicapped children. I. Nagler, Adam. II. Title.

HV888.N33 1997   362'.4083   97-930272-2

Cover design: Pekoe Jones/Multiphrenia
Text design: Tannice Goddard
Computer layout: Mary Bowness

Printed and bound in Canada

Contents

Acknowledgments

There are many people who have made important contributions to this book. First and foremost I would like to thank my wife, Sharon, who helped with the initial drafts, and my son, Adam, who literally wrote this manuscript with me. His constant evaluations and criticisms have helped to make this work an accurate representation of my thoughts.

I would also like to thank Anne Muegge, who helped with the initial research; Tracey Vanderkolff, for her assistance in producing the first copies; Ruth Ambros, for her careful proofreading; Mr. Archie Risebrough, who freely gave of his expertise on important financial matters for people with disabilities; and Mel Enkin, who came up with the title in no time at all.

A special thanks to all of the individuals who provided the case studies that have enriched this material. My teachers and my colleagues have always been very supportive; in particular, I thank Renison College at the University of Waterloo for giving me the time and the freedom to devote to this project.

I would like to thank my agent, Larry Hoffman, who directed me to write this book and provided a concise evaluation of the final draft. I am indebted to Stoddart Publishing for picking up this project and carrying it through to its conclusion. The astute observations of Lynne Missen, senior editor of Stoddart Publishing, enriched this work.

My spirit, to a great extent, has always been pushed to the limits by my parents, Ann and Leo Nagler, who provided the experiences which have guided my life.

I wish to acknowledge the constant support of my many relatives, especially Aunt Sabine Helman, who has always encouraged me to read, to participate, and to be involved.

Finally, I wish to thank my son David, who is always showing me the importance of attempting to win. As we both know, it is not the winning that is important, but the motivation to always try.

Chapter
1

You Can
Make It!

How do I know that you can make it through? Simple. Because my parents and I did. I was born in 1939, the first child for Ann and Leo Nagler, a furniture salesman and a housewife who lived in Calgary, Alberta. My father was twenty-five and my mother was twenty-two. It was an apparently uneventful birth, although the forceps marks that were left on my head were later considered to be an indication of possible head trauma, and a lack of oxygen to the brain is thought to have caused my disability.

Two months after my birth, my seventy-eight-year-old grandmother observed that I was "different": I was very stiff and didn't move like most babies. She had ten children of her own and eleven grandchildren and I was the most difficult baby to feed that she had ever seen. At first, my parents were reluctant to acknowledge this and believed that she was merely an interfering grandparent. But after talking to friends who had children, and their family doctor, they did realize that they had extreme difficulties in feeding me, that I was slow to roll over, and, later on, that I was slow to sit up and crawl. My parents' trauma and anxiety increased during the first six months of my life because of my noticeable spasticity — they did not want to admit to themselves or to others that I was different.

In 1939 and 1940 in Canada, my condition was misdiagnosed as polio, mental retardation, and a host of other conditions. While attempting to confirm a diagnosis and a treatment plan that would address my problems, my parents consulted many doctors, wrote letters, and made phone calls to specialized clinics, university medical schools, and pediatricians in larger Canadian and American cities. It was not until three years after my birth that physicians at the Mayo Clinic in Rochester, Minnesota, diagnosed my cerebral palsy.

The prospect of raising a child with a disability was devastating to my parents. As far as they knew, there were no children on either side of the family who had disabilities. They had to admit to my grandmother and to the rest of the family that something was wrong with me. My parents' family and friends were very supportive and offered to do anything they could to help: my aunts and cousins filled in as baby-sitters and later on as "therapists" to help strengthen my muscles.

After the doctors at the Mayo Clinic finally confirmed that I had cerebral palsy, they told my parents never to expect too little and always to push me to do the best that I possibly could. The physicians were concerned that I was affected by spasticity and was unable to walk. The physicians outlined patterns of therapy my parents could provide. These exercises were designed to increase my strength, establish my balance, and teach me to walk. But they also suggested that by the age of five or six, I should be left in Rochester for two or three years, arguing that this would allow the Mayo Clinic and its allied facilities to provide the treatment that would maximize my potential. My parents decided that I would remain at home.

With the assistance of many family members, friends, and employees at the family store, my parents provided the physical and occupational therapy that was needed to enhance my development. I was not able to walk until the age of five, but with the aid of special homemade walking devices, I was quite mobile. As there were no companies that specialized in technology that helped people with disabilities, my parents and family members had to make the devices themselves.

Amongst my earliest memories are my parents, their friends, and my friends holding me by both hands, moving my legs in all types of exercises; pedaling a tricycle; doing water exercises; and using walking supports. As soon as I learned to walk, my dad told our friends and family that I would soon be riding a two-wheel bike. Everybody thought he was crazy because I had very poor balance. In fact, at the time I had no balance skills at all, and for years I would trip and fall down while walking. By the fourth grade, however, I was riding a two-wheeler and playing baseball, football, and hockey with my friends. I never learned how to ice skate, but I did play goalie with the support of three or four defensemen.

My physical development was slow, but my parents and others were encouraged by my quick response to all non-physical activities. I was counting and reciting the alphabet and nursery rhymes before the age of two. When I was four,

I was playing board games such as Snakes and Ladders, Steeplechase, and Checkers. At five years of age, in 1944, I was concerned about when the Nazis would be beaten.

The effort by my parents to keep me at home required innumerable hours and was extremely exhausting. In addition to all of their concerns about me, they faced the stress associated with contemplating having more children. But cerebral palsy is not a genetic condition and my parents later had two healthy children.

Although it was sometimes difficult for them, my parents included me in their activities. Every Sunday night I was taken out for dinner and I remember waiters and other people asking my parents why they had to feed me. This hurt my parents as much as it hurt me. Most of my friends were helpful, but I was often embarrassed and ashamed by the effects of my disability. Occasionally this anxiety was increased by the remarks and taunts of peers and strangers.

Sometime before I was ten years old, a relative suggested that I not tell anyone that I had cerebral palsy, as "cerebral" meant brain problems and mental illness. Instead, I should explain that I had contracted polio shortly after birth. He felt that this would be a good enough explanation.

My relative was wrong. Having cerebral palsy does *not* mean that you have a mental illness, but I didn't know that at the time, and I was so devastated by the thought of having brain problems that I did not share the incident with my parents until I was in my early twenties. And so, throughout my school years, I often used polio as an explanation for my condition to avoid the stigma of having "mental problems," and, most of all, to avoid having to explain what cerebral palsy was. Even today many people are unfamiliar with the condition. I am sure that I have said the same thing thousands of times, and whenever I do, I often feel the pangs of shame that I associate with my youth.

My parents were told that although my physical development left much to be desired, I had exceptional verbal ability. The Mayo Clinic physicians said that all signs indicated that I was smarter than average and should be given every opportunity to participate in all activities. Even though I had cerebral palsy, they said that I should be mainstreamed — that I needed to attend school in spite of the fact that I would probably never be able to write.

Despite all this encouragement, my parents still encountered people who were reluctant to participate in my growth. Following our return from Rochester, they were advised by one physician to have me institutionalized, as they could, after all, always have other children who would probably be "normal." Needless to say, my parents rejected his advice. The doctors at the Mayo Clinic had instructed my parents to become advocates on my behalf as they would always face resistance from friends, acquaintances, educators, and therapists in trying to meet my needs. They were told never to take no for an answer, not to indulge me, and to include me in every activity they could.

Fortunately, my parents heeded most of this advice. Their journey was more difficult than yours may be, as in the early forties in Western Canada there were few resources available to aid parents whose children had disabilities. Between 1940 and 1945 there were only a limited number of clinics and therapists who were informed about cerebral palsy, and there were certainly no doctors who specialized in it. By their sheer determination, positive attitude, and, most importantly, their love, support, and encouragement, my parents created the conditions that today allow me to write this book.

My parents made me aware that many people would make fun of my condition and that both kids and adults might create embarrassing situations. When eating on my own I have been thrown out of restaurants because the owners or managers assumed that I was drunk or under the influence of narcotics. The former chairperson of a Sociology Graduate Department at a prominent university told me I should go home and live with my parents as I would never make it as a professor. Twenty-eight years later I am still proving him wrong.

My father taught me a very valuable lesson about how to deal with these sorts of people. When I was eight years old, he told me that I was a person just like anyone else, and that I should never accept actions that were inappropriate, discriminatory, or prejudicial. He told me that when you have asked legitimately many times for things that would improve your life, and when people have failed to cooperate, or if they treat you disrespectfully, they will always respond to "F.U." This does not always have to be a torrent of swear words directed at the offending party; it can involve threatening legal action, unfavorable media exposure, a complaint to a worker's superior, or any number of other suitably aggressive actions. It is an attitude of demanding what you need, rather than passively sitting around waiting to get it. I think I was in the fifth grade when my dad informed me that this rude response was sometimes necessary, especially for people who were narrow-minded and biased. Unfortunately, on rare occasions, I still encounter these types of people.

I have experienced the life of a child with a disability. The outcome of my life reflects the activities, concerns, and beliefs of many people — especially my parents. What they did was not always perfect, but they always did their best. Through trial and error, hard work, and experimentation they were able to find solutions and programs where none had existed before, and they were able to use and alter existing resources to help me learn, develop, and grow as a person. What your child's life will be like depends on your attitudes and values, as well as those of medical and paramedical personnel, relatives, peers, and occasionally even strangers. I have passionate ideas about what can be done, what should be done, and what should *never* be done in caring for children with disabilities, and in this book I will share these ideas with you.

If you have a child who has a disability, **you must take control!** You have the opportunity to maximize your child's *habilitative* or *rehabilitative* potential. Everything that your child may accomplish in the next year, five years, or five decades will be a reflection of the efforts and strategies that you adopt. With the help of conscientious parents, medical personnel, and many other caring individuals, people with disabilities can and do lead rewarding and productive lives. The majority of people whom society views as "disabled" have many recognizable and even superior abilities, and many people with disabilities have made extraordinary contributions.

The first requirement for successful parenting is to **love and accept your child.** There are children born with Tay-Sachs disease (a congenital disease that attacks the nervous system of a newborn child within the first year of life) or a variety of other conditions that have a short-term, terminal prognosis. These cases are painful not only for the children, but also for the children's parents. No matter what condition affects your child, you must give him or her all the love and support that you are able to muster. If your child dies prematurely, you can continue to live with the knowledge that you did your best and that your child was loved, protected, and cherished.

This is easier said than done. If my parents had heeded the advice of well-meaning relatives, friends, physicians, and other so-called experts, I would have been locked up in an institution. In such an environment it is unlikely that I would have survived to my present age of fifty-seven. Institutional environments usually provide the physical necessities to support life, yet they often lack the emotional resources that are needed to ensure that an individual will not only survive, but also enjoy the support needed to achieve maximum possible growth.

When a child is born, most parents are hoping to have the ultimate success: the high school valedictorian, the Olympic medalist, or the distinguished professional. In some cases, this will happen for children with disabilities. There are many instances where people with severe disabilities have achieved remarkable success. The lives of Helen Keller, Stephen Hawking, Rick Hansen, and former U.S. president Franklin Delano Roosevelt are shining examples of individuals with disabilities who have maximized their potential. Their accomplishments were a direct result of the efforts of their parents and other caregivers who provided them with the opportunity to enjoy rich and productive lives.

Creating the environment necessary to achieve a full and rewarding life for your son or daughter is not always easy. Children with disabilities and their families often encounter a series of barriers and stumbling blocks that appear to be overwhelming. It is frustrating to have long-term expectations that may never be met or that will require extraordinary lengths of time to accomplish. Grandparents and relatives can sometimes ignore the children who are "different." Parents of children with disabilities have a divorce rate that approaches double the North American average. Not only are these parents subject to the ordinary stresses that may lead to family breakdown and divorce, but they are also frequently subject to depression, potential drug abuse, and severe financial strain. When the stress of raising your special child begins to mount, you must remember that there are many resources and people available to help you, and that **you can and will make it through!**

It can be very difficult to know what to do after an expert has told you that you are expecting the impossible. My parents expected it. Many other parents of children who happen to have a disability spend years seeking it. For many, a goal that was once deemed impossible *is* attainable; for example, some young people with little or no hearing are now obtaining Master's and doctoral degrees from universities or specialized schools such as Gallaudet, a university that educates those with hearing impairments. For others, complete success is partially attainable, and for some it may be extremely difficult to obtain any recognizable measure of improvement. No matter what the initial diagnosis, it is important to realize that experts may not always recognize the true potential of children with disabilities.

As parents of children with disabilities, you may be required to reject some medical hypotheses and to seek out others, as finding an accurate diagnosis and effective treatment plan can be difficult, especially in the early stages of your child's life. Despite not knowing what the future will bring, thousands of parents have raised their special children in an atmosphere of love and support. Many children who are

diagnosed with the most severe disabilities such as quadriplegia and other complete lower extremity paralysis have been
able to become independent, self-supporting people. Whether
or not this happens is a direct result of the parents' ability to
guide their child's development.

I know an extraordinary individual in her mid-twenties
who has Down syndrome. When she was born, her parents
had many questions. "What potential does she have?" "What
opportunities will she have?" "What will her life be like?" In
many instances, these questions were impossible to answer,
but her parents took control and raised their daughter to the
best of their ability. This young woman now has a full-time
job as a factory worker, and functions independently. Among
her accomplishments are a Life Saving Certificate from the Red
Cross. Twenty years ago, if her parents had dreamed of such a
result, their hopes would have been viewed as unrealistic.

Another remarkable young woman danced a portion of a
ballet as part of the competition in which she became Miss
America. She achieved this honor in spite of the fact that she
had a severe hearing impairment. Most people would find it
hard to believe that it was possible for someone with such a
profound hearing deficit to become an accomplished dancer,
much less win the title of Miss America. This amazing woman
and many of her peers who are affected by a wide range of
disabilities have achieved, and will continue to achieve, many
admirable accomplishments. Their quality of life is a reflection of one major factor — the efforts of their parents in all
areas of their lives. **Parents have the power to make a positive
difference in their children's lives.**

My parents were strict when I was growing up. Initially, as
a youngster without full comprehension of what was taking

place, I did not appreciate the extraordinary commitment they made. As long as I live, however, I will benefit from the results. When your child is growing up, it may seem that they do not, or cannot, appreciate your hard work, sweat, and tears, but when they grow older you will be rewarded not only with their gratitude, but also with their success. In many instances, the problems that you encounter will be minor, and at other times the difficulties that you must face may appear to be catastrophic. It may get to be so hard that it can make you question "Is it worthwhile?" **Always remember that IT IS!**

A number of individuals encouraged me to write this book because I have not only had the lifelong experience of living with a disability, but because I am also a sociologist. I have taught disability-related courses; provided counseling to individuals with disabilities, their families, physicians, therapists, social workers, educators, employers, members of the clergy, and others in all aspects of life that impact on people with disabilities; and participated at international conferences on disability. In addition, I have been involved in organizations that function as support groups to people with disabilities and their families. Finally, I have organized and worked with advocacy groups that seek to improve the lives of people with disabilities. This work has given me a grasp of the resources that are available to children with disabilities and their families, and has allowed me to pass this valuable information on to you.

The topics covered in this book reflect my background as well as the results of a questionnaire given to 130 individuals with experience in the community of people with disabilities. This group includes people with disabilities, parents of children with disabilities, doctors, educators, social workers, prospective parents, and other people who have had contact with people with disabilities. The questionnaire asked that respondents identify their primary concerns related to the birth of a child with a disability or with conditions that later led to a disability. This book is written in the sincere belief that the vast majority of families have the ability to effectively cope with a disability and improve the life of their special child.

By reading this book you are undertaking an educational program and training yourself to become an "expert" in parenting a child with disabilities. To become a teacher, doctor, or social worker, for example, a professional goes through an organized program to develop expertise. You are now required to do the same. If you approach this task in a committed way, you will develop the skills to effectively provide and obtain the necessary care for your child's special needs. At the same time, these efforts will enrich your quality of life and that of your family.

The following questions and many more are explored over the course of this book. These questions identify the areas of concern expressed by parents of children who happen to have disabilities.

What is a disability and what is a handicap?
Why did the disability happen?
How will the disability affect my child?
How can I avoid being an overprotective parent?
How will my child's disability affect me and my relationships with friends and family?
How will I cope?
How will my child feel?
What will my child's life be like?

What is my role in caring for my child?

What resources are available?

How do I select the most appropriate caregivers, treatments, and environments for my child?

Should I consider an institution?

Where do I go for information?

Who is there to help me?

What are my legal rights?

What is the role of advocacy?

How should my child be educated?

What are my responsibilities to service providers?

What is this going to cost me?

Where can I go for financial aid?

Where should my family live?

How do I plan for my child's future?

Can my child become independent?

Not all of these questions are of equal importance. Nevertheless, they express the spectrum of concerns raised by people who are responsible for children with disabilities.

I have written this book in clear, nonmedical language so that it can be appreciated and understood by everyone. The goal of *Yes You Can!* is to provide a framework for action, as well as the best available information that will allow you to assist your children to become active, independent human beings.

While we will be discussing different types of disabilities, this book is not a complete blueprint on how to cope with every facet of a specific disability; it may not answer all your questions or concerns. You can learn more about the treatment of your child's condition from your family physician, medical specialists, support groups, or from books focusing on specific diseases and disabilities. An up-to-date list of these organizations and books can be found in Appendix 2 and the Bibliography, respectively. *Yes You Can!* provides the strategies for you, as a parent of a child who has a disability, to follow in order to ensure that your child enjoys and participates in life to the fullest. It addresses the wide range of challenges faced by parents of children with disabilities, and some solutions to these problems. Whether your child has cerebral palsy, diabetes, Down syndrome, or any one of hundreds of disabilities, it is up to you to develop and maximize your child's potential. This book will provide you with the knowledge and the tools to enhance the quality of life of your whole family, no matter what disability you are confronting. After reading *Yes You Can!*, you will have a more complete understanding of what is required to raise your special child to be a confident, happy, and successful human being.

Chapter

2

Finding Out Your Child Has a Disability

Finding out that a child has been born with a disability, or that a previously healthy child has suffered an injury or disease that causes a disability, can be the most traumatic moment in a parent's life. Shock is usually the first thing people experience. It can temporarily paralyze you, preventing you from taking action, or even making rational decisions. In this difficult first period it is always wise to take the counsel of professionals and family members with experience or others whom you trust, while always maintaining the right to make the final decision yourselves.

DEALING WITH THE SITUATION

After coming to grips with the shock of their situation, many parents come to feel that their expectations have been dashed and that they are failures as parents. They think that their world has come crashing down upon them, and that their family has been destroyed. Parents worry about hundreds of questions that have few immediate answers and about horror stories and negative images that they have gained from the media. This can lead to an unbalanced and overly bleak view of the opportunities, potential, and joy that can be found in raising a child with a disability.

The reaction of these parents to the situation they faced is typical:

"I looked at my child. He was beautiful. He appeared normal. He was everything we ever wanted. He was just like our previous children, so I thought. But Frank was different. We didn't really notice that anything was wrong, until seven months after he was born. He was gasping and at times had trouble breathing. He was not as heavy as other children his age and was more difficult to feed. Other than that, he was a happy, bright child who was smiling and recognizing all of us.

"The family physician examined him closely and sent us to a cardiac pediatrician (a physician specializing in children's heart problems). After an examination, the cardiologist told us that our child had a heart condition and it could be a valve or one of many other difficulties. It would require a number of sophisticated tests, including putting a dye through his heart.

"Our world crashed. We had had healthy, normal children, and our new baby, all of a sudden, was different. We cried. We were depressed. The realization that our child could possibly die before treatment, or at a very young age, became a tragic reality. We did not know what to tell our young kids. For a while we thought we did not know anything — what to do, what to think, what to believe, and who to trust."

These emotions are normal, and going through feelings of confusion and depression are part of a "mourning" process that many parents of children with disabilities go through. If you have these feelings, remember that you are not the only ones who feel this way, and that you *will* get over them. The family mentioned above was very fortunate. Their pediatric cardiologist was bright, sensitive, and caring. He not only diagnosed the heart problems, but sat with the parents and fully explained their options and how to deal with the emotions of knowing that their child may not survive. His compassion and support helped them on their first step toward successfully dealing with the devastating problems that they encountered. (You'll find that many of the medical professionals you are involved with will have the same ability to help you cope.) After five years and three operations, their child is happy, active, and healthy.

Some parents feel that they can deal with any challenge they face right off the bat. They realize immediately that a disability in the family does not have to be a negative, and view disability as simply one more barrier to be overcome. My parents were concerned about what I had, and how to deal with it. Although initially shocked, they quickly viewed the disability as a series of problems to be solved. I was already a member of the family, and they believed that as an individual I was entitled to a "normal" or "near-normal" life. They were prepared to do whatever it took to overcome my disability.

Most parents will not be able to move straight into a problem-solving mode as soon as their child's disability is diagnosed. They will need a period of adjustment that can take anywhere from a few days to a number of months. You can adjust more quickly by obtaining accurate information, sharing your feelings openly with others, seeking professional counseling, and, most importantly, having open discussions with all members of your immediate family. Nothing that you feel is the "wrong" emotion. Your feelings are deep and real, and a natural reaction to a very difficult (and stressful) situation. With time, love, and support, any negative emotions you feel can be replaced by positive ones leading to productive actions that will benefit your child.

My parents were fortunate to have the unqualified support of their entire family, a massive group including fifteen aunts and uncles, and ten cousins. Some people will have a large extended family that lives nearby and can provide help and support, but others, who might be isolated from their families, can look to other sources of support (these will be discussed later on). Extended families can be tremendous sources of strength and help, but remember that it is the immediate family members — you — who are the most important. The task is yours, and despite the tangle of emotions that you might feel when you find out about your child's disability, you will be able to persevere and help him[1] live the *best* life that he can.

Uncertainty

Most people want instant answers to their problems. In many situations, however, immediate solutions are difficult, if not impossible, to obtain. Getting the proper diagnosis and treatment for your child may require time, experimentation, travel, and disappointment. The stress of not knowing what it is that is affecting your child is different from the stress of finding

---

[1]   In the interests of gender equality, the pronouns "he" and "she" will be alternated from chapter to chapter. Children of both genders are meant to be included in these categorizations.

out immediately that your child has a disability. In the waiting period of finding out exactly what is wrong, many parents
become angry and frustrated with one another. This frustration can take the form of shouting matches, withdrawing
from the other partner, resorting to alcohol or other drugs,
and sometimes even physical abuse. These negative reactions
do not have to happen. They can be avoided by taking a
mature approach to the situation, by being open with your
partner, and by seeking counseling if any of these trouble
patterns start to emerge. Short-term feelings of hostility
are common reactions to the stress of a child's situation, but
if the feelings of hostility are carried over a longer period of
time and nothing is done to eliminate them, they can have
serious and tragic effects on the rest of the family. You have
to allow yourself a period of adjustment, but after a certain
point you also have to move on.

Blame

Whenever a child is born with a disability or suffers a disability after birth there is a tendency to attach blame, even when
there is none. Looking for someone or something to blame is
a common human reaction, but try to avoid it, if you can. A
four-year-old boy who was in the kitchen with his mother
pulled a pot of boiling water off the stove and was severely
scalded. The boy suffered third-degree burns to his face and
upper body and was hospitalized for over seven months. In this
trying situation the parents supported one another, even though
the husband's parents told him that his wife was responsible
because "children should always be closely supervised,
especially when they are in the kitchen." The husband never
even thought about blaming his wife, and reprimanded his

parents for their attempt to make her a scapegoat. His view was that accidents do happen, and that while his son did suffer a tragic injury, supporting his wife was the best and only thing he could do.

In another case, a friend of mine contracted polio and was partially paralyzed. Although it could never exactly be determined where he had caught the disease, his father attributed it to the fact that his mother allowed him to swim in the river, where some other people who had gone swimming had also become ill. Because he attached sole responsibility for his son's disease to his wife, the father became resentful of his spouse, who subsequently felt a tremendous amount of guilt and anxiety. They started fighting more frequently, and they eventually separated. Through counseling they were able to overcome their difficulties and get back together, but the need to blame, even when there was no clear justification for it, temporarily tore the family apart. By seeking counseling, the father could have addressed his feelings, and prevented the separation entirely. The various avenues through which you can seek support and counseling are discussed in detail in Chapter 6.

Jealousy

Some parents also feel jealous of people whose children do not have disabilities. This, too, is a perfectly normal reaction. Jealousy can lead some parents to avoid being around other children, as they serve as constant reminders of what might have been. Young friends of mine were looking forward to the birth of their first child with great excitement. The child was born with extensive brain damage and was never able to demonstrate any signs of progress. During the first three years of the child's life, his parents refused to be involved in family celebrations where there were children present. As the mother said, "It was too difficult to see children enjoying themselves."

Fortunately, most parents are able to come to terms with their own child's difficulties and cease feeling inadequate when they come into contact with children who do not have disabilities. If you experience these feelings, try to confront them. By interacting with other children with or without disabilities you and your child will develop a sense of self-esteem and a range of experiences that could not be gained in isolation.

IT'S NOT THE END OF THE WORLD

When you realize that your child has a disability it is *not* the end of the world. Many families have become stronger, more loving, and more closely knit because of a disability in the family. The disability gave them the opportunity to work together to help out their loved one. A disability can become a challenge that the family faces together, and the entire family shares in the gains that are made by the child. This sense of accomplishment is tremendous and can't be reached by many families who do not face such obstacles. Many of the negatives that parents imagine will go along with having a child who has a disability simply do not occur. Raising a child with a disability is *not* a prison sentence that will deprive you and your family of the joys of life. While you'll have to make some sacrifices, you will still have time for your friends, family, and hobbies. After a while, many of the activities that you once viewed as sacrifices will come to be seen as part of everyday life, rather than as an exceptional burden.

One parent remembers discovering her daughter had a hearing problem, and how she and her husband learned to deal with it:

"I remember seeing the movie about Helen Keller. There was one scene in particular when the mother realized that her child could not hear. She clapped and yelled in front of her child, and saw that there was no response from the baby. My child was five or six weeks old, and for some reason I thought I'd try the same thing. To my shock, horror, and surprise, when I came up loudly behind my baby she didn't even seem to know I was there. I could yell and I could scream but the baby made no reaction. I suspected that she had a hearing deficit, and this suspicion turned out to be correct.

"I could not believe that this beautiful child could not hear. I always thought that she was normal. I knew a family who had a child with a serious handicap, and we knew the work that they were required to do. At that time, the last thing I ever envisioned was raising a special needs kid. Initially I was ashamed and embarrassed. Perhaps these feelings are not rational, but it is strange how some people react to shock.

"However, it is wonderful to be living in Toronto, as all of the facilities that we could possibly ask for are available. After I found out, I contacted our doctor, who put me in touch with a special hearing clinic. At a very young age my daughter learned how to lip-read. This was a very difficult process, but by the time that she was twelve years old, she was able to communicate normally and went to public school. We had to make certain that the teachers would always talk directly to our child. When teachers face the blackboard, no matter how loud they are talking, the entire course is lost on our daughter. Her fellow students have been very helpful. We have also had a lot of help from the local hearing association, and from parents' groups. The resources out there are just incredible, but you have to be aware of what there is.

"Even though we had more services than we needed, it was always very difficult for us. In fact, after my husband found out, he almost became an alcoholic. People respond to difficulties in all sorts of ways. We are now living with it and it looks like our daughter is going to live a very normal life."

THE DIFFERENCE BETWEEN A DISABILITY AND A HANDICAP

Many people believe that a disability and a handicap are the same thing, but this is not the case. A disability is defined as a physical or psychological impairment that may interfere with a person's normal functioning on a temporary or permanent basis, while a handicap is a physical or psychological impairment that *prevents* regular functioning. **A disability does not have to be a handicap!** People with disabilities may have to do something differently from people without disabilities, but they can achieve many of the same results. A child may have a disability, but he need not be significantly handicapped by it. With technologies such as computers constantly improving, children with special needs can find many opportunities for social, economic, and psychological integration and independence.

There is a wide range of disabilities (see below), but they all fall under two basic categories: visible and invisible.

VISIBLE AND INVISIBLE DISABILITIES

One widely used system classifies disabilities as follows.

1. **Locomotion Disability:** Problems with mobility, posture, and the manipulation of objects (e.g., quadriplegia).
2. **Visceral Disability:** Problems with ingestion and excretion (e.g., spina bifida).
3. **Visual Disability:** Partial or total loss of sight, perceptual disorders.
4. **Communicative Disability:** Receptive and expressive disorders (e.g., autism).
5. **Intellectual Disability:** Retardation or memory impairment.
6. **Emotional Disability:** Psychoses and behavioral disorders.
7. **Invisible Disability:** An invisible disability is a disability that is not obviously apparent (e.g., metabolic disorders, epilepsy).
8. **Visible Disability:** A condition that is apparent to most observers (e.g., a cleft palate or paraplegia).

These descriptions provide an easy way to classify disabilities, but no matter how a disability is classified, the important thing to remember is that there are strategies to overcome most difficulties a condition may create.

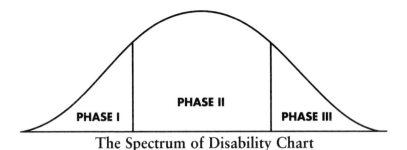

The Spectrum of Disability Chart

THE SPECTRUM OF DISABILITY

The spectrum of disability chart illustrates the range of severity of disabilities, as well as the outcomes that may be expected when a person has a specific disability. Positions in the spectrum are not static, as individuals that are classified as having Phase II disabilities frequently achieve Phase I status. It is important to remember that the labels of Phase I, II, and III are used to make classification easier. A specific phase suggests what range of options might be used, but it does not limit what an individual can achieve.

Two people with the same physical condition may be considered in different phases because of the way in which they respond to treatment. For example, a child with a severe facial deformity may withdraw from socializing with his friends because of the ridicule he is experiencing. Another child with the same condition may say, "accept me for what I am — not what you see." The child who is able to adapt and respond to treatment would be classified as having a minor disability, while the child who withdraws from his peers would be classified as having a more severe disability. In the movie *Mask*, which was based on a true story, the main character suffered from a condition that causes extreme facial deformity. However, he had a wide group of friends and a caring family, and was able to live a "normal" life. Although his physical disability was significant, he was able to successfully adapt.

Phase I Disabilities

Phase I of the chart depicts disabilities that are significantly alleviated by treatment. In Phase I cases, the disability will not usually dramatically intrude on a person's life. Some Phase I disabilities can be entirely alleviated through early therapy and surgery, and drugs may ease or control seizures such as those associated with epilepsy. Phase I disabilities are the least severe in the spectrum, and with significant rehabilitation and treatment their effects can be all but eliminated. For example, numerous cases of stuttering completely disappear when treated in the early years of a child's development. Surgery may alleviate many of the difficulties associated with a cleft palate. And lots of children participate in sports in spite of having artificial limbs. Clearly, a Phase I disability does not prevent someone from living a *normal* life.

Despite suffering through polio, scarlet fever, and double pneumonia as an infant, Wilma Rudolph won three gold medals at the 1960 Olympics, in 100-meter and 200-meter sprints and the 4x100-meter relay. Rudolph had lost the use of her right leg as a result of the polio, and was forced to wear a leg brace until the age of ten. With the help of therapy and motivation from her family, teachers, and coaches, she was able to overcome her disability and achieve international fame.

Phase II Disabilities

Phase II of the spectrum of disability illustrates conditions that often respond to treatment. To a large extent, the rehabilitation potential of individuals with Phase II disabilities is dependent upon two things: the available therapy and the person's motivation. There are many examples of children with significant disabilities who graduated from high school and university and who became professionals in a variety of fields. People with cystic fibrosis, muscular dystrophy, and a host of other severe conditions are often able to achieve exceptional accomplishments.

As a teenager, Canadian Terry Fox contracted cancer in one leg, which had to be amputated. Three years later in 1980, he courageously attempted to run across Canada in an effort to raise money for cancer research. The cancer resurfaced in his lungs after he had reached the halfway mark in his journey. He died in 1981, but he inspired a nation, and annually Canadians participate in Terry Fox Runs to raise funds for cancer research.

Phase III Disabilities

Many children are diagnosed with severe Phase III disabilities. In spite of this diagnosis, some children still achieve remarkable gains. A number of individuals with severe cases of cerebral palsy, for example, cannot speak or walk or write, but with the support of modern technology and a committed support network, they complete secondary and postsecondary education, and become able to support themselves.

My Left Foot is the story of Christy Brown, an Irishman who was severely incapacitated by cerebral palsy. With the help of a dedicated family, Brown became a noted author, poet, and international spokesperson for the rights of people with disabilities. *My Left Foot* is available at any local library or video store, and provides a valuable example of how someone with a severe disability can work toward achieving a productive existence.

In 1995, a major American television network dramatized the life of a developmentally delayed man (portrayed by Mickey Rooney) who had spent the first few decades of his life in an institution. With the help of a committed caregiver, this person was able to become relatively self-sufficient. There are numerous cases of individuals who have been confined to institutions because their parents were unable to care for them. After many years of institutional life, a few of these people have been able to demonstrate that they were capable people with many abilities. However, only a small number of them have been rescued from the confines of an institution.

THE IMPORTANCE OF AN ACCURATE DIAGNOSIS

In establishing the precise nature of the disability affecting your child, it is very important to establish an accurate diagnosis, so that your child can embark on the proper path of treatment as quickly as possible. Some parents refuse to accept the reality that their child may have disabilities. Initially they may blame ineffective teaching for their child's slow progress. Some even refuse to consult experts as they believe that their child is normal, and avoid labels, diagnoses, and early treatment. These parental reactions may have long-term negative effects for some special needs children.

It is very easy for a child with a disability to be misdiagnosed. For example, intellectual disorders are sometimes attributed to people with cerebral palsy. In fact, the majority of people with cerebral palsy do not experience intellectual difficulties. In cases such as these, an improper diagnosis prevents early intervention and can cause serious harm to a child's development.

Keep in mind that in a few cases it is difficult for physicians to recognize the nature of some conditions. Numerous disorders require sophisticated testing, and some of these disabilities are difficult to recognize in the early stages of life, such as sickle cell anemia, HIV, diabetes, many heart and lung problems, and learning disabilities. These situations can be frustrating for parents as well as physicians. You must be determined and persistent to ensure that your child receives the most appropriate treatment available. Believe it or not, the experts are sometimes wrong. For example, some children who are initially diagnosed as slow learners are subsequently diagnosed as having hearing impairments. Once the diagnosis is corrected, many of these children are able to function at their expected levels. Parents and others committed to the progress of children with disabilities have been responsible for the extraordinary gains of children who had been defined by the experts as having limited potential; if you do not agree with your doctor's opinion, you have every right to seek another one. Everything you are doing is for the benefit of your child, so don't be afraid to step on toes.

Once the nature of their child's disability has been diagnosed, most parents ask, "Why does my child have a disability?"

THE CAUSES OF DISABILITY

A disability can result from a number of factors, including genetic causes, illness or injury to the mother during pregnancy, trauma during birth, radiation, pollution, other environmental factors, and viral infections before, during, and after birth. In some cases it is impossible to determine why a disability has occurred.

Congenital Factors

Some disabling conditions are a result of congenital factors. This means that one or both parents carry a gene that causes an inherited condition, such as sickle cell anemia, Turner syndrome, Down syndrome, muscular dystrophy, and cystic fibrosis. In the case of Tay-Sachs disease, both parents must be carriers of the gene for their child to be affected. You can be tested to see if you are a carrier of any of the genetic diseases. If couples are aware of family histories involving congenital conditions, they might consider genetic counseling.

Genetic counseling establishes the probability of a child being affected by an inherited condition. If one or both parents know that they have a family history involving genetic disorders, they may elect not to have children. However, a person who is a carrier of a genetic disease may also give birth to a child that is perfectly healthy.

Even if the counseling demonstrates that a congenital defect may be a distinct possibility, a couple can still decide to have children. For example, if both parents are carriers of Tay-Sachs disease, there is a one in three or a one in four chance that their child will have the disease. Many parents are prepared to assume the risk of having a child with Tay-Sachs, knowing that they will also be able to bear healthy children.

This sort of counseling is usually done by family physicians or specialists in genetics. These specialists are aware of the conditions that can be transmitted genetically and fully inform parents of the risks they are facing and of the various courses of action they can pursue. If you are worried about genetic conditions, you can call your family doctor to set up an appointment or to have you referred to an appropriate specialist. Genetic counseling can be very beneficial. Tay-Sachs disease among Orthodox Jews in New York City, for example, has almost disappeared after widespread genetic counseling.

Maternal Injury or Illness
If a mother suffers severe physical or emotional trauma during pregnancy, it may have a negative effect on her child. A car accident, falling down the stairs, or periods of high stress are all serious, and merit attention. Wife abuse is also responsible for a startlingly high number of birth defects. Reliable statistics are very difficult to assemble, but all experts agree that pregnant women who are physically or sexually abused have a much greater probability of giving birth to children who have breathing difficulties and slower than average physical and mental development.

During pregnancy, mothers may contract measles, chicken pox, or other diseases that can affect the fetus. A disease may cause brain damage and other birth defects such as misshapen or missing limbs. Appropriate vaccinations prior to pregnancy can protect many mothers from illness, although there are some diseases that affect the fetus, such as herpes and AIDS, for which doctors have not yet found a vaccine.

Environmental Factors
A disability may also be the result of environmental factors such as exposure to x-rays, high-powered voltage lines, insecticides, and other contaminants. The decision to use an oil-based paint in the house during pregnancy is also perilous,

as the oil-paint fumes can damage the fetus. Airborne and waterborne toxins such as lead and mercury can also cause severe problems such as heart defects and other developmental disorders. To avoid this type of exposure, dentists have recently been advised to stop giving mercury-based fillings to pregnant women or to women who may become pregnant in the future. The children of many Gulf War veterans suffering from Gulf War Syndrome have been born with birth defects, and an unusually high number of their babies have been stillborn. If a mother has consulted with her physician and is cautious over the course of her pregnancy, however, many of these problems can be avoided.

Alcohol, Drugs, and Smoking
Pregnant women should avoid the use of alcohol, legal and illegal drugs, and tobacco, as these products are potentially dangerous and even deadly to the fetus. Studies demonstrate that women who smoke give birth to lower-weight babies, who are more likely to have a disability. A significant percentage of all babies born to alcoholic mothers suffer developmental delays and may have deformed limbs, small heads, and heart defects. In the 1960s many women took thalidomide, which was deemed to be an excellent anti-nausea medication. However, it caused many children to be born with stunted limbs and other medical problems. Thalidomide was subsequently pulled from the market. Even over-the-counter drugs should be avoided during pregnancy, as they may affect the fetus. Always consult your physician before taking any drug during pregnancy!

Trauma During Birth

A number of complications can occur during, and shortly after, birth. Babies have been injured during delivery through the improper use of forceps. Many women wish to avoid epidurals (local anesthetic) during birth as they believe that it may subsequently affect the child's development. Many others believe that epidurals have no negative side effects, but neither side has conclusive evidence to support their position. Breech births, multiple births, and premature births can also potentially create problems such as cerebral palsy and developmental delays. Ask your pediatrician or family physician for more details.

PRENATAL TESTING

Amniocentesis and other prenatal tests can frequently determine whether or not a fetus has been affected by a disease or other conditions. Sometimes these early tests produce fantastic results, since some conditions, including heart and kidney problems, can be identified and treated — even surgically corrected — prior to birth. Some children with cleft palates have also had their conditions surgically corrected prior to birth with a minimum of scarring. However, the intervention of various tests carries with it the possibility of prenatal injury. The advantages and disadvantages of prenatal procedures must be carefully weighed, and the nature and result of these sophisticated procedures should be thoroughly discussed with your physician.

WHAT OUTCOMES CAN BE ANTICIPATED?

Some disabilities, such as Down syndrome and cleft palate, may be immediately recognizable. In other cases, a disability may not be properly diagnosed for days, months, or years. Slow development in speech may reflect a hearing deficit, not a developmental disability. A stuttering condition, if treated early, may be alleviated before it affects your child's life. It is impossible to obtain an accurate measure of an infant's intellectual potential. Some children with severe disabilities are able to exceed the expectations that are predicted by medical and paramedical personnel.

Many parents and teachers tend to give up on children who have Tourette's syndrome, a genetic condition characterized by tics and inappropriate vocal outbursts. This need not, and should not, be the case. A couple of years ago, a Toronto newspaper profiled a Canadian physician who has Tourette's, but it does not affect his ability to practice medicine. He and thousands of others have been able to triumph over disabilities that were perceived by other people as overwhelming.

HOW MIGHT THE DISABILITY AFFECT MY CHILD?

Most children with disabilities experience the stress and alienation of being isolated and, in some cases, totally excluded from many of the activities in which they would like to participate. Many teenagers with disabilities are excluded from social and recreational programs, even though they are included in educational programs. This exclusion is often painful.

Some children with disabilities become totally dependent on their parents. They are reluctant to integrate with their peers, fearing ridicule, isolation, and embarrassment. It is important, therefore, to build your child's self-confidence — while children are still young, families should encourage them to take chances, and to be receptive to new ideas, activities, and people. An open-minded attitude promotes acceptance, participation, and inclusion.

My earliest and most treasured memories are of family get-togethers in which my cousins and other relatives made me feel that I was completely accepted and integrated. But I also remember vividly my first feelings of rejection. My mother and I were coming home from Banff on the train, when a waiter asked in a half-mocking tone: "Why can't your three-year-old feed himself?" I believe it was from this point in my life that I began to fear interaction with strangers.

If you can arrange conditions so that your child is directly integrated into classrooms and recreational settings, he is likely to develop the courage necessary to become a part of the larger society. If it is impossible to achieve complete integration, try to enable your child to participate at some level. If you explain to teachers, playmates, fellow students, and others the nature of your child's condition, they will usually try to include your child in most activities. But remember that there are times when your child may be excluded for reasons such as safety and security. For example, all children, but especially those with disabilities, should not be allowed to swim or engage in activities such as rock climbing or playing in treehouses without competent adult supervision. Your child should be included, however, if all reasonable precautions have been taken.

Some children are reluctant to describe the exact nature of

their disability. This is because they are embarrassed by their disabilities and, as a result, develop strong feelings of inferiority. If children cannot discuss the nature of their problems, it may increase their anxiety. These feelings can probably be alleviated — although not eliminated — by sensitive parents and others. You must make the point to your child that **it is not his problem** if people cannot accept him because of his disability; **it is their problem**.

This reality is difficult to convey to a child. People with hearing deficiencies, for example, are sometimes accused of being stupid, just as people with cerebral palsy and epilepsy are accused of being intoxicated when they experience involuntary movement. Confusion and misunderstanding on the part of people unfamiliar with a child's condition may lead the child to believe that he is wrong, or that he is somehow at fault for whatever may occur. Understandably, many parents want to insulate their children from the difficulties they might experience. In this attempt to shield the child, however, some parents become overprotective. (The consequences of overprotective parenting will be discussed later in this book.) When I was growing up, I discovered that you never know when people will act in a hurtful way toward a person with a disability. Even today, I am occasionally devastated by the actions of strangers and people whom I thought were friends. Parents and relatives will also be disappointed by the reactions of others, as they share in their child's pain.

It is strange that just because you have a disability, and are therefore defined as being different, that you are often expected to accept compromising and deprecating behavior with good humor. It is like saying, "you are a member of a minority, know your place, and be grateful." This is totally absurd.

THE IMPORTANCE OF A POSITIVE ATTITUDE

Developing a positive attitude is very important for everyone involved in raising a child. All children feel success, disappointment, and failure, and although children with disabilities will inevitably become aware of their limitations, they should always be encouraged to take on new challenges. This is sometimes difficult as children with physical limitations may be reluctant to participate in physical activities out of a fear of failure. Despite these fears, both the child's and the parent's perspective should be "have fun, and do your best."

In some cases, the limitations encountered by a person with a disability are imposed not by their physical condition, but by the incorrect assumptions of others. Occasionally both professionals and parents are convinced that a child's difficulties are insurmountable, when, in fact, they can be overcome to varying degrees. It is important to be optimistic while remaining realistic in forecasting the opportunities for progress and integration. Some children may be responsive in spite of being affected by a severe condition or by multiple disabilities.

The case of Helen Keller is a sterling illustration of what can be accomplished when a child is diagnosed with a Phase III disability. Before she was two years old, an illness left Helen Keller blind and deaf. She was unable to communicate with her family or understand the world around her. When Helen was seven years old, a talented young teacher named Anne Sullivan came to work with her. Miss Sullivan attempted to reach the girl's mind through the sense of touch and to teach her a manual alphabet by having her connect objects she could feel through words being spelled into her hand. Miss Sullivan's early efforts failed to produce any response, but at last there came a day when Helen understood — she realized the cool liquid pouring over her hand from the pump meant the word "water," which Miss Sullivan was spelling into her other hand. By nightfall of that same day, Helen had learned thirty words, and her education had begun. She went on to become a famous author and lecturer. If Helen had been limited by the expectations of others who believed that she would never be able to communicate with the outside world, she would not have become an inspiration to millions.

In addition to misdiagnosis, which incorrectly defines and treats a condition, incorrect labels are often responsible for the waste of life experienced by some children with severe disabilities. Incorrect labels can damage the self-esteem of a child who is defined as something they are not (e.g., when a child with an auditory processing disorder is told that he is an idiot). Some children have exceptional problems, but they still have **potential!** This potential must be recognized and developed so that these children can experience a positive quality of life.

My mother and father were told by many physicians that I would probably never be able to write. In spite of this assessment (which turned out to be correct), my parents focused on the importance of education. My dad told me that when I was seven or eight years old, he and my mother were assured that writing was not necessary for scholastic success, and that if I were properly motivated, I could obtain a Ph.D. (and they were right!). They were determined to provide me with every possible advantage that would allow me to become independent.

WHEN A FAMILY CANNOT COPE ANY LONGER

Some families discover that they are unable to cope with the consequences of having a child with a disability, and feel that they have no choice but to give up caring for their child. This is one of the most heart-wrenching decisions a parent can make. The decision to stop taking care of the child at home should be made by both parents, with the help of family, friends, and professionals. It is not a decision to be taken lightly, and it is my opinion that all other options should be exhausted before you give up your child. These options are covered later in this book.

Sometimes it becomes physically impossible for parents to care for their children. As parents age, it becomes very hard for them to provide all of the physical and psychological support necessary to raise someone who may be the size of an adult. It is one thing to diaper a baby or a young child, but it is another thing to care for a thirty-five-year-old person who is incontinent.

If you are unable to care for your child at home, it does not mean you are a failure as a parent or as a human being. Many parents cannot even cope with the responsibilities of raising a healthy child. In many cases, parents decide that their child can best be cared for outside of the home because they are facing a situation that is too much to handle. Familial, economic, social, and psychological factors may accumulate until one or both parents decide that they can no longer continue with the family unit intact. In these situations, institutionalization, adoption, and foster care may be considered as alternatives.

Institutionalization

By and large, institutionalization can meet a child's physical needs, but his emotional or social needs are seldom met. I have never met a person with a disability who was institutionalized who was subsequently able to become a totally independent person. Sometimes we hear about people who have been institutionalized at birth and then many years later had their potential recognized. In rare instances these people are able to leave the institution and enjoy life to varying degrees. Even committed caregivers working in institutional settings seldom have the time to develop the emotional relationships necessary for the growth and development of a young child. Many institutions are seriously understaffed and abuse has been recognized as an all too frequent occurrence.

I would recommend against institutionalization unless your child has a condition that requires specialized, around-the-clock care which cannot be adequately provided in a home environment. Short-term institutionalized care, however, may be productive for children with disabilities who live in rural areas, and who do not have access to the most advanced medical care and therapy.

If you decide to put your child in an institution, you should visit him as often as possible so that you can maintain your loving relationship with him, and to make certain that he is receiving the appropriate care. Day trips, dinners, family reunions, and if possible, vacations can all maintain an institutionalized child's sense of belonging in the family. Sometimes it is advisable to bring a caregiver from the institution along with you on these outings in order to provide the appropriate care. If families determine that they cannot provide for the requirements of their special child, they could consider having their child adopted, as there are some couples who are willing and able to provide a wonderful home environment with the support systems necessary to care for a child with a disability.

Adoption

You or your physician or case manager may be able to locate an individual or family who wishes to adopt a child with special needs. Many people cannot have children, and they are sometimes willing and able to provide a caring environment for a child with a disability. If you sincerely believe that you lack the capacity and the resources to provide for your special child, you may wish to consider this option. From my perspective, in many cases this is preferable to having your child institutionalized. If you do choose to take this step you should be aware that adoptive families should always be carefully assessed for their warmth and capacity to care for your child. Family physicians, public and private agencies, and the clergy are often able to locate such suitable families. Even when you are certain that you do not wish to care for your child, you will still want to ensure that she receives the most appropriate and loving care possible.

Foster Homes

In almost all communities, workers in social services can locate appropriate foster homes for the care of these children on an interim basis. In some instances, foster parents develop a special attachment to a child under their care, and proceed to legally adopt the child. Foster parents also usually have specialized training, and like adoptive parents, foster parents may be assessed by a number of agencies. These measures will give you the assurance that the care being provided for your child is more than adequate.

Some parents of children with disabilities are unable to have their special child live at home with them, but the vast majority of families with children who have disabilities are able to successfully manage within the home. The most important factor in these families' success is the motivation to succeed. While most adults can motivate themselves to succeed, most children require role models. If a child realizes that his parents always encourage success and will not be satisfied with anything less than his absolute best effort, he will be motivated to succeed. Never settling for failure becomes part of his character, and his self-esteem will be enhanced and maintained.

There is a wide range of disabilities that affect children, but the constant emphasis on always trying your best, reinforced in an atmosphere of warmth and support, will help any child with a disability triumph over the challenge that he will face. Instilling this confidence is a most important task as a parent, as it will allow your child to have faith in himself and work on his own behalf throughout the course of his entire life.

Chapter

3

You Are Your Child's Advocate

Advocacy is a vital task. Once you have mastered the strategies of advocacy, you will be able to successfully deal with all of the problems encountered by your special child. Advocacy means representing your child with vigor and commitment, whether with medical personnel, teachers, employers, friends, or relatives. This will be your most important task as a parent, as it will have an effect on all aspects of your child's life. Advocacy can ensure proper medical diagnosis, treatment, integration, accessibility, and independence. You must be prepared to push physicians, therapists, schools, community groups, politicians, and organizations on a regular basis to ensure a reasonable and adequate accommodation of your child's needs.

Advocacy must always be child directed and instruction based. All efforts should be made for your child's benefit, rather than what is easiest for professionals or for you. It's best to have a concrete strategy of what you want to achieve and how you want to achieve it. Decide on a definite plan or goal, and draw up a list showing what steps you need to take in order to best meet your child's needs.

WHAT IS THE PURPOSE OF ADVOCACY?

The main objectives of advocacy are:

1. To promote respect for the rights, freedoms, and dignity of the persons (children) served, both individually and as part of a group.
2. To ensure that your child's legal and human rights are recognized and protected.
3. To assist your child to receive the health care and social services to which she is entitled, and which would most adequately ensure her integration into society.
4. To enhance the autonomy of your child by advocating on the child's behalf both individually and collectively (you not only want your child to have access to all services, but you also want all children with the same disability to receive the same benefits).
5. To assist your child to lead as independent a life as possible, or to live in the least restrictive environment possible.
6. To help protect your child from financial, physical, psychological, and social abuse (this is vital not only within the confines of your home, but also within community organizations such as schools, churches,

and other communal groups, or in the institutional environments in which your child may reside).

Advocacy is designed to promote security and well-being in all areas of your child's life. Advocacy will open up new possibilities and opportunities for your child by empowering her and enhancing her acceptance into society. Better treatment will lead to higher self-esteem, and greater opportunities for employment and independence.

GROUP ADVOCACY VS. INDIVIDUAL ADVOCACY

There are two successful approaches to getting what you need: (1) group advocacy; and (2) individual advocacy. Group advocacy allows parents to join forces. If the services that your child needs are not available, it is quite likely that other parents will be seeking similar services. If you are concerned because your child is denied equal treatment, other parents will surely feel the same way. By working together you will be able to gain access to services and win new rights. Group advocacy leads to changes in the entire system.

For example, parent groups for mobility-impaired children have had significant success in getting school boards to make schools accessible by installing ramps, stairway lifts, and elevators and creating innovative class rotation schedules (where the teachers move from class to class instead of the students). When these parents banded together to make their voices heard, the school boards responded. Motivated by legislation already in place, school personnel will usually find funds to make schools accessible to children with mobility impairments.

If you live in a small community, or if you feel that your problems can best be worked out on a person-to-person level, you may choose individual advocacy to solve your problem. Individual advocacy focuses on your child's specific needs, in your specific setting. Individual advocacy does not require the same level of organization to get started as group advocacy, but you have fewer allies, and a smaller voice. That does not mean, however, that it will be any less effective. One person's efforts *can* make a difference!

One parent was able to persuade a local community center to establish special swimming programs for children who are unable to walk. She informed the center's administration that the community had six children who had spina bifida and cerebral palsy, and that these children should be given the same opportunities to enjoy community center programs as children who did not have disabilities. Initially the mother faced resistance, but she showed that there was a need for the program, pointed out that their staff included a number of well-trained swimming instructors, and enlisted the help of two local service clubs to provide funding. The program was successful and was subsequently adopted by three other recreation centers in the community.

WHAT ARE THE DIFFERENT KINDS OF ADVOCATES?

There are nine varieties of advocates, each dealing with a different range of problems and solutions. You may encounter some or all of these advocates, depending on your needs and the causes with which you are involved. Many of them are resources to be called on when you encounter problems in obtaining services.

1. **Parental Advocate:** As the name implies, this term covers all advocacy undertaken by a parent or guardian. For you, this will be the most important kind of advocacy. Because this child is your flesh and blood, your commitment to her will be deeper than anyone else's. Your child does not yet have the ability to speak for herself, to lobby, or to challenge the system; you must become her voice. All your efforts on her behalf, from lobbying for a special water fountain at school to building an access ramp to developing a new school program, are examples of parental advocacy.

   • *How Parental Advocates Can Help:* Until the late 1970s, summer camps were primarily for youngsters who did not have disabilities. Individuals and parent groups have been successful in getting many camps to accommodate children with disabilities. Through their hard work parents were able to provide a mainstream camping experience for their children with special needs. Camping associations in larger communities throughout Canada and the United States will provide lists of the camps that offer suitable programs. You can access these groups through your local YMCA, YWCA, or social service agencies.

2. **Self-Advocate:** Self-advocacy covers all efforts made by an individual on her own behalf. While your child is

growing up, she will probably not have a sufficient understanding of her rights and requirements to become a full and total self-advocate. You can, however, teach her from an early age to push for accommodation of her needs. As your child grows older she will become increasingly independent, and with the help of the advocacy skills that she has learned, she will be better able to cope in the real world.

• *How Self-Advocates Have Helped:* In England, children who have severe hearing impairments have demanded inclusion in school orchestras, as they are often able to enjoy and play percussion instruments through vibrations. These children demonstrated their ability and showed their teachers that they were able to participate along with their fellow classmates.

Self-advocacy is a crucial life skill that your child should be introduced to at an early age. If she knows how to advocate on her own behalf, it will alleviate many of the barriers that many children with disabilities continue to encounter. Your child should always be encouraged to go for it, to take a chance, and to demonstrate to others that she is capable of participating in activities often thought to be the exclusive domain of children without disabilities. Self-advocacy is an attitude and a skill that will permit participation, inclusion, and even leadership in many pursuits. While you will be the strongest voice for your child as she is growing up, once she has left home she must have the skills she needs to be independent.

3. **Citizen Advocate:** A citizen advocate is a volunteer who works to defend the rights and interests of a person with a disability. A citizen advocate can also lend emotional and practical support, and can be a friend, family member, or volunteer from the community.

   • *How Citizen Advocates Have Helped:* One individual initiated a wheelchair basketball program in the city of Toronto. He also arranged to take many children with special needs to professional baseball, hockey, and football games on a regular basis. For him, it was a valuable and fulfilling activity. Other citizen advocates have worked with families on a one-to-one basis. These volunteers provide recreational opportunities, respite care, physiotherapy, and other care that is often required. Citizen advocates are also very active in encouraging others to become involved in these activities.

4. **Case Manager:** A case manager is a person who provides parents with the necessary information for the proper care of their child, by directing them to specialists and facilities. Case managers can be infant specialists, parents of children with similar conditions, physiotherapists, occupational therapists, medical doctors, preschool teachers, school teachers, counselors, or members of the clergy. The case manager also serves as an advocate when families face problems in obtaining service. If you are just starting out as an advocate, it is a good idea to consult a case manager to point you in the right direction. Case managers have years of experience in solving problems

for their clients and they can be an invaluable resource in your advocacy efforts.

Most parents serve as their children's actual case managers. In the early stages of child care some parents attempt to obtain support and information from physicians, other parents facing similar situations, and paramedical staff. These individuals often suggest that parents consult or hire the services of a case manager. If you feel confident and capable of advocating for your child on your own, a case manager is not necessary. If, however, you are at first somewhat unsure about what you have to do, it might be a good idea to retain the services of a case manager.

• *How a Case Manager Has Helped:* Two parents from a rural community had a five-year-old daughter with hearing impairments. They felt that their child could benefit from a temporary stay in an institution, but they were unaware of what facilities were available. They were also worried about the negative consequences of having their daughter away from the family for an extended period of time. The parents consulted a case manager, who suggested the parents enroll their daughter in an institution for the hearing impaired for a six-month period. At the same time she arranged free lodging for the child's mother in the community close to her daughter for four of the six months. This helped to alleviate the trauma experienced by the child, who was separated from her family for the first time. During this time the child was able to learn to lip-read effectively and was subsequently registered in a regular school program in her own community. Without the case manager's help, the parents would not have found the institution or its speech therapy program.

5. **Social Work Sponsored Advocate:** This type of advocate is a social worker who usually works for a community agency such as a hospital, community clinic, or community social service office. Social work sponsored advocates ensure that your child receives appropriate treatment. They are able to provide advice and expertise in specific areas with which you may not be familiar.

• *How a Social Work Sponsored Advocate Has Helped:* A social worker encountered a family who was very distressed because their child had been diagnosed with muscular dystrophy. Upon further investigation, the social worker discovered that the physician in charge was a dictatorial individual who created severe social and psychological stress for the entire family. The family felt intimidated whenever they inquired about the adequacy of the pattern of treatment that was prescribed for their son. The social worker suggested another specialist who had a warm personal approach. In a short period of time, the family was able to begin coping in a very positive way.

6. **Legal Advocates and Legal Clinics:** In some instances the system may not respond to legitimate requests made by individuals, parents, and advocacy groups. In these situations, it is usually advisable to obtain legal advice from lawyers who specialize in human rights cases or from legal aid clinics that represent the

needs of special interest groups. A legal advocate provides representation in litigation or legal negotiations regarding advocacy issues. If you have a family lawyer, she may be able to perform this function for you. If she does not feel that she is the most capable attorney for your specific case, she may refer you to a specialist in advocacy issues or in the rights of people with disabilities. Legal aid clinics may also be able to provide you with the necessary advice. Some legal clinics provide free advice on disability-related issues, or offer financial support for legal challenges on disability issues.

• *How Legal Advocates Have Helped:* The parents of a child with cerebral palsy were frustrated by the fact that a school board in a small community refused to accept their child into the local public school because of the difficulties associated with his condition. The legal aid clinic undertook this case without cost to the parents. After one appeal the legal challenge was successful and the child was integrated into the community public school system.

7. **Special Advocate:** Special advocates focus their efforts on advocating in a single, specific area. You will find special advocates, for example, in the areas of education, medical aid, and occupational therapy. These advocates will be valuable allies in your attempts to achieve specific gains. Psychiatrists, psychologists, physiotherapists, and occupational therapists frequently serve as special advocates.

• *How a Special Advocate Has Helped:* A fifteen-year-old girl with autism had functioned for the first seven years of her school life in a public education system with the constant support of an attendant who always accompanied her to the classroom. After the student began to menstruate, she was totally repelled by the sight of her own blood and by the requirements necessary to contend with the situation. During her menstrual period she was extremely agitated, and someone else was forced to deal with her hygienic requirements. No classroom assistants would continue to work with the girl because of their fear of contracting the AIDS virus. The student was taken out of school for six months and counseled by a committed psychologist who was able to help her overcome her fear associated with having her period. After counseling was completed, the psychologist successfully lobbied the school board to allow the student back in to regular classes.

8. **Advocacy Groups:** Advocacy groups are composed of parents and professionals who are concerned with the rights and opportunities of people with disabilities. You can draw upon the support and knowledge that advocacy groups provide as allies in your advocacy efforts.
   • *How Advocacy Groups Have Helped:* Advocacy groups have lobbied local, state, provincial, and federal governments to admit students with severe disabilities into regular classrooms with support systems that have not traditionally been a part of the education system. They were also instrumental in having the Americans with Disabilities Act (ADA) made into law.

9. **Social Action Groups:** Social action groups are organizations designed to achieve the acceptance and integration of individuals with disabilities. These groups include the American Civil Liberties Union (ACLU) and the Canadian Civil Rights Association. By supporting politicians who support disability issues, social action groups are very effective in getting disability-friendly legislation passed.

• *How Social Action Groups Have Helped:* Social action groups frequently work for politicians and political parties who promise to put disability-related concerns at the forefront of their agenda. Former U.S. president George Bush realized the power of the American community of people with disabilities and their allies by promising the Americans with Disabilities Act, which expanded the legal rights of people with disabilities. According to pollster Louis Harris, 60 percent of Bush's margin of victory in 1990 was attributable to the support he obtained from the disabled community and their allies.

WHAT IF I AM DISSATISFIED WITH THE OTHER ADVOCATES FOR MY CHILD?

Advocates are supposed to represent the best interests of your child. Occasionally, however, these people may have their own agendas. They may be committed to therapies that have worked in similar cases, or they may have ideological interests that might interfere with your child's welfare. Your role is to evaluate the effectiveness of every advocate who is working with your child. If they are not doing a satisfactory job, it is your right and responsibility as the parent to change the advocate's focus or to find other individuals who will be better able to act on your child's behalf. First try to discuss your concerns with them. If an advocate refuses to acknowledge these concerns, you should find alternative sources of support.

WHAT PROTECTION DO WE HAVE UNDER THE LAW?

The law is now on the side of those who have disabilities. The Americans with Disabilities Act in the United States and the Charter of Rights and Freedoms in Canada assure people with disabilities equality of opportunity, full participation, access to independent living, and economic self-sufficiency. The laws regarding disability focus on mainstreaming and integrating people with disabilities, moving away from dependency and segregation.

In spite of legislation, however, people with disabilities remain at a severe disadvantage. A staggering 58 percent of all men with disabilities and 80 percent of all women with disabilities are unemployed. A large number of buildings and facilities are not accessible to the mobility impaired, and there is frequent discrimination against people with disabilities. This is not a result of deficiencies in the legislation, but in the willingness of people to comply with the legislation.

HOW CAN I USE THE LAW?

You can use the law in many ways. First of all, the mere threat of legal action may be more than enough to have school boards and other groups cater to your needs. Legal clinics and law schools will frequently provide reasonable, if not free, legal advice on how to obtain the benefits that you desire. For a major legal undertaking you may have to engage a lawyer in order to obtain the rights to which you and your child are entitled. Remember that it is frequently a very expensive and exhausting undertaking to become involved in a formal legal struggle; try to satisfy your needs through the processes of counseling and mediation before embarking on such a course.

Areas of the Law
The law can establish benefits, rights, and opportunities in medical treatment, education, employment, accommodation, transportation, medical care plans (Medicaid and Medicare), protection, recreation, human rights, and government support benefits. It is important that you recognize each of the above areas and determine, possibly with the assistance of your case manager, advocacy group, or support group, how to obtain the necessary entitlements.

How to Expand Rights
Your child may require specialized educational support, computer devices, or other equipment that may have to be individually designed. Your support group may be able to put you in touch with an individual or organization that can meet your needs. If this is the case, then it's a waste of time for you to try to reinvent the wheel. If, however, there are no estab-

lished policies for granting your benefits, then you must learn how to expand your rights.

The first step is to approach the authorities that have the power to grant your requests with a well-documented presentation illustrating the legitimacy of your child's needs. Your presentation needs to convince the people in power that not only are your child's needs legitimate, but so too are the needs of all those with disabilities who find themselves in similar circumstances. If you can persuade the decision-makers that your child requires specific accommodations, and that these accommodations will improve the lives of a significant number of children within the community, then there is an excellent chance that your needs will be met. If you are dealing with politicians, it is a useful strategy to convey to them that you have supported them in the past, and that you and your support group plan on supporting them in the future. Politicians will usually do their best to meet your needs, especially when they realize that they can obtain support from a variety of groups in the community.

If this initial approach is not successful, you may want to undertake a public education and public influence campaign by writing letters and making follow-up phone calls to members of the media in your community. Successful media exposure can alert entire communities to your cause, gain added support, and put pressure on the people in charge to take the action that you have requested. At this point, it may be advisable to contact a university faculty of law or a legal clinic. The faculty or clinic can sometimes offer strategies to help you obtain your requests. If these groups are unable to provide you with satisfactory guidance, it may be necessary to seek professional legal help. Usually, the effective use of media pressure and advocacy efforts will allow you to achieve your goals without having to rely on the court system.

Mounting a Legal Challenge

Because legal action can be expensive, it is strongly recommended that you work with support and advocacy groups in order to share the costs. A large group of people with the same needs will have access to a wider base of resources, and will usually be able to amass more powerful allies. This will make your task much easier and financially affordable. Fighting a month- or year-long court battle by yourself can be an exhausting experience. Fighting the same battle with tens, hundreds, or thousands of others can make it much easier.

It is difficult to establish legal precedents, as in many cases the traditional system is firmly embedded and some groups are reluctant to grant the requests of people who have disabilities. In the last twenty years, however, advocacy organizations and local, national, and international groups have clearly had an impact. Children with disabilities and their parents have made substantial gains, and it is hoped that these positive changes will accelerate as the grassroots movement of people with disabilities becomes more sophisticated, stronger, and more effective. The legal community has been successful in influencing landlords to rent apartments to people with disabilities and to have sidewalks ramped to make communities accessible to children and adults in wheelchairs. While each individual case to further the rights of people with disabilities must be evaluated on its own merit, the law now clearly favors granting rights to those people who have justifiable needs.

Legal and ethical issues concerning disability will continue to emerge as a consequence of your needs and of the changing values and laws that society adopts. It is almost inevitable that as parents of children with disabilities, you may encounter barriers that frustrate your attempts to achieve integration and progress. As you can see throughout this book, however, real achievements and gains have been made because of the determination of parents, support groups, and advocacy groups who believe that their special children should have the opportunity to be integrated as much as possible into their own societies. **The name of the game is power.** If you have the backing of support and advocacy groups, you will discover you have the power to obtain the significant changes that will allow your child to enjoy the benefits to which she is entitled.

When I was young, I discovered that many individuals, teachers, and others were initially reluctant to make the effort to provide the necessities that I required. Their excuse was that it was too difficult or that it took too much time or that it wasn't a part of their contract. In many cases all they needed was a nudge from those in authority to get them to make sure that my needs were met.

From grades two to ten, I was on many school teams, despite my lack of athletic ability. Although I was seldom put into a game unless our team was "way ahead," I was a loyal and strong supporter of every school team and represented a fighting spirit on the bench. One of my parents' physician advisors told them that my inclusion on school sports teams could create a lifelong positive attitude. My doctor feared that if I were excluded, I would not develop the necessary social skills to function independently. By speaking up on my behalf, my parents ensured that I would make new friends, have new experiences, and enjoy a normal childhood.

I also learned that there are proper times to make special

requests. Many years ago I realized that it is inappropriate to ask stewardesses to cut up my food in mid-flight, as they are usually overworked and called on to solve dozens of different problems on each flight. It is better to contact the airline in advance to make them aware of your special needs. That way meals are delivered as requested, with a minimum of inconvenience to anyone. Even in relatively minor efforts at advocacy, it is important to see both sides of the coin, to ensure that everyone is satisfied with the result.

In restaurants, never be reluctant to ask the waiter to deliver the food as required. When I was invited to birthday parties as a child, my mother always contacted the host family ahead of time to avoid embarrassment and to make sure that my needs were met.

WHAT DO I NEED TO BECOME A SUCCESSFUL ADVOCATE?

There are many ways to advocate on your child's behalf. Some means are simple, and some are more complex. The key to success in any type of advocacy is to gather the proper information and to combine this knowledge with a large dose of commitment. The application of these two attributes will lead to skill at advocating, which you will gain with experience.

Knowledge
To deal with the difficulties you will face, begin by obtaining all the available information. This includes: a detailed knowledge of your child's needs, and how best to meet these needs; what personnel and services are required for your child, and if they

are available in your area; what the costs of your child's care will be, what financial resources are available to you, and where you can obtain these resources; and a full and complete knowledge of your legal rights and those of your child.

You can gather this information from physicians, nurses, therapists, social workers, other sources, such as support groups, libraries, colleges, and specialized institutions that represent the interests of people with disabilities, as well as individuals with the professional experience to advocate effectively for your children. Writing to national, state, provincial, or local organizations that represent your child's disability is another means of obtaining information (see Appendices 1 and 2). These organizations can provide information about effective patterns of treatment and lists of specialists, clinics, and support groups. In addition, you may wish to contact home and school associations, religious groups, service organizations, and local, state, provincial, and federal departments of health and of social services, which will frequently provide information and personnel who can meet the needs of your child.

Take note of the names and numbers of all of the people with whom you are in contact in order to build up your advocacy directory. In establishing this advocacy support system, contact people by phone and by letter. In many cases you will also be able to use fax machines and e-mail. This may require a considerable amount of time, but once you gain the relevant information, you will be able to participate in, and even organize, strategies that will meet the needs of your child.

Commitment
I cannot emphasize enough that you will always be the best advocate for your child. While the vast majority of health care

professionals are qualified, dedicated, caring personnel, they will not always be able to provide your child with the time and services she deserves. While they will work hard on your behalf, your child will often be one client or patient among many, all of whom have numerous needs that must be fulfilled. Volunteers, friends, and members of the community can all provide invaluable help, but keep in mind that they also have many other commitments they must meet.

Budget deficits, staff shortfalls, and the extra training that your child's accommodation may require are not your problems. As an advocate you are working solely for your child's benefit. Difficulties that may arise in the course of accommodation are the responsibility of administrators. You will probably be able to sympathize with them, but as a parent, your job is to **always put your child first**. Others may have the best interests of institutions, budgets, or other people at heart. As a parent your child is Number One.

You have a very unique bond with your child. You and your spouse are the individuals most responsible for your child's future. As such, you have more motivation than anyone else to get what is best for your son or daughter, and to ensure that he can succeed. This commitment is a necessary element that will always drive you to push for what is best for your child. Raising a child with special needs is a difficult task requiring many hours of hard work, but you will find the rewards of successful advocacy to be worthwhile, not only for your special child, but for your entire family.

Expertise

You cannot expect to be an expert advocate for your child right off the bat. You will learn the techniques that are most effective with time, practice, and hard work. While the techniques for dealing with specific disabilities vary greatly from case to case, there are some basic, common sense principles that are helpful in all cases.

- **Be Open-Minded:** There are often many solutions to a single problem. Always be receptive to new information, new technology, and alternative strategies.
- **Choose Carefully:** Multiple sets of opportunities often present themselves at the same time. As each option may be valid, it is important to weigh the costs and benefits of each one separately.
- **Mix and Match:** If you feel that elements of several different plans are valid, don't be afraid to pick and choose the parts that you like best. A competent professional will usually be more than happy to accommodate you.
- **Be Ready to Change:** Not all treatments work for all people. If something is not working for your child, don't be afraid to change it. After a reasonable trial period, if one approach isn't working, consider trying something else.
- **Move Forward:** Don't dwell on missed opportunities — learn from them and apply what you've learned. Hindsight is always 20/20, but no one has eyes in the back of his head.
- **Focus on the Program:** Occasionally a professional caregiver assumes dominance in a child's care. Out of loyalty or intimidation some parents feel bound to allow a professional to continue a specific program. Always look at the content of the program, not at

who the caregiver is. Doctors who assume total control over your child's care may provide the best possible care, but then again, they may not.

- **Always Ask Questions:** Questions should *not* be confined to your child's care. You should inquire as to how many journals your physician reads on a regular basis, how many seminars he or she attends, and whether or not he or she teaches. This will assure you whether or not your physician is at the leading edge of knowledge in his or her field.

COMMON PROBLEMS

When advocating you may run into numerous roadblocks. If you are aware of the possible difficulties beforehand, you will be better able to overcome them.

Resistance
Advocacy has created resistance and negativity among many individuals and groups. This negativity has arisen because of two reasons: First, a lack of understanding of the concept of advocacy; and second, because of the manner in which some individuals advocate for their clients. Some organizations are reluctant to provide services because they feel the services will make them inefficient, or that they will be too expensive. Many educators will say, "This is the way it is," and will refuse to change their policy to accommodate children with special needs. Many social welfare agencies may claim that they do not offer the services that you require. In these cases you may have to fight for innovation and change.

Lack of Understanding

When dealing with people who are not familiar with your child's disability, you should always be ready to provide an explanation of the disability, and what it entails. This will allow people to better understand where you and your child are coming from, what you need, and why you need it. Having to repeat the same story over and over again can be very trying, but you have to recognize that people who are not familiar with your child's situation may also need a little bit of understanding. Once they are fully aware of the situation many people will be willing to help you out.

Distrust

Advocacy should not be primarily adversarial in nature, as you will gain very little through an overzealous and abrasive approach. A confrontational stance usually leads to distrust on both sides, and it can make advocacy more difficult for you, and have a negative effect on what subsequently happens to your child. Unreasonably aggressive action may foster the belief that you are demanding unwarranted expenditures of money and time. It is more effective to attempt to work together with the professionals responsible for your child's accommodation than to work against them. Remember that most of the people that you encounter through advocacy will be willing to work out a solution. Bringing them into a **partnership** to solve a problem is far easier than trying to solve the same problem with them as an enemy.

Dictatorial Professionals

Some physicians will maintain that they know everything and that you should always follow their directions. They may see you as interfering or meddling in areas where you do not belong. Their attitude is wrong. While you may not have all of the answers, **parents should always be part of the team.** You know your child best, and you should always be consulted when important decisions are being made.

Lack of Resources

Frequently, especially if you live in a small community, you will find that the required personnel, technology, and programs are not available. These shortages may be a result of oversight, lack of demand, or lack of financial resources.

Lack of Time

Most people cannot do everything themselves. We all need breaks at one time or another. Single parents are usually at a particular disadvantage because they do not have the ready-made support system of a "nuclear family" to help in the activities required in raising a special needs child. That is why it is important to use support groups to help alleviate your burden. They will be able to ease tension, obtain funds, services, and support. (Chapter 8 deals with support groups in more detail.)

HOW TO SOLVE THE PROBLEMS

These problems do not have to deter you from your goal. There are numerous nonconfrontational ways of dealing with the situations above.

Write Letters and Make Phone Calls

You can begin advocating by writing letters and making phone calls to the appropriate personnel. If you can establish that you have a legitimate concern, you will usually receive a positive response. When writing letters requesting significant change, send copies of your letters to senior bureaucrats, government representatives, and sometimes even local media. The more attention your cause receives, the better.

It may also be valuable to contact your local school trustee, alderperson, councilperson, state, provincial, or federal representatives, as they can obtain favorable publicity by responding to the needs of children with disabilities. Pressure from superiors is a very effective way to get professionals to change their point of view.

Use Allies

You should not underestimate the importance of using support groups and other parents with similar concerns as a resource. Their experiences and abilities will be an invaluable aid in accomplishing your goals.

Demonstrate Your Interest

If you illustrate that you are aware of the issues being discussed, your doctor may be more willing to include you in his or her decisions. The deeper your understanding and the greater your expressed concern, the better your chances of being involved in the decision-making process. Reading the relevant books and articles will help you in this quest. Your local library should contain most of the books you need. If not, then ask your doctor. They will probably be impressed by your initiative.

Ask Questions

This is the best way to learn about your child's condition. Asking questions will allow you to gain a better understanding of the medical side of your child's disability. You can also develop a closer relationship with the physician, and you may even be able to detect a possible flaw in the course of action being taken. If you don't ask, you will never know.

Make Constant Notes

Keep a record of everything that has been done and everyone you have contacted on your child's behalf. By keeping track of every letter you write and phone call you make, you guarantee that the person or organization with which you are dealing is held accountable for their action or inaction. If, for example, you have a written log indicating that you spoke to so and so on such and such a date about installing a ramp in a local recreation center, they will be unable to claim that your conversation never took place. Be comprehensive; write down all names, dates, times, and nature of contacts.

Keep Track of Your Child's Medical History

A complete and up-to-date case history will enable you to provide the necessary information to anyone who begins working with your child. This record should include every symptom of the condition and all the therapies that have been used. Record your child's reaction to individual people, drugs, and treatments. The medical history should also include standard medical concerns such as allergies, vaccinations, and hearing and sight tests. At a moment's glance it will allow you to examine which therapies have been beneficial, which have been ineffective, and which types have been left untried.

Keep an Educational Log

A collection of your child's individual education programs (see Chapter 7 for details) will be a valuable resource in planning her future education. This collection will help show teachers and administrators what your child has accomplished in the past.

Keep Track of Recreation

Remember what activities your child enjoys, where she has had a good time, what the facilities were like, and what the cost was. After several years you should have an impressive collection of things to do on a lazy Sunday afternoon.

Find the Appropriate Sources

If the program or item you seek does not exist because there has never been a need for it before, it is often a simple matter of making a request to the proper authority. The sources are there; you just have to locate them. Local support groups will often help you locate the proper source. For example, school boards will deal with most education-related expenses, while municipal or state governments will deal with requests for access to public parks or buildings.

Get Help

If you need new or unavailable technology, it is often possible to get a local engineer or carpenter to build it for you. Local doctors, universities, and social workers can sometimes aid in developing a new rehabilitation or educational program. If the things you need are expensive, there are often funds available from a wide variety of sources. (See Chapter 11 for advice on financing.)

Advocacy is a strategy you can use to ensure that your child has the most appropriate opportunities in all phases of her life. By using advocacy you will become informed about your child's disability and you will learn how to select the personnel who will be most beneficial to your child. Advocacy will provide you with organizational skills, a clear focus on what to attain, and the confidence that you will achieve the best possible care and treatment for your child.

Chapter

4

All in the Family

A disability or serious illness affects the entire family. When a family is able to cope **effectively** with a disability, the process can be enriching for all family members. If, however, the family unit fails to provide the supportive environment needed to successfully manage the challenges, a child's development can be inhibited. Adjusting to a child's disability can be frustrating, painful, and at times depressing, but in the long run, successful adaptation rewards the whole family.

THE IMPORTANCE OF THE FAMILY

The family is traditionally a child's best source of support. A child's accomplishments, self-respect, and self-esteem are all molded by his family. The family should always provide a refuge where the child is loved and supported. This atmosphere will encourage the child to be independent, creative, and active. This is what all parents want for their children. When raising a child with special needs, this family atmosphere is doubly important. While strangers, acquaintances, and even friends may sometimes let the child down, the family should always be there for him.

The family not only includes parents and siblings, but also aunts, uncles, cousins, nieces, nephews, grandparents, other relatives, and even close friends, who can all help with the social and emotional growth of your child. Your extended family can play an important part of your **support network**. By surrounding him with love and affection, your child will grow up knowing that he has an important place in the family and in the world.

WHAT TO TELL YOUR FRIENDS AND FAMILY

Many people will not know how to respond to your needs. Sometimes friends, grandparents, and even your own siblings may ignore you. It might be a simple process for these people to relate to "normal" children, but they can become reluctant to see you, and perhaps even hostile, when they feel that they are expected to participate in the care of a child with a disability. You may discover that your relationships with many relatives and friends become strained or even severed. Some people just do not possess the sensitivity, knowledge, or capacity to care that is required. It has been said that in times of crisis people discover who their real friends are. Convey to your friends that you not only hope for their emotional support, but you would also appreciate it if they could help you in other ways. Often when they are provided with the appropriate information and made aware of your needs, they will change their attitude and become a source of strength for you.

In spite of your efforts, however, there may be some people who are unable to provide the support you need. If they are unwilling or unable to provide help or understanding, there's not much you can do, and there's no point in worrying about them. For some of your friends and family, time may be an important factor, and some people who are initially unable to help you may over time come to be relied upon as an important resource. Don't refuse someone's offer of help just because it did not come immediately.

Whenever a new child is born into a family, other siblings feel somewhat neglected. When a child with a disability is born, this feeling is often enhanced because of the extra attention and time that is required to care for the child. Understandably, at this early stage older siblings often feel left out. You must go out of your way to assure them that **they are loved and needed.**

If you do have other children, they should be informed of the difficulties being experienced by their sibling as soon as possible, as they, too, will be involved in loving and caring for the child. Try to make your other children feel that they are very important — not only for themselves, but for the help and the support that they can contribute. If the other children are not made aware of their brother or sister's condition, they will feel isolated and separated. Consult them on most important issues, as in many situations they can contribute valuable ideas to be used in the care of your new child. By involving your children you give them a sense of importance and maturity, and make them feel that they are a valued member of your family. Many parents set aside a special time each week to discuss all problems that have arisen within the family and the ways to deal with these difficulties.

ADAPTING TO A DISABILITY

Giving birth to a child with a disability is often perceived as a crisis. The same feelings occur when a child suffers a disability through injury or disease. Stages similar to the ones social scientist Elisabeth Kübler-Ross pioneered for dealing with the death of a loved one, can be used to reflect typical reactions to the diagnosis of a disability for your child. The stages of family adjustment most often noted in response to a child's disability are: **withdrawal or rejection, denial, fear and frustration, and adjustment.**

Not everyone goes through every stage, nor are the stages always experienced in sequence. Some families do not encounter any of these stages, and proceed directly to meeting the challenges of caring for their child.

Rejection or Withdrawal
The first stage of adapting to a disability is rejection or withdrawal. Parents, relatives, and friends usually celebrate birth, which is traditionally an opportunity for warmth, love, and friendship. If a child is born with a recognized disability, this period may be transformed into one of anxiety and distress. Some parents withdraw physically and emotionally from their baby, and miss out on bonding, that formative experience between parents and child. At this early stage, they may feel

that they have to institutionalize their child, or they may be advised to do so by well-meaning physicians, clergy, relatives, or friends.

Bonding with the child is vital, as physical and emotional cues are established that are critical for the relationship between the baby and his parents. Many parents assert that at this initial stage, their capacity to create an atmosphere of warmth and security was instrumental in their acceptance of the child, and in the child's subsequent development. Many studies have shown that a child's physical growth and social development are enhanced when he is a part of a warm, caring family atmosphere.

Accepting a baby with disabilities is made easier when the mother and father and other family members are able to hold and envelop the child in physical warmth. Sometimes it may be difficult to establish this physical contact, as many children born with serious disabilities are initially placed in incubators. But even if an infant has to spend the majority of his time in an incubator, physical and social contact can still be sustained. Stroking, singing lullabies, and talking gently are all effective means of creating a bond with your child. Opportunities for physical contact should be taken at the earliest possible moment. This will provide your baby with a sense of warmth and you with a sense of attachment and belonging. This constant contact is regarded as crucial to a child's growth and recovery. Most hospitals now provide overnight beds so that parents can be with their children.

Feelings of withdrawal or rejection at this stage are understandable, as parents have had their image of the ideal child compromised. They may be very disappointed, frustrated, or angry. These reactions are normal in such circumstances and should be expressed. It may be comforting to know that most individuals are surprised that they are able to cope even in the most difficult of circumstances. During an infant's initial development, never give up hope, as a precise diagnosis of the capacities of the child may not yet have been clearly defined. Similarly, children or adults who suffer serious disabilities as a result of an injury or disease may subsequently live fulfilling and productive lives. The first stage of adjusting to a disability is often perceived as being overwhelming, but try to continue to love and encourage your child, despite any feelings of rejection or withdrawal.

Denial

The second major stage is denial. People exhibit this reaction when they are shocked by a dramatic event that they refuse to accept. "This can't be happening to me." "It can't be my child." "Their diagnosis is wrong." "They don't know what they are talking about." These are typical statements made by someone in denial.

Denial may lead to a positive response. Many parents refuse to accept a negative diagnosis and consequently pursue physicians, strategies, and patterns of therapy that will generate rehabilitation and integration. Denial can also have negative effects. Some parents may spend thousands of dollars in fruitless attempts to locate a therapy that will make the child "normal." There are many dubious therapists and clinics offering parents false hopes and dreams. Denial may prevent acceptance of the diagnosis and subsequent treatment. It is important to accept the situation and to move forward in an effort to find a solution.

Fear and Frustration

The next stage is fear and frustration. Most parents experience some levels of fear, anxiety, and frustration as they cope with the problems of raising a new child. These feelings are legitimate responses to the unexpected disappointment of not having a healthy child. Counseling is often very helpful as it allows families to cope with these normal reactions. Parents usually expect their family physicians to provide information, strength, and direction. While most physicians lend valuable support to parents who encounter unforeseen situations, some doctors are overwhelmed by the extent of their professional obligation, and do not have an adequate amount of time or skills to provide parents with the explanations and comfort that they need.

At this point it may be worthwhile to solicit advice and support from close friends and family members. Social workers, psychologists, and case managers can also provide valuable reassurance and guidance. Most parents are inclined to believe that they can handle their situation without the intervention of others, but this belief is often false. There are usually supportive and helpful roles that professional caregivers and others can play for families in distress.

Adjustment

The final stage is adjustment. In raising a child with a disability, remember that adjustment is an ongoing process, and in order to maintain the adjustment phase, it is essential to maintain **open communication** between all family members. Husbands and wives should feel free to express their feelings, and relevant issues regarding their child's education and medical treatment. Complete adjustment is very difficult to achieve, **but it can be done!**

A major part of adjustment involves conveying a positive attitude to your spouse and all of your children. Maintaining a positive attitude means including the other children in discussions and activities involving the special needs of their sibling. It also involves creating time for the other children as well, so that they know that they are important beloved members of the family.

Some parents set aside time each week to spend with each child for recreational and other activities. This may include attending sporting events, concerts, going out for ice cream, and many other activities. All successful parents realize that each child is special. You cannot rely only on schedules, but try to always be available, as children encounter situations in which attention, encouragement, and reassurance are needed at any time. Emphasizing the importance of every member of the family makes the process of adjustment easier.

COPING WITH LOSS

Some children with disabilities die shortly after they are born. If your child has a terminal disability or dies as a result of injury or disease, you must allow time to mourn for your loss. If you have other children, you must take the responsibility of comforting them, as well as dealing with your own mourning. In this very difficult time, grief counselors, psychiatrists, psychologists, and religious leaders can be invaluable sources of support and comfort. Although many parents feel that they can deal with their loss on their own, it is usually advisable, especially for their children, that an outside resource be involved.

In the long run, professional grief counselors are crucial, as the loss of a child is frequently a major factor that leads to family breakdown. Spouses are sometimes inclined to blame each other and to act out their grief in other ways that include drinking, social isolation, refusal to discuss the problem, or fixation on the death. If these actions take place, they can create serious difficulties for the other spouse and surviving children. Grief counselors are fully aware of the short- and long-term consequences of loss, and can provide valuable strategies for maintaining the integrity of the family in stressful situations.

Grief counselors can be contacted through your local house of worship, social services agencies, hospitals, family physicians, relatives, and friends. Group counseling is a new and fast developing resource in this area.

NEGATIVE COPING

We've seen the importance of coping positively with your child's disability, and at the stages parents may go through in adapting to it. Within these stages, individual family members can exhibit many types of behavior that have negative effects on how the family copes as a whole. Parents can be overanxious, passive, depressed, overprotective, rejecting, isolating, withdrawn, or aggressive. Siblings are often jealous or withdrawn. The child with a disability can display anxiety, depression, withdrawal, aggression, undesirable behavior, and temper tantrums.

Negative Coping for Parents

- **Overanxiety:** When parents suddenly find themselves responsible for a child with special needs, they are often overwhelmed. They lack direction, purpose, and initiative. They feel self-pity and dwell on the tragedy that has happened, instead of looking at ways to alleviate the problem. These feelings can lead to excessive worry about every aspect of the child's life. They become afraid to make a decision and develop a tendency to withdraw. These feelings can prevent effective planning of the strategies necessary for their child's care.

- **Passivity:** Many parents feel overwhelmed by the task of raising a child with a disability, and for a few weeks, months, or even years, they are unable or unwilling to shoulder the responsibility of being fully involved in their child's care. Passivity is often linked to feelings of ignorance and a lack of confidence. By educating yourself in your child's condition and by consulting advocacy groups, experts, and other parents with similar problems, you can overcome most tendencies toward passivity.

- **Depression:** Like overanxiety, depression is a common reaction to the birth of a child with a disability, or to the consequences of an accident or disease that may bring about a disability. For a short period of time, depression is an understandable reaction, but it is necessary to overcome it. Depression often leads to inaction, and if you feel that you are experiencing lingering feelings of depression over your child's disability, you should seek counseling.

- **Overprotection:** Many parents are inclined to be over-protective of their child, and shield him from any experience that might be *potentially* harmful. It is important to combat this tendency as soon as it arises, or else your child may be prevented from fully growing up and developing.
- **Rejection:** Some parents reject their children who have disabilities; they cannot cope with the embarrassment they feel. In other cases, parents do not have the emotional maturity or financial resources to undertake their difficult task. Therapy can frequently ease these feelings of rejection. If these feelings cannot be eliminated, however, the use of a foster home or possibly an adoption agency should be considered.
- **Isolation:** Some parents and siblings isolate the child with disabilities, feeling reluctant to include their special child in routine family activities such as recreational outings, shopping, vacations, and social gatherings. Isolation denies a child the opportunity to be accepted, to participate in family life, and to develop social skills. Often we don't realize that we are, in fact, keeping one part of our lives separate from the rest — the isolation is subconscious and unintentional. Take a look at what you do as a whole family. Are there any activities in which you don't include your special child?

Several years ago, a young woman in one of my classes became engaged to a fellow student. His family resided in a rural community some fifty miles from Waterloo. Over the course of several years of their relationship, his parents visited the couple on a weekly basis, but the young lady was never invited to the family farm. She finally insisted on visiting the farm, and discovered that her fiancé had two siblings with Down syndrome. He and his parents had never mentioned the existence of these children. The young woman was overwhelmed. She indicated to me that the children appeared to be loved, well cared for, and motivated to do as much as possible on their own, but she could not comprehend that the existence of these children had never been mentioned to her. Her fiancé's family's shame at having two children who were not "normal" had prevented them from including the children in family activities. This type of behavior is not unusual. The fact that it exists, however, does not mean that such behavior is acceptable.

- **Withdrawal:** Many parents are inclined to cut themselves off from their traditional social and recreational activities in the belief that they have overwhelming responsibilities for their special needs child. However, you can and should participate in as many social events as you can, and include your child with disabilities whenever possible.

- **Friction and Aggression:** Friction and aggression can result when parents blame each other for their child's disability. It can also occur when one parent does not believe that the spouse is doing his or her fair share of the work in caring for their child. This inability to cope can take the form of emotional or physical hostility, social isolation, alcoholism, drug abuse, separation, or divorce.

Negative Coping for Siblings

- **Jealousy:** Sibling rivalry is present in every household. It is particularly difficult for young children to understand the fact that children with disabilities will usually require more time and specialized care. As a result, other children often experience feelings of anger and jealousy. Try to explain as clearly as possible to your other children why their brother or sister needs special treatment. You should also try to spend as much quality time as possible with your other children.

- **Withdrawal:** Children may have similar experiences to those of their parents in terms of withdrawing from friends and activities. A child's withdrawal may, however, have more to do with embarrassment over having a brother or sister with a disability than with a sense of responsibility. If you see evidence of this type of behavior from one of your children, talk to him and encourage him to stay involved in school and leisure activities, and not to move away from his friends. Emphasize that there is nothing wrong with having a sibling with special needs, and that there is nothing to be ashamed of. You may also want to encourage him to bring his friends to your home so that these friends will not be uncomfortable around a child with a disability. Your children should always feel free to bring their friends back to your house; having a child with a disability should not prevent your home from having a warm, welcoming atmosphere.

Negative Coping for the Child with Disabilities

- **Anxiety:** Children with disabilities often display

anxiety, especially in new or strange situations, and withdraw from their surroundings. Each situation will be different, but you can alleviate some of the anxiety felt in new settings by explaining his condition to his classmates, teammates, or others. This can be done in the classroom, at birthday parties, camps, or in any other setting where the child is encouraged to be on his own. This will help lead to a sense of independence and self-esteem. You must emphasize to your child that it is okay to be different and that he has done nothing wrong. If your child can develop the confidence to explain his condition to every new acquaintance or gathering of people, this will also help alleviate his feelings of anxiety.

Strangers and younger children are prone to stare and occasionally make fun of people who are different. Even asking questions about why a condition exists often creates anxiety for the child who has a disability. You will not always be there to comfort your child; he must develop his self-confidence so he can deal with these situations **on his own.**

It is important to tell your child that he will often be subjected to rude and unacceptable behavior. It may be useful to **act out** these situations so that your child will learn how to effectively confront uncomfortable experiences. Role-playing these situations with a sense of humor will allow your child to enjoy while he is learning. Playing the role of a rude or insensitive passerby in an exaggerated manner will illustrate to your child that the people who treat him rudely are not worthy his concern. This is a difficult process, as a rude comment made in jest while acting is very different from the real thing. Your child will learn that some people are not well informed, and others are insensitive. Explaining to him that he should just let insults roll off his back is good advice, although this knowledge will not always alleviate the hurt. You can ease these hurt feelings by providing constant encouragement and support. The anxiety that accompanies a disability is a life-long problem, and while it can never be eliminated, any steps that you can take to minimize its impact will be worthwhile.

- **Depression and Shame:** A child with a disability will experience depression and shame for many of the same reasons that he experiences anxiety. Not being able to participate and accomplish the same things as his peers is hard. Children with disabilities are often not included in athletic and social pursuits, and being left out increases their feelings of inferiority. You can alleviate some of these feelings by providing support and building self-confidence. Including children with disabilities in all family activities and getting them to participate in a wide range of activities with other children will increase their sense of independence, self-esteem, and security.

- **Behavior Problems:** Some children demonstrate behavioral problems that are related to their disability. For example, some autistic children and some special needs children with attention deficit hyperactivity disorder may be inclined to misbehave without any apparent provocation. This problem can be alleviated, but not eliminated. Counseling, drug therapy, support, love, and encouragement can be used as treatment, but they may not always be effective. When a child's disability causes undesirable behavior, it's important to be very patient. The child is not willfully misbehaving, but the disability may make it seem so. It is important, however, to distinguish between misbehavior which is a result of the disability and which the child cannot control, and unacceptable behavior which the child can control. There is a significant difference between a child who swears and yells because of Tourette's syndrome, and one who swears and shouts because he is angry.

- **Temper Tantrums and Aggression:** All children may throw temper tantrums at one time or another. This is especially true for children under the age of ten. In addition to factors such as fatigue, which may induce temper tantrums and aggression, children with disabilities continually experience frustration because they are "different" and in many areas their disability can inhibit their regular participation. As such, some children with disabilities are even more likely to have temper tantrums.

  Aggression at later ages largely stems from the same feelings of frustration, isolation, and anxiety that caused problems at younger ages. In some cases, drug therapy may be appropriate. For instance, children suffering from attention deficit disorders often act out; Ritalin has been used to alleviate their behavior, allowing them to participate in regular school programs. Always be very careful in assessing the effects and side effects of drug therapy and the reasons why the therapy is prescribed. Many children suffer from overmedication, which can have further serious psychological and physical side effects. Any medication should be constantly supervised. Behavior modification and other therapies have also been used to diminish children's aggression. All of these options should be considered if your child continually misbehaves.

A FAMILY'S SUCCESS STORY

It is difficult to appreciate the extra work that is required to raise a child with serious disabilities. I know a couple who has three boys between five and eight years of age, who have multiple disabilities including attention deficit hyperactivity disorder (ADHD), Tourette's syndrome, obsessive compulsive disorder, allergies, and fine muscle weaknesses. They are very concerned about their sons because many children who exhibit the behavioral and academic problems that result from ADHD face an uncertain future as young adults, and often become involved in delinquent activities. The story of this couple's hard work and dedication is a fine example of the intensity of the commitment made by parents who make the effort to raise their children to become self-sufficient adults.

The family's day begins at 6:30 a.m. when all of the children must be woken up and given their medication, including Ritalin and clonidine. According to their mother, "They're f***ing nuts until the meds kick in — completely off the wall." The children have to take their medicine every three hours and need to be very carefully monitored for any side effects. One of the children, for example, developed an erratic heartbeat.

The children are washed, dressed, and given breakfast before they have to be taken to three different schools. It is not uncommon for fights and disturbances to break out during breakfast. The oldest child has been both verbally and physically abusive toward the middle brother. While this behavior has recently changed with these two becoming friends and beginning to play together, the middle child has started to abuse the youngest brother. This continuous conflict has caused no end of trouble for the parents.

One day, when driving the boys to school, one of the boys was hitting another with a bat. The mother told her son to stop but he refused. The mother then stopped the car and slapped the boy on the cheek, leaving a small mark. When dropping this child off at school, she advised his teacher that she had hit her son, alerting her that he had a difficult morning and might act out later in class. The teacher, by law, had to advise the school principal and then report the information to the Children's Aid Society. The CAS did the necessary follow-up by telephone. (Reporting to the CAS is now mandatory in many areas because of the focus on the abuse of children with disabilities. When there is an indication of abuse in any form, all people in positions of authority are required by law to report the incident to their local CAS.) The mother was upset and embarrassed.

The mother visits all three schools regularly and spends many hours a week in the boys' classrooms. The schools have placed two of the boys in special programs, and one boy has had the support of a part-time teaching assistant in the regular classroom. Another boy is taken to the home of a specialized teacher for tutoring several times a week. The cost of this tutor is $40.00 an hour. For the last year, the schools have had to cut back on support programs due to funding cuts. In light of the decreasing number of services available, both parents have learned to become advocates for their sons. They try to read everything available on their children's conditions, and if the educational programs their sons need are not in place, they develop alternatives. This involves a time commitment of many hours each week.

The mother felt that one of her most important sources of support was the local chapter of the ADHD parent group. The parents' group advised her on how to access the best medical and resource personnel, and the best educational and recreational programs. As she became more knowledgeable about her children's disabilities, the need for regular support group attendance diminished. After several years of hard work and learning, she discovered that she had become an advocacy expert. The parents are constantly examining new programs, medical interventions, and innovations in drug therapy. The children see a staggering number of professionals, including pediatricians, pediatric cardiologists, psychiatrists, psychologists, Tourette's specialists, social workers, educational specialists and teachers, hearing specialists, and occupational therapists. The parents assess each professional carefully, as they want to make sure that each specialist will treat their children with sensitivity, competence, and compassion.

In addition to therapy and school, the children are involved in recreational programs that include karate and gymnastics. The boys' potential is also being developed through their work with computers, which the two older children have become quite adept at using. They are able to work and play on it together, lessening the conflict between them.

While the boys are getting along together better, all sorts of loud disturbances can erupt for little or no apparent reason. The parents have placed outside locks on the boy's bedrooms to provide a secure environment for each of them during the brief periods when they become unmanageable. Being "unmanageable" means fighting with or hurting a brother, having temper tantrums, throwing toys or being otherwise destructive, and cursing. The boys have few friends and some of the neighbours show a distrust of the children and isolate the boys. The mother maintains that it is important to be open about the children's disabilities so that visitors can understand the behavior that they might witness.

Individually, the boys demonstrate an ability to behave quite well. One of the children spent an overnight visit with a friend and said it was the best night that he had ever had. When they are together, however, the boys feed off each other and create constant turmoil.

Both parents are highly educated. The father comes home each night after a hard day's work and still finds the energy and time to help with dinner, play with his sons, read them stories, and help put them to bed. In addition, he accompanies his wife to many of the necessary appointments regarding the children.

The main source of assistance for these parents comes from their support system. The boys' grandparents help out on a regular basis even though they live in different communities. They have regular baby-sitters who know the children and who are given reliable back-up plans should emergencies develop. The mother attends support groups, concerts, and movies with friends during the week, and on the weekends she spends quality time with her husband. Frequently, they get away for an evening at a motel close to home.

This mother is a very open person. She said, "I have had to become the boys' case manager. My main job is to get them what they need to become productive and to constantly monitor their medications, physical health, and school programs. In addition, I must be a mother, wife, and homemaker. There is a need to be on top of things all the time."

Recently, the parents found an overnight camp specializing in providing programs for children with attention deficit disorder. The camp provides a competent staff at a two to one camper ratio. The camp provides programs in all recreational activities designed to increase the children's self-esteem and independence. Programs take place in a noncompetitive atmosphere where encouragement is given for cooperation instead of winning. Campers have the opportunity to work with computers and engage in a well-rounded series of games, plays, and overnight canoe expeditions. In addition to the benefits provided to the children, the parents are provided with a three-week respite period in which they can relax, spend some time alone together, or go on a private vacation. The only downside to the camp is that it is very expensive, at $2,800.00 per child.

These parents are committed to their children and to each other. Their marriage is solid and the family unit is strengthened by the support network they have put together. This does not mean that the parents do not become frequently exasperated. The mother expressed distress as a result of the incident in which she admitted to slapping her child, but this illustrates the extreme anxiety that parents under such stress can experience. On occasion, the mother goes for a long walk in the neighborhood. On one of these 5 a.m. walks, she could hear her sons shouting inside her house from a block away. Even though the neighbors are aware of her sons' difficulties, such noisy disruptions create continuing embarrassment. She does not, however, let these embarrassments get to her, as she and her husband love their children very much and refuse to be deterred by people who do not understand their situation.

It can be very difficult to be responsible for one child with a disability, and the workload spirals when a parent has two or three children who require specialized care. With the help of a strong support system, these parents have applied the courage, strength, and devotion required to conscientiously undertake these responsibilities. They are special people, like many others who raise children who have disabilities, and their experiences serve as an example of what can be accomplished with the proper preparation and dedication.

The strength that your family shows will have the greatest impact on your child's long-term success. Maintaining close relationships with all members of your family requires sensitivity, intimacy, privacy, time for recreation, and openness. Each relationship is special, and you must make the effort to strengthen the bonds within your family so that you are able to meet and overcome the challenges posed by your child's disability.

Keep in mind that there is no one right way to raise your family; every family has its own way to meet its needs. A family's own strategies to cope work just as well, if not better, than what anyone else could suggest. Have faith in yourself, but don't be afraid to ask people outside your family for help — that's what they are there for. Always have the confidence that your family will succeed. Families have a lot more strength to adapt and cope than you might think!

The Responsibilities of Parenting a Child with Disabilities

Having a child with a disability presents additional parenting responsibilities and issues that you may be unprepared for. Not all parents will have to meet all of the challenges in this chapter, but if you are ready for them and have a plan to deal with them before problems arise, it will make your life much easier. By anticipating the physical, emotional, financial, and other needs of your child ahead of time, you will be better able to manage your time, and share in the joy your child will bring. It may not be easy, but it will be worthwhile.

DEALING WITH PRACTICAL PROBLEMS

The practical problems involved in raising a child with a disability cover everything from the physical to the financial.

Sleep Disturbances

Dealing with sleep disturbances is difficult for everyone, particularly working parents. In many instances you may have to obtain the support of volunteers or employees to successfully administer the necessary therapies, especially when there may be regular interruption of sleep.

Children with cystic fibrosis and asthma must be carefully monitored during their sleep, and electronic devices have recently become available that will sound a warning should a child experience breathing problems. Physicians and other medical experts are now directing parents to have their babies sleep on their backs to avoid Sudden Infant Death Syndrome (SIDS).

Physical Burdens Relating to Care

Many children with disabilities need help in toileting and in most, if not all, of their personal functions. This can be physically and emotionally demanding. It is one thing to change the diapers of an infant, but it is quite another to take responsibility for the toileting of a fifteen-year-old who cannot perform this function by herself. Many younger parents are able to care for children who require extensive physical care, but it becomes difficult as the children and parents age. In some instances parents desire to maintain "high-level care," but are unable to do so as they experience physical injury as a result of lifting and other required activities. Not all parents need to perform the same types of physically demanding tasks, but over an extended number of years the challenge of meeting their child's needs can become increasingly difficult. You may have to consider engaging help for tasks that you were once able to do yourself. This help can often be found among volunteers in the community, especially among high school and university students.

Parents experience increased emotional stress when they have to take part in repetitive, monotonous therapies to train their special needs children to progress through developmental stages. My parents spent hundreds of hours teaching me how to walk, and the boredom of the task and the uncertainty of success or failure was emotionally draining.

Complicated and Specialized Diets

Dietary requirements are often very important to a child's health. As children do not always eat at home, constant monitoring is difficult, but for some children it must be done. For example, an exposure to the slightest amount of peanut oil can have fatal consequences for a child who has a strong allergy to the substance. For children with some other conditions, such as infantile diabetes, the consumption of excess amounts of sugar can lead to serious health problems.

Read the ingredients of packages carefully; if you are eating out, let the restaurant staff know what your child is allergic to and ask questions concerning the ingredients, for example, including what oil they cook with, and what kind of nuts are in an item. If the ingredient lists are vague or if a waitperson is unsure of an ingredient, it is better to avoid the food, rather than take a risk. If your child is on a special diet, tell others who may have the temporary responsibility of providing meals for her exactly what food substances your child cannot have. It may be necessary for you to provide something for your child. For instance, if your child cannot have sugar and she is invited to a birthday party, you may have to send along an alternative treat for her to eat instead of the birthday cake.

As your child matures, she will be able to monitor most of her diet herself.

Extra Housecleaning

For children who are incontinent the extra care requirements are often quite tiring. Some children have extreme allergies to dust and other substances, and as a result their environment must be closely monitored and controlled. It's a good idea to always use "environmentally friendly" products and avoid agents such as lemon oil, ammonia, and most oven cleaners, which are toxic. Consult an allergy specialist for more specific advice about your child's situation. For example, many of these experts advise parents of children with breathing difficulties to avoid aerosol products, carpeting, and new paint. You might consider hiring someone to assist you with housecleaning. This will free up some time for you to spend with your child.

Modifications to the Family Residence

Houses often need to be made accessible for children with disabilities. For children in wheelchairs, it may be necessary to have ramps installed; for children who are hearing impaired, it is often advisable to have different lighting systems so that they can be aware of a doorbell, a ringing bell, or a fire alarm. Similarly, you can modify showers or bathtubs by installing handgrips, non-slip "grids," and specialized seats for those who have mobility impairments. Faucets permitting controlled temperatures are also available, and portable shower heads make bathing easier for children with special needs.

If you are handy with tools you may be able to undertake these projects yourself. If not, you can enlist the help of a local carpenter or an organization that specializes in building devices for people with disabilities. Contact your local support group or your family physician for names of these organizations. Many local engineers, contractors, and builders are developing an interest and talent in this area.

Relocation

Most families want to keep all of their members together, but children with disabilities who live in rural areas are often at a disadvantage because they do not always have access to medical personnel and rehabilitative facilities. As a result, parents may choose to move to areas where the necessary facilities are available. If moving the entire family is difficult, one parent or another family member may accompany the child to a setting where special facilities are available. Organizations such as Ronald McDonald House, which operates across North America, supply rooms for parents from rural areas for free or a minimal cost while their children are receiving treatment nearby. A directory of Ronald McDonald Houses can be obtained by writing to Ronald McDonald Charities, whose address is available in the directory in Appendix 2.

The Unpredictability of the Disease or Disability

Diseases and disabilities often take unpredictable turns, causing setbacks in recovery or therapeutic progress. This unpredictability demands emotional strength for maintaining optimism and stability in the family. Many children with severe disabilities make remarkable progress to reward the efforts of their family. Because this progress may take months or years to develop, it's important to keep your commitment to a rehabilitation process that might be very successful. On the other hand, some children do not make notable progress in spite of the best efforts and commitments of their families. As previously mentioned, some children become worse and others die as a consequence of their diseases and disabilities. Remember that you did everything possible to make the life of your child as fulfilling as possible.

The Financial Obligations
The costs of raising a child with a disability can sometimes grow into the tens of thousands of dollars and beyond. The consequences of this burden, and the ways in which you can alleviate it, are outlined in Chapter 11.

Discipline
If your child has been assessed as "trainable," try to undertake a compassionate but consistently firm approach to discipline. It is suggested that you use the strategies of positive reinforcement to motivate your child, even when she may not understand why her behavior is unacceptable. Complimenting, hugging, and stroking are all means of exhibiting positive support. Caregivers must also be taught and given permission to use these techniques to avoid potential abuse.

Don't be reluctant to discipline your child just because she happens to have a disability. If you do not teach your special child how to behave properly, she will have difficulty in establishing and maintaining friendships and in her academic and social pursuits.

If your child throws a tantrum, you must handle it in an appropriate way. It is always difficult to deal with a three-year-old who is kicking and screaming in the fresh produce section of the local supermarket. Disciplining the child verbally or by holding her may be necessary. Sometimes it is simply appropriate to let your child wear herself out. After your child's tantrum is over, sit her down and explain why her behavior was unacceptable, and perhaps dock her allowance or send her to her room. A child should always understand why she is being disciplined. I am *very* reluctant to suggest physical punishment because in many instances when parents resort to physical punishment, they themselves are out of control. Contemporary research on child-rearing maintains that physical punishment is considered to be unwarranted, no matter what the circumstances. Your child should learn the consequences of her actions, but she should not become fearful of her parents. She should understand that her parents are disappointed by the fact that she has behaved badly. She should learn not to misbehave because what she is doing is wrong, not because she fears punishment.

Treat a child with a disability with the same firmness and fairness as you would other children. If you have to punish her, it is important that you make clear the reason why she's being punished, and why her behavior is inappropriate. If she does not understand why she is being reprimanded, it is likely that she will repeat the same behavior. This will create many difficulties in her acceptance and progress.

If you do not treat your special child the same way that you treat your other children, she may become spoiled, as she knows that whatever she does will be accepted "because she has a disability." This should never happen. A child with a disability should be held to the same high standards of behavior as anyone else. As long as she understands her behavior, she should be held accountable for it. Not disciplining one child can also lead to resentment among brothers and sisters, as they will perceive you as acting unfairly. Allowances can be made for a child with a disability, but she should not be treated as a "Golden Child" who can do no wrong.

SHARING THE JOY AND SHARING THE PAIN

Have you ever contemplated being a member of a group that was different, excluded, and isolated due to conditions over which you had no control? Being a member of this group would cause you physical, social, and psychological anguish. Members do not choose to be a part of this group, but they are still affected by physical pain, institutionalization, social and psychological segregation, rejection, exclusion from public places, undereducation, and discrimination in employment. This is what it often means to be a person with a disability.

The child who has a disability often experiences testing, probing, examination, pain, and embarrassment. It is difficult for an adult to respond positively under similar circumstances. How difficult do you think it must be for a baby or child? Being exposed to these things is difficult for a child to understand. Most adults realize that injections and uncomfortable examinations are occasionally necessary to alleviate the pain that can come with disability or disease. However, many children, particularly young children, will disguise any pain in order to avoid the discomfort of further examinations. As a parent, you have to realize that your child does not necessarily reason in the same way that you do and that they deal with the world as children, not as adults. They often view their parents as members of the other side, holding them down, screaming at them, forcing drugs into their mouth, and forcing them to comply with painful treatment.

It is difficult to make a young child realize that treatment is for her own good. Her fear, her pain, and her suffering are very real. Teenagers have run away from home to avoid the effects of chemotherapy and radiation used to treat cancer. Recently, a fifteen-year-old cancer sufferer ran away from home because he believed he had experienced too much pain as a result of the chemotherapy and radiation. He felt that his parents were forcing him to undergo the therapy, which produced many painful and embarrassing side effects. The young man believed that he had the right to forgo therapy, and that he would rather die than be exposed to more of the resulting side effects. His parents turned to the media to help search for their son. After being made aware through a newscast that he was the object of a nation-wide search, he contacted his parents and returned home to continue his treatment.

It's important to discuss the nature of a disability and disease with children so that they are able to understand the difficulties they will encounter, and to accept the treatment. Parents often find it hard to treat their children as adults, but the time comes when you have to grant your children a measure of autonomy.

What Can I Do to Share the Pain?

Children facing the dilemmas associated with disability require allies. Sometimes medical personnel are not sensitive enough to the pain many children with disabilities feel. As a parent it is your job to alleviate as much of your child's pain as you possibly can. What your child needs most of all is the secure knowledge and trust that her parents will do everything possible not only to aid in rehabilitation, but also to protect her from all the types of physical, social, and emotional pain she may encounter.

Easing the Physical Pain

Doctors will normally prescribe standard painkillers for your child, but other, more unconventional, methods of pain relief are also effective. Rubbing a sore limb with topical anesthesia (often available from your pharmacist without prescription), a procedure not widely used, can ease much of the pain that comes with inoculations and injections. Your family doctor will be able to prescribe creams, ointments, or medications that are specifically designed to lessen the pain associated with many procedures. Hypnosis, yoga, acupuncture, chiropractic, and homeopathic medicines are all innovative methods that can be used to make a child's experiences less painful. You can obtain information about these alternative treatments in larger urban centers where these disciplines are practiced, as well as from libraries and the Internet. Before proceeding with any alternatives, consult the primary caregivers to make sure they are compatible with already prescribed therapies.

Again, when your child is undergoing treatment, try to explain that she is suffering pain for a reason. Tell her that all the needles, pokes, and prods she is going through now will make her feel better in the future — that they are trying to help her walk better, or stand straighter, or join a regular classroom. The ability of your child to understand this information will vary with her age, but it is important to emphasize at an early age that **there will be a benefit** to undergoing the treatment.

It may also be appropriate to treat your child to something special after a particularly painful appointment. Take her out to a movie, treat her to ice cream, or buy her a toy or a book as a reward for being a good patient. If you can build a positive incentive into therapy that will make your child a more willing and enthusiastic patient, these efforts will certainly have been worthwhile. Constant reinforcement in the form of encourage-ment, love, and inclusion in all activities will usually motivate them to continue to deal with the discomforts of treatment.

Easing the Social and Emotional Pain
Physical pain is not the only discomfort associated with disability. Children with disabilities often have to confront social and emotional pain. No one likes being isolated, laughed at, or rejected. As difficult as this is for adults, it is worse for children, who often lack confidence and are easily hurt. Realizing that one is different and has a disability can be crushing to children's self-esteem. They experience the frus-tration, awareness, and consequences of being set apart and excluded from regular activities. Children with disabilities frequently miss school programs because of the requirements of therapy, are not invited to birthday parties, and are forced to stay home from trips: all of these exclusions can have neg-ative impacts on a child's identity.

Another type of pain children with disabilities experience is known as anticipatory pain. Many children with disabilities will anticipate uncomfortable situations and avoid them, as they do not want to endure any suffering. A child may fake a stomachache in order to avoid attending a birthday party. She is afraid to say, "I don't like being teased, laughed at, stared at, and being alone in a group where others are having fun," and instead will invent symptoms that will allow her to avoid a potentially uncomfortable situation. Frequently children without disabilities will ask, "What's wrong with you?" This request may be nothing more than a desire for an explanation. However, a child with a disability may feel uncomfortable if everyone is looking at her, and that giving an answer to the question is a public admission of inferiority.

What Is My Role?

As a parent, you are there to share your child's pain. You are a positive part of her identity, and share in many of her activities. Hopefully you will always be a supportive part of her life. In addition to sharing the pain, you should also employ innovative techniques to motivate your child to participate and enjoy all the activities that are available to her. Explaining to a child at age five, ten, or fifteen why she is different, and how she should deal with this difference, can be very hard. You must start early, and your child must believe from day one that you, your family, and your friends are striving to maintain an atmosphere of love, trust, security, and integration.

The attitude that you want your child to adopt is "Accept me for who I am — if you can't, then that's your problem, not mine." This attitude is difficult for anyone to adopt, especially a child. Nonetheless keep pushing her in that direction. Very seldom do the problems for children with disabilities occur because their parents have encouraged them to "go for it!" Most of these problems are created by people who are ignorant and influenced by traditional (and invalid) stereotypes of people with disabilities.

In many cases you will be able to understand the pain that your child is experiencing. You will not, however, be aware of everything that she is going through. Be open to the fact that your child's frustrations and anxieties may increase, and that she may cope with these experiences in a variety of ways. Try to be sensitive to all of the efforts she makes to deal with the barriers she faces.

Later on, your child will probably realize what you as parents went through and voice her appreciation of the efforts that you have made on her behalf. Most children do not appreciate the sacrifices that their parents have made until after their teenage years. And most parents are not looking for gratitude, as they feel success when their child advances. My parents always told me that the highlights of their lives could be gauged in my successes — high school graduation, a B.A., an M.A., and finally my Ph.D. My father said that he could not have been prouder if he had obtained the degree on his own. When I published my first book, my parents were in ecstasy and gave copies to many of their friends. I published my seventh book before my father passed away, and dedicated it to my parents. My mother and dad never dreamed of such success, and they claimed that my accomplishments were their accomplishments. I had more than fulfilled their dreams. My accomplishments demonstrated to my parents that their efforts had given me the opportunity to live and enjoy a very rewarding life.

You don't want your child to feel that "she owes you." You want her to feel that she is a secure member of the family, and that she will be loved unconditionally. If you can make it clear to your child that her success will mean more than anything that she can say or give to you, and if you push her to the best of her abilities, then you will have done your job well.

DISABILITY AND THE OVERPROTECTIVE PARENT

Many children with disabilities, like their adult counterparts, are reluctant to take on new experiences because of the embarrassment and other negative emotions that come with it. This reluctance is sometimes encouraged by overprotective parents, who may be concerned about the difficulties that their children will encounter, especially when the parents are not present to offer security and protection.

My parents told me that everybody gets hurt at one time or another, and always encouraged me to participate — so I did. The first time I broke my nose I was sliding down an ice-covered hill on my feet — an activity that is dangerous for anyone. The second time, my nose was smashed during a soccer match. I was playing goalie, and as I was lying on the ground pulling the ball toward me, someone kicked me in the face with a square-toed soccer boot.

Some children with disabilities want to experience absolutely everything possible. I have met many children in wheelchairs who are always willing to jump into a pool or onto a mat in order to enjoy themselves. This is not the typical reaction of children in wheelchairs, as many kids tend to regard the chair as a symbol of security they should never leave. But as one nine-year-old in a chair stated, "Lift me and carry me anywhere, as I want to go where the chair can't." Taking risks allows children to participate with their friends and to be open to new and challenging experiences. Horseback riding, wheelchair basketball, golf, and the Special Olympics program are but a few of the many activities that are now open to children and adults with disabilities. I met a man at a conference on disability who was born without feet and who climbed mountains and flew his own plane. His perspective was "I did it, and I will always have the courage to go for it." This same spirit has led me to mountain climb and try white-water rafting.

This fearless attitude is often scary for parents; it's hard to let a child be independent — especially if there is a possibility of the child getting hurt. Overprotection, however, is more dangerous, as it may prevent a child from enjoying experiences that will increase her self-esteem and encourage her to exceed her limits. If all reasonable safety precautions have been taken, I recommend that you encourage your special child to pursue these kinds of activities, whenever she shows an interest. Everyone should be realistic about their limitations, but within those parameters they should take chances and enjoy the rewards that will result.

AVOIDING UNNECESSARY RISKS

I'm always amazed at the large number of serious accidents that occur in the home. Falling down stairs, electrical shocks, spills from the stove, and poisoning from household objects are all dangers that face children daily and can be largely avoided. As a parent, take every reasonable precaution to ensure your child's safety and well-being both in and out of the home. This is particularly true for children with disabilities, who may be more prone to have accidents or who may experience difficulties in unfamiliar situations.

Follow the same commonsense safety preparations that you would do for any child. Keep all household cleansers, dish detergents, and other toxic substances out of your child's reach. All medications should be properly labeled and out of your child's reach. Fire can be a deadly hazard to children with sight or hearing impairments; install smoke and carbon monoxide detectors on every floor of your dwelling (there are available special sight and vibration detectors for the hearing impaired). Also, teach your children what to do in case of a fire or other emergency.

Bathtub safety can be ensured by always testing the water temperature before putting your baby into the water, and through constant supervision. Even leaving a child alone for one or two minutes to answer the phone can be potentially fatal. Put gates at the top and bottom of all your stairways. Avoid any toys that are small enough to fit into your child's mouth, and suspend any mobiles high enough above your child's crib that they face no danger of choking. Check all beds and cribs for pieces that could possibly be chewed off and choked on. Plug up all electrical outlets when not in use, and check all cords to make sure that they are not frayed or have any wire showing. In the car, place your child in the rear seat, in an appropriately sized car seat, and any young child in a wheelchair should be buckled in.

Keep emergency numbers by the phone, as well as the number of your family doctor. A knowledge of cardiopulmonary resuscitation (CPR), may also come in handy, especially if your child suffers from respiratory or seizure problems. The Red Cross, local hospitals, and even some schools and community centers offer CPR courses.

Not all accidents can be avoided, of course, but if you are careful and thorough you can minimize the risks of any accidents occurring in your home. When I was twelve years old my parents took me to a resort. As I had had three years of swimming lessons, my parents assumed that I could look after myself, especially in a supervised pool. Halfway across the pool I had a panic attack, and I might have drowned had I not been rescued by three swimmers who were close to me. A child with a disability may normally be able to accomplish many tasks independently, but they may also be more vulnerable to such incidents. You and your child's other caregivers should always be aware of the potential for accidents, but you should not worry so much that you prevent your child from enjoying themselves and attempting new experiences.

WHEN CRISES ARISE

Make no mistake about it, caring for any child can be *very* difficult, and there is often increased stress involved in raising a child with a disability. In many instances emergencies occur, and parents and other caregivers may be required to act instantaneously. These crises can be emotional, psychological, physical, organizational, social, and/or financial. For some, crises occur regularly (e.g., seizures related to epilepsy and other conditions) and for others they develop from particular circumstances. For example, children with diabetes or breathing difficulties related to asthma may go into shock. This reaction requires treatment and in some cases immediate hospitalization. It is necessary, therefore, that you understand what to do in these situations and anticipate when they might occur so you'll be able to respond to them in an appropriate way. Also, teach these requirements to other competent caregivers so that emergency treatment can be given in your absence.

If it is appropriate, provide your child with a MedicAlert bracelet, as she may be in an environment where people are unaware of her difficulties or allergies. Some children with malignant hyperthermia (a genetically influenced condition that causes some children to be highly allergic to certain anesthetics) can only tolerate certain types of anesthetics, and may also have life-threatening reactions to extreme changes in temperature; a MedicAlert bracelet will ensure that medical personnel find this information readily available.

As children with disabilities, diseases, and allergies get older, it is crucial to involve them more closely in their own care whenever possible, as they can recognize the warning signs before anyone else. If your child is completely familiar with her own condition and she acts responsibly, she will usually be able to avoid or avert crises on her own. A child with a fatal allergy to peanut-related products can be taught to ask about the ingredients of what she is eating, and thereby avoid any dangerous foods. Some children as young as six years old carry serum to protect themselves from insect stings to which they are allergic. If children are made aware of their own needs they can respond appropriately if a crisis occurs and ease the pressure that their parents encounter.

SEXUALITY AND DISABILITY

It is very important to be able to communicate openly with your special child, so that you feel comfortable discussing any topic with them. Many parents have difficulties discussing sexual matters with their children. Even though you may feel uncomfortable with discussions of this nature, it is important that teenagers and adults with disabilities receive accurate information about sexuality so that their sexual feelings can be accepted and handled properly. While children gain some information from the mass media and from their friends, you should be there as a trusted resource that is available to provide them with understanding and support.

Sex education for all children begins at an early age. Many excellent books designed for children of all ages are available in most public libraries. Try to either read these books and share the information with your children, or provide the books for your child to read. Respond to all of their questions in an open, supportive manner.

If you feel uncomfortable discussing sex-related issues with your child, you can refer their questions to a doctor, nurse, sexual planning counselor, friend, relative, or member of the clergy who will be more prepared to help solve their problems.

Problems That Are Faced in Sexual Relationships

Because they are "different," teenagers and adults with disabilities often experience extra pressures and difficulties in sexual relationships. Many adolescents with disabilities experience isolation and rejection. In some cases teenagers with disabilities, especially females, find themselves in exploitive dating situations where they are told to submit to advances or their relationship will end. Thus, not only do you have to provide knowledge of sexuality, but you have to teach your child how to say no and how to avoid situations of potential abuse. Teach her what sort of behavior is and is not acceptable, and how to refuse unwanted advances. This is closely tied to the process of developing and maintaining your child's self-esteem, so that your child will feel good enough about herself that she will not feel the need to get involved in a potentially harmful relationship.

It is a common misperception that people with disabilities cannot or do not want to experience sexual pleasure. In most cases people with disabilities have the same needs, drives, and desires as everyone else. People in wheelchairs and those with severe cerebral palsy and other disabilities can and do experience positive and fulfilling relationships. Sexuality does not only have to involve intercourse, as it can include love that is given and received in many ways, including touching, holding, and being touched. Trained counselors can help men and women who are paraplegics or face other difficulties to enjoy love and warmth through alternative measures. The field of specialists in sexual counseling for people with disabilities is rapidly growing, and these counselors can provide the information, support, and techniques that are necessary to help your child lead a more fulfilling life. Specialists in sexual counseling can include doctors, nurses, psychiatrists, psychologists, social workers, case managers, or teachers. Take advantage of their knowledge and skills, or encourage your child to get guidance from them whenever possible. If you are feeling uncertain about what advice to give your child or how to answer your child's questions, it may be helpful to discuss matters of sexuality that relate to your child with these experts. You may also find that members of your parental support group can provide helpful and caring advice.

Although none of the responsibilities that I have outlined in this chapter is easy, neither is it insurmountable. By going one step at a time and breaking down what you have to do into manageable parts, what can at first seem like a tremendous burden can become a part of your daily routine that you manage with ease. Try not to dwell on what you *have* to do for your special child, but instead think of what you love to do with them. You will share joy and pain with your child, but if you are well prepared to meet their needs at all times, the moments of joy will far outnumber the moments of pain.

Chapter
6

How to Handle Stress and Avoid Burnout

Raising a child is stressful, but the added responsibilities of raising a child who has a disability create different challenges from those faced by parents of children without disabilities, and can lead to increased stress. Because of these extra pressures, parents of children with disabilities are especially susceptible to burnout. Thus it is very important that you be aware of what stress is, what causes it, and how to best cope with it.

WHAT IS STRESS?

According to Dr. Peter Hanson, in his excellent book *The Joy of Stress*, stress is an individual reaction. Stress can come from your job, from your family, and even from the news on TV. If you handle stress poorly, it can be fatal, but if you channel stress into the right areas it can help you accomplish your goals and even help you live longer. Limited amounts of stress can increase your efficiency by heightening your level of attention and pushing you to work harder. The positive effects of stress can be seen in the electric performance of an actor on opening night and in-the-clutch shooting of a basketball player in the closing minutes of a championship game. However, if you experience too much stress your efficiency falls rapidly, and you can even become counterproductive. Dr. Hanson advises that you learn to ignore what you can't control, and learn to manage what you can. If you take control of the areas in your life that cause you stress, you will be able to deal with the problems of raising your special child in a more efficient manner.

Signs of Stress

As a parent of a child with a disability the added tasks that you may have to perform can lead to an increase in stress. Irritability, depression, anxiety, insomnia, aggression, and all types of abuse are signs of mismanaged stress.

These emotions and behaviors can have a dramatic impact on the family. If you notice that you or any other member of your family begins to exhibit some or many of these behaviors, there may be a need for outside intervention.

Sources of Stress

By identifying the sources of stress in your life, you will be better able to control their effects and live a healthier, more productive life. Stress evolves from many situations. The most prevalent forms of stress occur in the following areas:

1. **Personal Stress:** This is the stress experienced by parents when they learn that their child has a disability, and through their everyday coping with it. The life that parents may have envisioned for their child often becomes dramatically compromised when they realize that he may have to overcome serious physical and emotional barriers. All the other sources of stress are part of this stress.

2. **Stress Between Parents:** This is the stress that accumulates between parents as a result of disagreements, frustrations, and difficulties faced in the raising of a child with special needs. You must protect your marriage by maintaining an honest and open relationship in which you are always willing to discuss the issues. If resentments and grudges are not expressed and allowed to fester and grow, they can lead to unnecessary problems.

3. **Stress Between Parents and Other Children:** As we saw in Chapter 4, younger children often feel ignored and isolated when a sibling has a disability, because they do not receive as much attention and affection as they had grown accustomed to. As a consequence they may become extremely jealous and misbehave. Older children may become resentful because of the added responsibilities they must shoulder. They, too, have a tendency to act out or rebel. Obviously, this misbehavior adds to the stress experienced by a parent.

4. **Stress Among Extended Family Members:** Many members of the extended family may ignore the fact that your child has a disability. People often experience isolation from relatives who are uncomfortable around a child that is different. Other family members, on the other hand, will rally to your support. They may even provide positive stress by pushing you to do the most for your child. You must be forthcoming with all of your family members and explain your child's situation. You can minimize the stress among the extended family members by clearly describing your family's needs and requirements in raising your special child, and by trying to include them in your family's life.

5. **Stress of Diagnosis:** Some diagnoses are easy to obtain, but others may take months, if not years to make correctly. Because the first signs of scleroderma (a serious disorder in which the skin hardens and internal organs break down as the result of an inflammation of the skeletal muscles, the heart, and other internal organs) are unclear, it can take up to five years to diagnose, and it is often misdiagnosed as rheumatoid arthritis or muscular dystrophy. The extended period of waiting and uncertainty obviously produces stress. While it is impossible to avoid worrying completely, do not dwell on something over which you have no control. Focus only on readily available ways to deal with the problem, and be ready to work with professionals once a diagnosis is made.

6. **Stress of Unknown Outcomes:** There are many diseases and disabilities for which the long-term outcome is initially unknown. For instance, cancer can be fatal for some children, yet others make a full recovery. The inability to forecast the future need not prevent you from creating a positive, loving atmosphere for your child. Not knowing what the result of your child's condition will be can serve as a motivating factor. As the outcome is unknown, you have the opportunity to change it. By channeling your uncertainty into hard work on your child's behalf, you can make the stress of unknown outcomes a positive stress.

7. **Stress of the Possibility of Painful, Terminal Conditions:** If you know that your child may have only a short period of time to live, you may want to enlist the support of counselors, doctors, relatives, and friends who can help to provide you and your family with a warm, supportive atmosphere. Your spouse and other children will require your love, your support, and sympathy at this time more than any other. It can become incredibly difficult to attempt to meet their needs while you are also suffering. It is at this time that professional counseling can be most helpful.

8. **Stress of Ongoing Tests and Treatment:** Many children with disabilities undergo painful treatments that often leave them reluctant to continue with their therapy. This puts a terrible burden on both you and your child. If your child experiences severe burns or

another disability whose treatment often involves severe pain and stress, you must give them all of the support that you can, and try to convince them that the treatment is necessary so that they will eventually be able to enjoy life more fully. In some instances, all that you may be able to do is be there with your child. At other times you may be able to bring gifts, toys, video games, and other treats. It can be very helpful to bring in relatives and friends to visit, as this will give him tremendous encouragement and support. If your child has been confined to a hospital or rehabilitation center for an extended period of time, bringing him home to visit for a weekend can often alleviate some of the stress he may feel.

Parents and caregivers often have to endure long waits in specialists' offices for diagnosis and treatment. This is difficult for both parents and their children. Usually, parents have to comfort their children during this time, and motivate them to undergo sometimes painful tests and therapies as best they can.

9. **Stress of Relationship Between Parents and Case Managers:** Many parents work with case managers who are experts in the management of the disability and who know how to obtain the support that is necessary for the best treatment of their child. In some instances, however, parents may feel overwhelmed by the personality and power of the case manager. It is always necessary to select a case manager with whom you can openly communicate. Some parents may choose to eliminate this potential source

of stress by assuming the role of their child's case manager.

10. **Stress of the Relationships Between Parents and Professional Care Providers**: This is similar to the stress between parents and case managers, yet unlike with case managers, most parents cannot undertake medical roles or the roles of educators and therapists. In cases where a relationship with a professional is not going smoothly, it is not always possible or advisable to change personnel. Try to remember that professionals are involved in many cases beside your own. Sometimes a brusque manner and cool personality merely reflect the fact that a doctor is involved with many cases and is just attempting to do his best. Some professionals, however, go beyond the bounds of what many parents feel is acceptable, and may insist on using drugs or other therapies that you question. Or they may not adequately inform parents of the nature and risks of surgical procedures, even though you must sign a consent form authorizing the surgery. Their explanations may sometimes be too short and couched in medical jargon.

If you feel that your child's physician has gone beyond these bounds, you may decide that it is appropriate to select another specialist. Changing to someone who is more open-minded and friendly, or who has more time for you, may solve your problem. If changing personnel is not an option, then a frank discussion with the service provider may alleviate the problem.

11. **Stress of Decision-Making:** As parents you will be required to make lots of decisions, many of them quite difficult. No matter how hard the choices become, remember that you know your child best, that you care for your child and love him more than anyone else in the world, and that you are always trying to do your best. Do not worry about choices that you have made in the past. If you do make a mistake, it is crucial to learn from your error and move on, rather than wallowing in regret. Always look to the future, not to the past.

12. **Financial Stress:** In most instances, a number of extra costs accumulate as a result of having the responsibility of caring for a child with a disability. See chapters 3 and 11 for ways to meet the challenge of funding. Remember that there are often resources available that can help you out.

13. **Stress of Ongoing, Unrelieved Responsibilities:** Caring for children is an ongoing responsibility. In assuming the special tasks required for the care of children with disabilities, it is important not to attempt to do everything on your own. Gather support and a commitment to help from family members, support groups, volunteers, professionals, and others. The more people with whom you share the work of raising your child, the less stress you will feel.

14. **Stress of Social Isolation Due to Responsibilities:** As illustrated, many parents and families experience

social isolation when it is known that they have a
child with a disability. This can lead to feelings of
alienation, abandonment, and inferiority. To avoid
these feelings, it is important to educate friends and
family about your child's disability, as well as to
make an extra effort to allow them to feel comfortable with you and your child. In some instances you
will not be able to attend previously scheduled parties, meetings, and work hours because of crisis
situations that sometimes result as a part of raising
your child. Therefore it is necessary that all your
friends and coworkers be aware of your responsibilities. But don't go into a shell after your special child
is born. A night out with friends for dinner or a
show can have a positive, rejuvenating effect, and
reduce the general level of stress that you feel.

15. **Stress of Relocation:** Any move is a source of stress.
    As medical attention and therapy may not be avail-
    able, some parents choose to relocate on a part- or
    full-time basis so that their child can benefit from
    treatment that is not available at home. Keep in mind
    the benefits that will be reaped by your child in the
    short and long term as a result of your move.

16. **Stress of Advocacy Roles:** As we saw in Chapter 3, it
    is difficult but productive to learn the strategies of
    advocacy. Being an advocate may involve added
    stress as you will be forcing others (in a legitimate
    way) to respond to your child's needs. By learning
    the strategies of advocacy you will improve your

child's opportunities and those of other children who have the same condition. Remember that the stress that you feel as a result of your efforts will be repaid many times over in your joy at your child's success.

HOW DO I COPE WITH STRESS?

People react to stress in many ways, some healthy, and some not. When dealing with stress, especially over an extended period of time, you can become angry. This is most likely to occur when you are tired, disappointed, frustrated, or over-worked. Sooner or later we all make mistakes, and we may react in ways that are socially or legally unacceptable. In frustration we may scream at caregivers, our spouse, or our children. When these situations occur, apologize. Most of the time your friends, family members, and professionals will recognize that you are going through a difficult period, and understand your reaction. By apologizing you will maintain their respect.

The following is a list of ways in which you can positively deal with stress:

- Talk about your problems with an expert such as a psychiatrist, a psychologist, a physician, clergyperson, or social worker.
- Calmly confront those who are causing you stress.
- Take a brief vacation (a nice dinner without the kids, a brief weekend out of town) to ease the pressure.
- Talk about your problems with a close friend or family member.

- Engage in a favorite leisure activity — go for a walk, take a nap, have a shower, read a favorite book, listen to music, write a letter, or play a sport.

COUNSELING

Whether a family is united or disrupted by the impact of a child's disability depends on a family's maturity, its coping skills, its recognition and understanding of the problem, and its physical and emotional strengths. Although most families gradually adapt to the situation, the process often requires the support of medical personnel and skilled counselors. These professionals are familiar with the stresses of dealing with a disability and are skilled in the physical and psychological techniques required for successful coping.

Counseling will not eliminate the grief associated with severe permanent disability or the death of a child, but it will allow you, your mate, your children, and your relatives to grieve and cope in a healthier manner. Counseling usually alleviates the anger and blame-placing that is often associated with these events. Going to a counselor does not in any way mean that you are inferior or incapable. There should be no stigma attached to taking advantage of counseling. It is merely one of the resources available to ease the difficulties of raising a child with a disability. If you were confronted by a legal problem, you would seek the advice of a competent lawyer. Similarly, a competent counselor will familiarize you with all of the strategies available to help you successfully raise your child.

Many factors, such as increased family tension, sibling

rivalry, and unresolved frustration with professionals and caregivers, may indicate the need for counseling, but there is no set guideline that dictates when counseling is necessary. Some parents are reluctant to rely on counselors because their initial exposure to them has been unsatisfactory. Don't give up on counseling after one bad experience. Even if one counselor has not met your needs, it does not mean that all counselors will be unable to do so.

Selecting a Counselor

Choosing the right counselor for your family is very important — in many respects it's like choosing a friend. Most social workers, psychologists, psychiatrists, members of religious groups, and others who offer counseling are competent, but it is important to work with a counselor with whom you have some personal chemistry. Some people "hit it off," while others discover that it is difficult to initiate a trusting relationship. With your counselor, everything must be open, and you must feel free to "put everything on the table." For many individuals, it is often difficult to establish this trusting relationship, but it is worth the effort, as everyone involved benefits from effective counseling. The counselor can be very helpful in explaining how the disability will affect a family, and can help to maintain a healthy family structure during times of stress.

The characteristics to look for in a good counselor are:

- compassion
- awareness of the strategies available to select medical and paramedical treatment
- willingness to discuss the available strategies with you

and involve you in the decision-making process
(you must always be able to provide **informed** consent)
- always seeking new strategies in situations where
diagnoses and prognoses are not clearly established
- desire and ability to provide counseling to your children, parents, and other individuals who desire to be
involved in the care and integration of your child.

FAMILY PRESSURES AND DISABILITY

The decision to care for a child with a disability involves a
long-term commitment. In some families the mother wishes to
assume the responsibilities, while the father is reluctant. In
other instances the father insists on caring for the child in
spite of his wife's reluctance. This conflict over the care of the
child will lead to an accumulation of stress that can be very
harmful to the strength of a marriage.

I know a couple who were married for ten years and had
one child whom they adored. A second son was born who
had Down syndrome. Initially, both parents assumed the
responsibility of caring for their child, but over the course of
his first three years, the parents' relationship deteriorated.
The mother became intent on having the child with Down
syndrome institutionalized. The father, after surveying the
available institutions, refused to do this, as he believed that it
was his obligation to care for his son. He felt that institutional
care lacked the warmth and caring he considered vital for his
son's well-being. The mother left her husband, taking her
older son with her, and for the last ten years, the father has
been a committed sole caregiver.

AVOIDING BURNOUT

Parents are sometimes overwhelmed by the work involved in taking care of their child with special needs. In performing this work, they often neglect their emotional responsibilities toward each other. It is important not only to share the responsibilities, but to continue to enrich your own relationship with your spouse, other children, and extended family members. Don't focus on the singular aspect of providing the necessary care for your child. The importance and vitality of other relationships must always be maintained and enhanced.

Not only are other relationships important to sustain, you also need to look after yourself. Many parents of children who have disabilities feel guilty if they take care of their own needs. But total concentration on your child at the expense of your own well-being is highly stressful and can be detrimental to your health. If you fail to meet your own emotional and physical needs, the stress that you experience can lead to anger, weakened family relationships, and a decrease in the quality of care your special child will receive.

Recreation, rest, and participation in social events are critical elements of self-care. In order to keep up your commitment to your child and a high quality of care, it is necessary that you take breaks so that you can regularly "recharge your batteries." These activities do not necessarily have to cost much money, as you can go for walks, engage in window shopping, read, or participate in a number of other activities that provide rest and relaxation. Taking at least one night off every week to see a movie or go out for dinner is important to allow you to keep up a high level of energy. A regular program of physical fitness is also important. You can go jogging, join a health club, a basketball league, or find a regular tennis partner. The specific activity is not important, as long as you **do something!** Plan your time off carefully and organize caregivers well in advance.

WHAT IS BURNOUT?

Every human being has limits. Burnout takes place when an individual or family literally cannot "take it any more," and they become physically and psychologically overwhelmed by the responsibilities of providing care. While people are sometimes aware of the stresses affecting their lives and are able to contend with them, they are sometimes overcome by stress that is unforeseen. People who experience burnout have far higher rates of divorce, alcoholism, headaches, and depression than the general population. Occasionally these individuals resort to bizarre patterns of behavior, including abuse and occasionally even the murder of their children.

In Canada in late 1994, in two separate instances, parents murdered their children who had cerebral palsy. One of these parents took her own life at the same time. In these tragic situations, it emerged that the parents did not have adequate access to the facilities and support that would have allowed them to maintain their child's quality of life. Both of these families lacked a sufficient back-up system that could have helped them deal with the pressures of raising their children. In these cases the community did not provide sufficient resources to allow the families to share their burden, leading to a buildup of stress and tension that ultimately had tragic consequences.

People usually suffer in silence for long periods of time

before experiencing burnout, and when burnout occurs relationships with other people such as case workers, the clergy, and friends become frayed, if not dissolved. The intimate relationships of parents under severe stress also deteriorate, and the people with the heaviest responsibilities feel isolated and depressed. Single parents are particularly vulnerable to burnout, as they do not have a partner with whom to share the responsibilities of their child's care.

How Do I Avoid Burnout?

One of the first strategies that you must adopt to avoid burnout is to create a "crisis support system." This system consists of a confidant or a group of individuals who will share the necessary responsibilities with you when emergencies occur. Their role is to give you reassurance, advice, and, in extreme cases, emergency care for your child. They will allow you an opportunity to work through your crisis. These confidants should also be available to other members of the immediate family.

Keeping up regular consultative meetings with all of the specialists involved in the care of your child is also important. Talk about the difficulties that you, your child, and your family are experiencing so that they can be dealt with in a positive manner before crisis situations occur. Taking care of your own physical and emotional needs is just as important as taking care of those of your other family members.

Have a regular time each week when you have a **family meeting** at which you encourage everyone to discuss everything that is going on concerning their own lives and the life of your special child. Deal immediately with any concerns that are raised so that no one believes that their difficulties are not important. You must do everything you can to maintain family togetherness.

Lastly, there will be times when you will have to be away from your children. These times might include a vacation or other important family events, such as a wedding. When you are planning these events, make sure that you have at least one backup other than your regular caregiver so that you will definitely be able to go. If you are unable to go to these special events because you can't find a substitute caregiver you may develop a sense of resentment toward your child for something that is beyond his control. By planning ahead you will be able to make sure that you get the relief that you need to help avoid burnout.

VACATIONS AND RECREATION

Sometimes a vacation with the entire family can also serve as a needed break from the routine of your life at home. While taking a vacation with a child who has significant disabilities can be difficult, it is getting easier all the time. The travel market for people with disabilities and their families is expanding at an unprecedented rate. There are four million people with physical disabilities in Canada, forty million in the United States, and another fifty million in Europe. Transportation companies, the hotel industry, theme parks, tourist attractions, and the entertainment industry have all recognized this large consumer group, and are in the process of making changes to accommodate those with disabilities and their families.

National, state, and provincial parks in Canada and the United States are now doing their utmost to ensure that their facilities are accessible to people with special needs. Thus people with disabilities can gain access to hiking trails, camp sites, and other recreational locations. It is always helpful to contact local travel planners and businesses to locate accessible facilities. The Automobile Club produces a valuable guide that can tell you which of these facilities are disability-friendly. Theme parks such as Disneyland and MarineWorld can make special arrangements for visitors with disabilities.

In the last two decades travel companies have organized trips all over the world for people with special needs. The tour's organizers ensure access to all facilities, including museums, restaurants, hotels, and special sites of interest, and they will also make arrangements for dietary needs, medical care, and specialized medication. The provisions made on these tours will allow you and your children to enjoy a family holiday that would have been exceedingly difficult to plan on your own.

One of the recent innovations in the barrier-free travel market has come from car rental companies: the availability of vans equipped with ramps for travelers in wheelchairs. And as a consequence of the Americans with Disabilities Act in the United States and a government program known as Access Canada, higher accommodation standards have been established and are being adopted by virtually every hotel, motel, and resort in both countries. Washrooms with grab bars, phones with devices for the hearing impaired, and other devices to aid people with disabilities are usually available upon request, as long as sufficient notice is given.

Organizations in many communities provide specialized vacations for children with serious diseases and disabilities. Some of these organizations, such as the Special Wish

Foundation and the Make a Child Smile Foundation, are supervised by professional personnel who are fully trained in taking care of children with disabilities. They usually take very seriously ill children (the majority are diagnosed with terminal conditions); however, they do accept some children who may have to undergo difficult or painful therapies such as radiation. If a child qualifies for one of these programs, their vacation is usually provided at little, if any, cost.

Separate and integrated camps also provide specialized care and a fun summertime experience for children with special needs. In addition to providing an enjoyable break for your child, sending them to a summer camp for a week or two allows you valuable respite time that you can use to rest and relax or to take a vacation with your spouse.

Preparing for a Vacation

There are some obvious precautions that you should take when your special needs child is at a separate facility. It is important to provide the personnel with any of your child's dietary needs, prescriptions, and any specialized care that may be required. You should also provide a list of medical personnel and other facilities that may be needed in an emergency.

If you are taking your special needs child with you on your vacation, write down ahead of time all the extra things you will need on your trip: the telephone numbers and addresses of doctors, clinics, and hospitals in the area you are visiting that are able to deal with your child's condition; a list of your child's current medications and dosages; a list of any allergy problems; and, if necessary, specialized insurance policies. Plan your lodging well in advance, arrange for the availability of medical care, medicines, and prescriptions, and bring with you a letter from your physician detailing any special treatment that your child may require. By planning your trip well in advance, you will be able to avoid any surprises and be able to handle any problems that may arise.

Because many children with disabilities face limits or constraints on what they can do and where they can go, a family or individual vacation can be a wonderful way to enrich your children's lives and introduce them to new experiences. Proper preparation can ensure an experience that the entire family will cherish and remember.

One parent relates her family's experience on vacation:

"Our daughter has always been in a wheelchair. She was born without the proper development of her legs and one arm as a result of thalidomide, a drug I took during pregnancy. We had many difficulties, but perhaps one of the greatest problems we initially faced was going on holidays. Before our daughter was born, we always visited family and they visited us. All the kids played together and enjoyed doing so. The cousins had a great relationship. When our daughter was born, you might have thought that she had a communicable disease, because our family really wanted nothing to do with us. The cousins isolated her. It was unfortunate, but that was just the way it happened to be.

"Vacations, as you know, are for fun and good times, but some people just can't relate to people with disabilities. In the 1960s, holidaying with a child with disabilities was always difficult, because nothing was accessible, but we got around the problem very well. We took our daughter camping. We went canoeing, fishing, and swimming, and the disability was not a problem. Our vacations were an important part of our family life and brought us closer together. Today the problems of access hardly exist. Modern buildings including hotels, office buildings, and other facilities are usually ramped and at least accessible. Families who have children with disabilities have a wide range of options that were unavailable to us back in the '60s, and they should take advantage of them!"

Your special child should never have the impression that he is the cause of problems within the family. In other words, your relationship with your spouse must be secure, and you must share your responsibilities equally. But while it will probably be impossible to eliminate all of the stress that you feel on a day-to-day basis, that is no cause for concern. No one lives a life free of stress, and it's unreasonable to expect that you will be able to do so. Stress does not have to be a negative force. It can be a positive tool that pushes you to function at the peak of your capacity. The key is to recognize the sign of excessive stress before burnout occurs and to do something about it. Remember that you are not facing this challenge alone — there are many people out there who can help you. Chapter 8 on support groups will elaborate on these resources in greater detail.

Chapter 7

The Education Question

Since World War II, people with disabilities have made significant advances toward being mainstreamed into contemporary society, especially in the area of education. In the past, people with disabilities found themselves barred from public educational institutions as a result of a value system that did not accept those who were "not normal." Children with disabilities were isolated and institutionalized — not identified as a disenfranchised minority who might make significant contributions. Their educational potential was minimized or ignored.

Most people with disabilities are no longer prevented from experiencing the full range of academic opportunities. This change can be attributed to three factors: advocacy, empowerment, and integration. Thanks to the efforts of people with disabilities, parents, and others who have taken an active approach to social change, and new research that is currently being conducted, society is recognizing the vast untapped potential that exists within the community of children with disabilities. Although the rate of change appears to be slow, never has so much attention been focused on the needs, rights, inherent dignity, and integrity of all those who experience disability.

The barriers facing people with disabilities are finally being removed or surmounted by new legislation. Along with continued activism, this legislation is changing negative social attitudes and helping to facilitate integration.

THE IMPORTANCE OF EDUCATION

Education is a most important component of your child's life. It is the key that will unlock all of her further achievements. Through education she will learn the basic social and physical skills to live independently, meet friends, and have fun. Your special child's education may in some respects be even more important than the education of a child without a disability, because your child may have to overcome additional barriers in order to learn. You can begin the learning process by teaching her at home at an early age. Early education at home may involve teaching her about her condition, advising her on how to explain her disability to others, and showing her how to do physical and rehabilitative exercises.

WHAT ARE MY CHILD'S LEGAL RIGHTS?

Under the Education for All Handicapped Children Act (EAHCA) of 1975 and the ADA of 1991 in the United States, and under various provincial guidelines in Canada, children with disabilities are guaranteed a free and appropriate public education. This means that your local school board *must* make the necessary efforts and expenditures to accommodate your child at his school. They are unable to say, "We don't have the necessary program." Or, "We don't have the money that would be required." Or, "We can't accept your child in 'our' school." If you face a reaction of this sort from your local public school, and it refuses to comply with the law, then you can take it to court, **and win!**

Public Law 94–142 was created by the EAHCA, and declares that your child has a right to:

1. a free, appropriate education;
2. a proper placement in the least restrictive educational environment;
3. aids and services as necessary; and
4. fair assessment procedures.

In Canada, the same basic rights are ensured under a variety of provincial laws. To protect these rights and to ensure that they are carried out, every school in Canada and the United States is required to develop a written Individualized Education Plan (IEP) for every child with special needs each year in cooperation with the child's parents. Furthermore, if you disagree with the school's course of action in the IEP, you can appeal their decisions all the way up to the state or provincial Department of Education, and even to the judicial system. IEPs will be discussed in more detail later in this chapter.

The law provides protection for your child's educational

rights, although you may face some difficulties in getting your child's school to implement the law properly. Normally school officials will be willing to work with you in order to accommodate your child, but occasionally they will provide direct opposition to efforts on your child's behalf. There are several common ways that schools fail to comply with their legal responsibilities:

- **Waiting Lists:** Large numbers of children who have been identified as having disabilities are kept waiting for the evaluation and services that they need. As a result the children may miss weeks, months, and even years of school. Teachers and administrators may plead they are understaffed, but that is no excuse. Your child deserves to have her needs met as soon as possible.
- **Denial of Related Services:** Children are frequently denied extracurricular services that are related to their condition, such as physical therapy, occupational therapy, school health services, and transportation. Sometimes schools will claim that students are receiving the services, or will receive them in a short time, when, in fact, the school has no plan to provide the service at all.
- **Exclusion:** Sometimes children with disabilities are not permitted into the classroom, and they are denied adequate and appropriate services.
- **Unnecessary Segregation:** Because the law states that children must be educated in **the least restrictive environment,** your child has a right to be educated in an integrated classroom. Studies have shown that most

children with disabilities learn more in an integrated classroom, yet many children are unnecessarily separated from a regular classroom, because it is easier for the teacher to do so. You can prevent this from happening.

- **Illegal Expulsion:** In 1994, parents from a small community in Ontario were very upset because their child was expelled from a public school. The teachers and school board officials felt that the student's extensive cerebral palsy made it extremely difficult for the child to learn in a regular classroom environment. The parents believed that the regular classroom was the best educational environment for their son. At my direction they contacted the Advocacy Resource Centre for the Handicapped (ARCH), a legal aid clinic for people with disabilities and their families. The family decided to pursue legal action, and as a result, the school was legally required to enroll the child on a permanent basis. This case is now under appeal.

- **Unsatisfactory IEPs:** Many children do not receive IEPs, or receive a prewritten IEP as a substitute for a truly individualized plan. If your child receives an IEP that is not up to your standards, you can appeal it and have the IEP redone.

- **Unnecessary Barriers:** Sometimes schools don't alert parents about their child's IEP meeting, or let parents know only the day before it takes place, or schedule it at an inconvenient time. By law, schools are required to give "prior notice" to parents. Prior notice means that parents are to be told the date of their child's IEP meeting well before it occurs and that parents are to be informed of their due process rights and procedural safeguards before any actions are taken or refused for their child. Many parents are not fully informed of their rights during the IEP meeting.

If you feel that your child's school officials have made one of these errors and they are unwilling to correct their mistake, then North American law has given you the recourse to protect your child. In the vast majority of all special education cases a legal appeal is not necessary, but if it is, **the law is on your side!**

THE ROLE OF THE PARENT

You are now in a position to guarantee that your special child will be educated in the best possible environment. This will ensure that your child has the opportunity to maximize her abilities. A realistic goal for many children with disabilities is to graduate not only from high school, but also from colleges and universities. The new opportunities available in the field of education will allow them to fulfill these goals and find a place in the workforce.

Next to your child, you will bear the most responsibility for her educational success. Teachers, administrators, trustees, and others in the educational world may not always be willing to make the necessary efforts to accommodate your child, even when the law is in your favor. In these cases, it will be your responsibility as a parent to lobby, prod, and pressure the school system into treating your child properly. If those steps are insufficient, you may be forced to take legal action. You must keep working for your child's success.

WHAT IS THE RANGE OF OPTIONS FOR MY CHILD?

To ensure that your child has access to the programs which best meet her needs, you must first be aware of your legal rights and choices. Modern educational philosophy centers on providing services to the student in the least intrusive setting, through the mainstreaming of every possible student.

Dr. Joel Hundert and Dr. William Mahoney of McMaster University recently completed a study of 1300 students for the Government of Canada. The key findings of their investigation show the advantages of day-care integration. Hundert and Mahoney found, however, that placement in integrated settings does not automatically lead to an increase in the interactive play of children with and without disabilities. The study showed that teacher skills combined with parent interaction can create social environments where children with and without special needs integrate socially, learning and playing together. This emphasizes the need for parents to involve teachers very closely in their special child's education. If teachers are unaware of the steps they have to take to make a child's pre-school experience worthwhile, then the child might not gain any significant benefit from the integrated setting.

One observation in the McMaster study is that children with severe disabilities demonstrated low developmental gains in specialized settings. This means that children with disabilities who were placed in institutions made very limited progress. While their minimal gains could be established and maintained by a staff of well-meaning people, the gains were in no way comparable to those that could have been made if the same children were pushed to their limits. Caregivers who have preset convictions and expectations for a particular child may not tap the full potential of students who have impaired capacities. It is important for children with disabilities to be constantly reevaluated, and to have goals set for them that stretch the limits of their abilities, not place limits on them.

Today, integration is the first choice of many educators for people with disabilities. While it is generally the best option, it's important to review all the options in the continuum of services. The primary factors to consider are the potential benefits to be achieved by integrated education and the available alternatives. Assessing these factors will allow you to decide whether a student with a disability can benefit from full, "supported" or partial integration, self-contained specialized education, or a separate program in which the student has full-time, one-on-one tutoring.

These different forms of integration are not mutually exclusive, as some special students graduate to more integrated settings as their needs and abilities change. Education is a continuum of service and an ever-changing process. Be prepared to examine a wide variety of these options in order to find the one that is right for your child.

Full Integration

A primary goal of successful education is to establish the ideal learning environment. It is vital to develop mutual understanding and respect among students with disabilities, students without disabilities, parents, and teachers. This promotes inclusion and the development and maintenance of self-esteem, and avoids the negative factors associated with the isolation, or "ghettoization," of people with disabilities. Full integration is the educational experience of being in a mainstream class-room and is the most desired form of schooling.

According to 1995 statistics, over 70 percent of children with disabilities are integrated into mainstream schools. Fifteen years ago, less than 20 percent of children with disabilities were placed in an integrated surrounding. This dramatic change reflects the acceptance of the fact that children with severe disabilities often thrive in an integrated learning environment.

For almost all children with disabilities, integration is the road to the future. In some separate educational environments, there is a widespread belief that because a child has a disability, she will not benefit from an education. Because of this belief, the child is not pushed to succeed. In most of these cases, the child will not succeed. This self-fulfilling prophecy defines the extent of the abilities that anyone with a disability may develop.

In an integrated environment these artificial barriers are rarely imposed. Even though students with special needs do not always obtain regular specialized programs in the integrated environment, they are usually supported by fellow students and teachers. In this type of setting, many students with disabilities achieve gains that are unanticipated by physicians, teachers, and parents. Other students may motivate special students and push them toward higher accomplishments.

Prior to the late 1980s, students in wheelchairs found it difficult, if not impossible, to attend community and post-secondary schools. Today, throughout North America, building codes have been changed to require educational institutions to be accessible. However, some communities find it financially prohibitive to install ramps and/or elevators. In these settings, teachers often change classrooms in order not to deny access to students who have mobility impairments.

Ironically, for decades it was thought that children with a spectrum of disabilities who resided in rural areas were at a disadvantage because they *couldn't* access specialized separate educational facilities. Because of the difficulty of amassing the necessary resources, these children were accommodated in mainstream facilities. However, authorities agree that this integration promoted the educational and social adjustment of most of the special children.

Partial Integration

In partial integration the special needs student attends the regular classroom, often with the support of an aide or resource teacher, for a specified part of the school day. During the remainder of the classroom time, the student attends a "self-contained" program, which augments the regular classroom experience by providing specialized education and therapy designed to promote the student's capabilities. Some of the students may graduate to a full-time regular classroom.

Many children with ADHD may be put into self-contained classrooms for their academic subjects, but integrated into regular classes with their peers for physical education, music, art, or such options as carpentry or cooking.

"Supported" Integration

Socialization and integration are crucial facets of any educational program. In many situations, a student with a disability will not be able to function in a mainstream classroom without some sort of assistance. Supported integration takes place when a student is effectively integrated into a mainstream classroom setting with the support of specialized staff and/or technological aids such as computers and enlargers. (Unlike partial integration, which may or may not make use of a teacher's aide or other personnel, supported integration always pairs a student with a resource personnel.)

Teacher's Aides

Teacher's aides provide the educational, social, and physical supports necessary for the integration of a student with a disability. You can obtain the services of a teacher's aide from the pools of substitute teachers through your local school board, from volunteers, and through support groups. Parents, teachers, and principals should identify the child's needs and then select the appropriate aide.

Traditionally some teachers have been reluctant to have educational support staff in their classrooms, but in many instances they have discovered that these personnel not only permit special needs children to enjoy their classroom experience, but also allow the teacher to undertake programs that they might not ordinarily conduct, such as photography (including the developing and printing of film) and field trips. The use of such technology as enlarged screens and Bliss boards can also let a student with a disability participate and contribute in the classroom.

A student with cerebral palsy who had a severe speech impediment and used a wheelchair required a teaching assistant to take notes for him and communicate his responses. With this support, which began in grade one, the child was successfully integrated into a regular public education program. He is currently enrolled in grade eight and maintains a B to B plus average. He has had the good fortune to have the same educational assistant for his entire school career. This student has made tremendous progress and has mastered language skills to the point where he can be understood by most individuals. The assistant still works with the young man, but she is no longer required to communicate the student's responses.

A parent shares this story about her daughter with cerebral palsy:

"We worked so hard when Ashley was born. She had cerebral palsy and was not able to write, although she has managed to use a computer. We lived in London, Ontario, where there are a lot of facilities for people who have disabilities, so we contacted a parent support group. They suggested that we move to an area of the city where our child could be educated in a wonderful school. When we first went to meet the principal, he was outstanding; he told us that the school had looked after a number of other children who had more serious difficulties than our child. He arranged for a teaching assistant who had worked in the school for three years to work with Ashley.

"The TA was a real professional. She gave our child all the encouragement that she needed to do well. She told us that the main problem in teaching our child in school would not be doing the academic work, but making friends. She came to our house for three weeks before school started and became a good friend of Ashley. When Ashley was taken to school, she was introduced, her problems were explained, and the children from that day on were extremely helpful. Our caregiver told us that when she organized things she would not be doing that much, as Ashley's fellow students would readily pitch in. Ashley has a wonderful collection of friends. She gets invited to their parties, and her friends really enjoy having her with them when they go for swimming lessons. It looks like Ashley is going to be able to learn how to swim."

Intervenors

Intervenors are personnel who receive specialized training to enable people with severe sight, hearing, and speech impairments to communicate. Using a combination of touch, computer techniques, and Braille, these individuals teach people with disabilities the art of communicating directly with their audiences. Intervenors are not merely translators — they interpret the voice inflections of their clients as well as their speech. In this way they are communication conduits, expressing the thoughts and emotions of people who have communication disorders. Intervenors are used in employment, and recreational and social pursuits, as well as in the educational process. Many parents are able to become effective intervenors by working intimately with their children so that they are able to recognize, translate, and communicate effectively. The profession of intervenors has been established at many schools during the last decade. See Appendix 2 for the addresses of national organizations that can provide the numbers of your local support groups; these groups can direct you to appropriate intervenors.

An intervenor was employed by the parents of a child who had extensive hearing, sight, and speech difficulties. Initially this child was classified as being mute. The intervenor had the skills to establish and develop communication, and was able to properly assess the child's potential. The parents had hired the intervenor when their child was three years old, because they were extremely anxious that they weren't able to communicate easily with their child. The intervenor established that the child, aside from her disabilities, had at least normal intelligence, and over the course of nine years she was able to enhance the child's communication skills. The child was subsequently enrolled in the school system with the constant encouragement and participation of the intervenor.

In addition to allowing the child to make significant strides toward achieving integration, the intervenor was also able to enrich the classroom experience for all of the students. The intervenor's presence allowed the teacher to use programs that required the involvement of at least two adults and the intervenor was also able to contribute her unique programming skills and sensitivity. The intervenor encouraged the other students to participate in the education of the child who had disabilities. This encouragement led the students to involve the child in activities outside the classroom as well.

Separate Accommodation

Other students with more demanding special needs may require separate accommodation for their education. Separate education can include institutionalization, individualized tutoring, or home-based education (which is usually provided by a parent). While it is difficult and extremely frustrating for teachers to work with children who are faced with numerous and severe physical and psychiatric difficulties, many students with profound disabilities have absorbed many important living and learning skills. Sometimes this can only be achieved in a separate educational setting.

One child with multiple disabilities that have impaired his communication skills, his mobility, and his hearing has spent his entire educational life in a separate educational facility. He used to get up from his desk and wander around with no apparent reason, and also threw paper darts, spilled paint, and provoked the students beside him. But in this facility, he has learned to behave in a manner so that his outbursts are becoming less frequent, and he has learned to dress himself, although he cannot tie his shoes or do up buttons. He responds to terms like cat, dog, and ice cream in a very positive way, although occasionally he will pat a dog while saying "cat." The separate environment appeared to be a feasible location for his education.

His mother and father try to include him in some family activities, but he has severe disabilities and it is very difficult to do so. His parents also employ people in their home to look after their son on a continuous basis. As the mother said to me, "Fortunately, we are middle class and we can afford to look after our son. We have always shuddered to think what would have happened if he had been fully institutionalized. He can take himself to the washroom, he can eat with us at the table with considerable difficulty, and we can see some change, although it is very slow. What is important is that we love him and he loves us. You can tell that when you hold him, and you experience the warmth that only a parent can know."

In a separate institution or learning environment, however, children with special needs often do not have the opportunities to interact with children who do not have disabilities. As a result, in separate environments, children with disabilities often experience the problems associated with the "ghettoization" of people with disabilities. In these situations it becomes more difficult for them to acquire the self-esteem and social skills to successfully experience acceptance and integration. They often find themselves with a very small group of associates and friends. In social situations, at least when young, they sometimes meet children for very short periods of time, but they fail to develop even basic relationships. Some children who grow up in an isolated environment even become fearful of other children, and would rather spend their time with their parents, other adults, and children who have similar disabilities.

Institutionalized Education

An institutionalized education can range from a separate day school for children with disabilities to an institution in which the child lives on a long-term basis. Sometimes a child will take part in an institutionalized education for only a short period of time so that she can develop specific intellectual and social skills for regular classroom attendance.

Self-contained educational facilities (institutions) must be closely supervised in order to ensure that the environment provides the most positive opportunity for learning. In many jurisdictions separate facilities are understaffed and under-financed. They are subject to frequent budget cuts, and very rarely attract top-notch staff. Some of these isolated special environments not only neglect the student's educational welfare, but also provide an atmosphere where the psychological and sexual abuse of students has taken place. This is not the case in the majority of institutions, but if you decide to enroll your child in a separate facility it would be wise to thoroughly evaluate the facility on a continuing basis.

I recently met an individual who graduated from Gallaudet University, an institution of higher learning specifically designed to educate students with hearing impairments. He told me that he had always been educated in a separate facility, since the public school system did not have the resources to accommodate him. He is a militant member of the hearing-impaired community who does not believe that individuals with severe hearing impairments should be involved with the hearing community, especially in their social pursuits. The advantage for him in being educated in a separate facility was that he was always with students who had similar needs, and therefore he did not experience the rejection and ridicule that often affects students with hearing impairments when they are educated in a regular facility. He maintains that people who are categorized as being severely hearing impaired belong to a unique and fulfilling subculture, and that it is not necessary to have them integrated with "hearing society."

Some students live and are educated in a separate institutional facility because their parents do not have the means or resources to place them in a mainstream classroom. These children are perceived to have extensive disabilities that make it difficult, if not impossible, to have them educated in a traditional classroom. Occasionally you hear of individuals with autism, for example, who have the opportunity to live in the "real world" after spending their lives in an institution. They have learned the necessary skills to cope with living in mainstream society. The majority of people who have been institutionalized since birth or shortly thereafter, however, are not given the opportunities to develop their abilities to the same extent as someone who is educated outside of an institution. The most meaningful things that a child does not receive in an institutional setting are the love, support, and motivation that come from the warmth of a family; the affection and security that the family provides are the most important elements of a child's growth and development.

Home-Based or Specialist Education

Some students with disabilities are educated either at home by a parent or by a specialist on a one-to-one basis. Hiring a specialist may permit your child to attain unanticipated levels of accomplishment, but it's usually very expensive. If you wish to educate your child at home, try to keep yourself abreast of the latest available innovations and support systems. Maintain a relationship with special education facilities and the local board of education in order to be aware of any mandatory educational requirements, as well as any outside support that could simplify your task.

One child sustained a severe spinal injury after falling from the loft of a barn and became a paraplegic. His mother and grandparents, who also resided on the farm, assumed responsibility for the young man's education, which was overseen by a local county inspector. His grandfather had been a high school science teacher, and with support from a number of outside agencies, his family was able to organize an educational program that met the state requirements. These requirements were tested in yearly examinations, which he was able to pass. The young man graduated from high school, and is now involved in a computer science course at a school of science and technology. This is the first time in his life that he has been away from home. His home-based education adequately prepared him for postsecondary education, but he had very few contacts with other students, and missed out on the social and recreational opportunities that going to an integrated school would have provided.

The young man is living in an independent living center for people with mobility impairments, and is enjoying the experience of being independent. A local service club is buying him a van that will be refitted, so he will be as independent as possible. For the first year at the school of science and technology he was forced to rely on a transportation system for the disabled in his community. Unfortunately, the system was not very reliable and he missed more than 20 percent of his classes during the final term. His case manager recommended getting the van so that Frank could get himself to classes and fully benefit from his educational program. Frank's success is an example of how people with disabilities can benefit from both separate and integrated learning.

WHERE SHOULD MY CHILD GO TO SCHOOL?

There are a number of factors to consider in establishing the best educational environment for your child:

- location
- attitudes toward children with disabilities
- specialized resource people available
- technological resources available
- child's intellectual potential
- child's physical requirements.

Professional educators and politicians often have to be reminded that from an economic perspective, it is usually most beneficial to have children with special needs educated within a mainstream setting. The cost of an assistant or of added technology is much cheaper than establishing another whole classroom for special students. Parents can also avoid the cost of sending their child to a private facility. There is a need for specialized educational facilities, but in most situations, such facilities do not provide students with the quality of education they would receive within the integrated setting — and these students rarely qualify for postsecondary education.

In attempting to locate the least restrictive and best educational environment, you will have to assume a proactive role. Try to distinguish among what is appropriate, what is necessary, and what is legitimate. You will probably find that there is not one option, but rather a series of placement options.

In some instances (e.g., children with severe physical disabilities such as extensive cerebral palsy and children who are severely autistic) integrated educational environments may not be appropriate, and occasionally, parents of children with special needs find that the only environment conducive to their children's education can be found in a separate setting. Justifiably, parents may experience anxiety in choosing the most appropriate environment for their child. The reality is that some conditions cannot be accommodated in a traditional educational environment; in these situations parents are doing their best for a child by having her educated in a self-contained environment.

WHAT IS AN IEP, AND WHY IS IT IMPORTANT?

If you do decide that your child can and should be integrated into the public school system, one of the first things that will be done is the Individualized Education Program (IEP), a written assessment of your child's needs and the necessary services. The IEP is used to create a personal educational strategy specifically designed to meet your child's needs.

The IEP must be reviewed on a regular basis by the classroom teacher, the special needs teachers, the principal or vice principal, as well as the parents and, occasionally, a case manager. Parents should give teachers a list of their child's special requirements, which will be incorporated during the meetings. They should also prepare regular reports for teachers on their child's progress at home, as well as any problems or frustrations that may have arisen as a result of their child's classroom experience. Constant feedback between parents and teachers allows for problems to be identified and solved as *quickly* as possible.

What Is in the IEP?

An IEP usually includes a statement outlining the child's current educational performance, short- and long-term goals, instructional objectives, and the required services. It also describes the extent to which the child will be able to participate in regular educational programs, individualized regular programs, and specialized group programs for children with similar difficulties and needs. IEPs are reviewed and updated on a regular basis, and therefore they should contain the projected start date and the anticipated duration.

In some cases it may be productive to include alternative strategies into the IEP in case the original program for educational development is not as successful as had been anticipated. The IEP may also include the need for specialized teachers in the classroom who will augment the regular teacher's role. In many cases the classroom teacher cannot meet the needs of children with disabilities while at the same time providing for the needs of the other students.

Creating an IEP is a multidimensional project that can include the input of doctors, therapists, educational professionals, speech therapists, social workers, nurses, and occupational therapists. At the planning stage there may be disagreements between parents and professionals over which strategies will meet the needs of the child and her family; for example, there may be financial concerns about the need for a full- or part-time aide, or a teacher may not want additional personnel in the classroom. It is often beneficial to name a case manager to oversee the provision of service generated by the plan. If a case manager is present at the regular IEP meetings, he or she may be able to suggest special techniques and insights that will maximize the child's response to her educational program.

Ten Strategies for an Effective IEP

1. **Be Involved:** Your involvement in your child's IEP is of the utmost importance. In most cases parents and case managers are aware of their child's capabilities and potential, as well as of the available resources. Usually the educational authorities will be committed to providing what they believe to be the appropriate IEP for your child. They are, however, often influenced by increased costs and traditional forms of classroom instruction. The potential difficulties that may arise from having specialized equipment, extra personnel, and a child with special needs in a regular classroom setting may lead to a different or more conservative IEP than you would prefer. Or, in other cases, teachers have recognized the potential of students with disabilities and have recommended strategies that exceeded the parents' expectations. By being involved you can ensure the best possible treatment for your child.

2. **Be Optimistic:** It is not unusual for both teachers and parents to underestimate or overestimate a special

child's potential. As a parent you should always believe that your child can succeed and can do well. Compliment and reinforce your child's successes and accomplishments, as this will build her self-esteem and motivate her to continue her efforts.

3. **Be Realistic:** While a progressive plan is always desirable, if an IEP is overly ambitious, your child will not be able to make significant progress and you and she will become frustrated. It is difficult to strike a balance between asking too much and expecting too little. A reasonable program that is within your child's grasp will enable her to succeed.

4. **Gain Total Access:** It is crucial that parents always have access to meetings, written assessments, and reports, and be involved in decision-making. Without this access, it is difficult to ensure that your child's needs will be met. It is your duty to make the school personnel aware of your interest and expertise in your child's education, your intention to be informed of, and involved in, meetings, and your expectations of regular updates regarding your child's progress. Ask for any written reports or meeting notes for your home file. Remember that it is your legal right to participate in your child's IEP. If you face resistance to your efforts to participate you can take legal action.

5. **Bring Support:** Try to bring another person to IEP meetings for support — your spouse, a case worker,

or an advocate. They will help you understand the recommended strategies and advise you on whether or not to accept them. Having other people to support you also influences the education professionals to abide by the decisions made in the IEP meeting.

6. **Take Notes:** Always take notes during the meeting. If you don't want to write, you may consider asking the members of the IEP team if they would allow you to tape-record the meeting for reasons of accuracy. A tape recording will be especially helpful during your first several meetings when you are in unfamiliar territory. It will allow you to go over the meeting in detail to be certain that you understand everything that was discussed.

7. **Be Prepared:** Go to an IEP meeting armed with information — including the nature of the disability, the child's abilities, difficulties, accomplishments, current drug therapy, and any known allergies or other problems that your child may encounter on a regular basis. Your knowledge is power, and it can create extra opportunities for your child. If you don't know or are unsure about some of these facts, you can obtain the necessary information from your child's physician, case manager, or advocate. A wealth of information will allow the teachers and administrators to design a program that is appropriate for your child.

8. **Consult Others:** Parents of other children with disabilities have already experienced the same

procedure that you are facing, some of them many times over. They have already been involved in the creation of IEPs for their children with similar needs. They can tell you what they did, how staff members at certain schools will act, and what to expect.

9. **Be Flexible:** Keep in mind that there may be a wide range of strategies to follow. If one strategy does not appear to be productive over a defined period of time, then you and the IEP group should be prepared to reevaluate your decisions and possibly adopt another strategy; children with similar conditions do not always respond to the same programs. Occasionally teachers will recognize something that parents are not aware of — they notice if a child exhibits sight, hearing, or perceptual difficulties. You must also be prepared to make compromises, at least on a short-term basis.

10. **Look at a Wide Range of Factors:** In assessing why a child responds or fails to respond to certain educational programs, it's important to consider a wide range of factors, including the nature of the educational program, the personnel involved, the support personnel, and the available equipment. A child's lack of response to certain programs may be due to cultural problems, the size of the class, or even the teachers' personalities.

What Happens When Problems Occur?

Constant monitoring of the IEP is crucial. The goal of the program is to provide a **creative, flexible, and innovative** curriculum. In most situations, this plan will respond to the needs of your child, but occasionally you may feel that the program is inappropriate and reassessment is required. What can you do to repair the problem?

1. **Contact the Classroom Teacher (or Aide) and Educational Specialists:** Explain to them your areas of concern and how you would like to see these areas addressed. It is always the best strategy to work directly with the teacher in a cooperative fashion. If you approach the problems as a team, and not as adversaries, you will have a better chance of finding a solution.

2. **Meet with Other School Resources:** Other resources include everyone who is present at your IEP team meetings, as well as educational consultants. If the teacher is uncooperative or refuses to see your point of view, this step makes it possible to enlist the support of other allies within the school.

3. **Discuss the Situation with the School Principal:** If the teacher is still unreceptive, the principal will often be a valuable intermediary in creating a solution to your concerns. In addition to mediating your dispute, the principal may also be able to put pressure on the teacher to accommodate you.

4. **Contact Outside Resources for Support:** These resources include your case manager, school board personnel, superintendents, medical personnel, social

workers, advocacy groups, and other professionals. If the principal is unwilling or unable to deal with your concerns, then members of the outside resources should be contacted. They will bring alternative strategies and opinions that can be used to address your concerns. However, keep on trying to resolve the situation without forcing a solution on the teacher.

5. **Involve the Political Realm:** If no one within your child's school is willing to accommodate your child's needs or bend to the pressure of your advocacy efforts, you can push for success by going to the teacher's and principal's superiors — the politicians. Political resources that you appeal to can include school trustees, health boards, other members of your local government, and even members of the legislature.

6. **Take Legal Action:** If the educators continue to be unresponsive, you can appeal to various legal bodies such as appeal boards and the court system. In many regions there are advocacy groups and specific legal clinics that can represent you in IEP meetings. In some situations a letter from a legal clinic will be enough to motivate a school system to provide the accommodation that you seek. Because the law favors people with disabilities, if you are forced to take legal action, you will probably be successful. However, be aware that if you have to resort to a legal settlement, it may create lasting bitterness and resentment on both sides.

It's usually not necessary to become involved in all six steps when you are working on your child's IEP, as most difficulties can usually be resolved through meetings with the classroom teachers and other school personnel. Steps five and six should only be used as a last resort, when all other avenues have been unsuccessful.

THE IMPORTANCE OF USING ALLIES

It is important to locate and work with allies who have the power or the potential to influence the system. These forces, combined with information you may obtain from organizations representing specific disabilities, will provide the strategies that you can use to further your child's education (see Appendix 2 for a partial list of these organizations). It is your responsibility to contact the organization that can provide the necessary information to support your child.

ELEMENTS OF A SUCCESSFUL CLASSROOM EXPERIENCE

A key component of classroom success for the special needs student is an educational environment that is conducive to cooperative group work and involvement. This can be contrasted with the traditional emphasis on individual achievement in a competitive setting. This cooperation is vital as students with special needs often benefit from the moral support, input, and motivation provided by fellow students. It's best when this spirit extends beyond the formal classroom so that the student with a disability feels that she is a legitimate part of the student body.

It's also important that the student, parent, teacher, and/or teacher's aide inform the other students in the classroom about the nature of the disability. This explanation will usually create a positive atmosphere and alleviate any worries or concerns that the rest of the students might have had about the new student. It will serve as an ice-breaker and might encourage some of the other students to help out.

My parents had to implore the Calgary public school system to have me admitted — and then encourage the school system and individual teachers to have me effectively integrated into classrooms. This integration meant that the teachers had to spend extra time in giving me oral exams. I was required to either dictate my exams to the teacher or to a secretary. Dictating turned out to be an advantage for me, except in the subjects of mathematics and statistics. Dictating allowed me to finish every exam that I "performed," and I was allowed to include an amount of material that even the fastest writers would not have been able to record. I also learned that when you are dictating to a teacher or a professor, you have to be accurate, and you cannot bluff your way through an exam. This system further helped me as I could occasionally tell from a teacher's expression that it would probably be useful to pursue another line of argument. I was also forced to prepare diligently for exams as I did not want to be embarrassed by my lack of knowledge. These learning skills and techniques allowed me to do very well, as I was able to maintain a B plus to A average in both high school and university.

And there was also the problem of how I was to take notes,

since, as I've mentioned, I don't write. Portable tape recorders didn't exist back in those days, so starting in grade seven, I carried a portable typewriter around with me. This, however, wasn't a satisfactory solution, as my typing speed was very slow. The answer was carbon paper. My friends would make carbon copies of their notes, and in some cases, even type them up.

It's hard to deal with all the problems at once, but having the support of my teachers and fellow students helped me immensely.

THE IMPORTANCE OF EXTRACURRICULAR ACTIVITIES

Students with special needs in an integrated setting often discover that they are accepted during the school day, but are often isolated and rejected in non-school-related activities. Some students require specialized transportation and some are in wheelchairs, but this should not exclude them from participation in athletic and social events. It is the responsibility of teachers as well as parents to take whatever measures are necessary to ensure that all students have access to extracurricular activities. This is the place where relationships are built. All students experience disappointment and rejection, but a disability should not exclude interaction with peers.

During elementary school a friend of mine who lived next door had a condition that caused a softening of the bone in his left hip. As a result he wore an extensive brace. This did not stop him from playing floor hockey and basketball or going dancing. He was always involved in school and social activities, and was perhaps the fiercest competitor that I have ever met. Disabilities need not prevent participation at almost any level of activity.

As I mentioned previously, I had a strong interest in sports, and from grade two on, I played many house league sports and was on many school teams. I later found out that my dad had spoken to many of the school coaches and informed them that it was very important for me to be on the team. I spent most of my time on the bench, but so did a few other players. During my junior high school years, I was on the student council and was elected sports convenor (with the assistance of teachers, the convenor organized all of the school sports and their practice sessions and clinics). When I was in grade nine, my school, which was the smallest in the city, won the city track meet. I remember arranging all of the practices for the events beginning in January, and by June, we had developed a successful team. I led the victory march through downtown Calgary in rush-hour traffic. I remember catching hell from the principal the next day, but it was worth it.

Students with disabilities should be given all of the opportunities that student social life has to offer; in allowing them to have these experiences, you are acknowledging them as *people*. It is up to you to raise your children so they know that not only are they special kids with special needs, but they are also human beings.

In a Christmas pageant at an elementary school in Waterloo, Ontario, a student who used a wheelchair played the role of Mary. At the end of the play, the audience delivered a five-minute standing ovation! This young girl showed that having a disability does *not* mean that you have a handicap. She served as an example of what can be achieved if students, parents, and teachers are willing to work together with an open mind.

THE COST OF EDUCATION

Many specialized programs involving teacher's aides and computer technology, for example, require substantial financial expenditures. Most parents do not have the economic resources necessary to provide for the needs of their children. If the school board will not or cannot pay for the support that you need, it is important that you do not give up hope. There are many community resources available, as well as a wide range of donors who may be willing to help you out.

- Service clubs will often provide for the specialized needs of students by providing grants.
- Specific groups for people with disabilities such as the United Cerebral Palsy Association and the American and Canadian Associations for the Blind will often be able to provide information that is necessary in handling unique situations.
- In some areas, volunteers from the community at large or from local home and school associations will provide the personnel and/or the funds necessary to accommodate children with special needs. These institutions regard special requests as opportunities not only for improving the quality of life of affected people, but for providing a more integrated educational environment.
- Private endowments and specialized funds can also provide for the needs of students who have disabilities. These organizations will support programs that emphasize the integration, mainstreaming, and accommodation of these students. In many instances

these endowments do not normally contribute to these types of needs, but you will find that they often may support unique requests. You can obtain lists of private foundations and specialized funds from your local library, service clubs, your support and advocacy organizations, as well as from the directory in Appendix 2.

EDUCATING TEACHERS

Educating teachers is of primary importance, as many teachers will go to exceptional lengths to provide the educational support systems needed to assist students with special needs. I know a teacher at the grade four level who was informed that she would have an autistic child in her class who had not been very successful during her previous five years within the school system, having failed one year. When the teacher was approached by the parents, she obtained extra information on autism, in addition to the parent's description of the child and her special needs. This highly motivated teacher not only provided herself with background material, but also took steps to properly inform the students that they would have a new student with special needs. The student was well accepted in her new class and was able to make significant academic and social gains. These gains were unanticipated by her previous teachers, her parents, and the teacher, a woman who admitted that initially, she was somewhat reluctant to get involved with "this new educational problem."

Some teachers are not aware of the specialized strategies that some students with disabilities require. Parents should take it upon themselves to inform the teacher of their child's special needs so that the teacher will be able to prepare him or herself adequately. Teachers can be fantastic resources if they are given the tools.

When I was in elementary school my parents would have my teachers and the principal over to our house for lunch three or four times during the school year. This created an atmosphere of trust, and my parents were successful in conveying to most of my teachers the legitimacy of their desire to have me actively involved in a regular school program. A good working relationship with my teachers and the school administration made my integration into the "regular" classroom much easier.

Educate yourself as fully as possible on all aspects of your child's disability so that you can become your child's educational advisor. In this role it is up to you to choose the strategies that will enable her to learn most effectively. In some situations your child may not flourish because of the attitude, personality, or ability of a particular teacher, rather than as the result of a particular program. You should be flexible and try to work with the people at your child's school to overcome any problems that are encountered.

Remember that it is often difficult to choose the right strategy. You should continually assess your child's accomplishments, her educational and social experiences, and the effectiveness of the educational environment. Make informed decisions based on your knowledge of your child's disability and on the available medical and educational advice. In some instances, parents prove the experts wrong. There are few, if any, experts that would have forecasted the accomplishments of Helen Keller and other people with disabilities. Like children without disabilities, these kids with special needs will reflect the spectrum of accomplishment. A few will make astounding accomplishments, but some will not. You should feel that you have provided your child with the best available opportunities, by selecting the educational program that is most beneficial. Take satisfaction in knowing that you have done your best.

Chapter 8

Lean on Me:
Support Groups

In the late 1950s and early 1960s, the civil rights movement in the United States became a powerful force. One of its key principles was to promote the legitimate integration of minorities into mainstream society. And one way this was accomplished was through the creation of support groups. These groups were coalitions of individuals who provided their members with emotional, financial, educational, and legal aid that allowed them to participate in the civil rights movement and to go forward in their own lives.

At the same time many people began to believe that it was important to have people with disabilities achieve the benefits of integration. Following the successful example of the civil rights movement, support groups emerged targeting people with specific disabilities, including spina bifida, sickle cell anemia, developmental disabilities, paraplegia, and quadriplegia. These groups provided information, counseling, technology, financial support, and other services, and were effective in alleviating many people's personal hardship. But it was not until the late 1980s that groups representing people with disabilities bonded together to work as a whole. This lobby group was successful in achieving the passage of the Americans with Disabilities Act in 1990, showing its new-found national power. In Canada, Section 16 of the Charter of Rights and Freedoms was added in 1994, guaranteeing the rights of people with disabilities.

The process of integration, however, is still by no means simple. Numerous pressures continue to face any parents or guardians who wish to have their special child accepted as a full member of society. In the attempt to meet your child's needs, local and national support groups can be invaluable resources that can make the tasks you face much easier.

WHAT IS A SUPPORT NETWORK?

A support network comprises a number of individuals or groups who will provide the direction, help, support, and respite that you may require to successfully care for your child. The network may include organizations such as a specific support group for your child's disability, advocacy groups, caregivers, medical or paramedical personnel, home and school associations, religious groups, community groups, and your friends and relatives who are willing and able to provide the aid that your family requires on a regular basis or during emergencies.

Why Are Support Groups Important?
In providing a total care system for a child who has a disability,

it is vital to take advantage of existing support groups and to structure your own network so that the help you require will always be available. By accessing your community support groups you will be taking the first step to creating a resource that will benefit your entire family. There is no question that once you learn the requirements of care, you, your spouse, and other family members may be the best qualified personnel to administer that care, but when families attempt to provide complete care for their child on their own, they risk many difficulties. Over an extended period of time, it may become too physically and emotionally draining for you to attempt to provide all of the care — especially if your child requires full-time attention. Parents who try to provide total care are at a very high risk of suffering from burnout.

THE COMPONENTS OF A SUPPORT NETWORK

Disability Organizations

These include organizations such as the Institute for the Blind and the Deaf and the National Organization for the Cerebral Palsied. Personnel in these organizations can provide you with the most current information available in terms of medical advice, rehabilitative opportunities, and other areas to meet the needs of people with specific conditions. They evaluate therapies; raise or access funds for group and individual programs; provide education for parents, caregivers, and the public; and often provide equipment such as wheelchairs, prosthetics, and computers either free of charge or, usually, at costs below market prices. They also provide the invaluable service of helping parents cope with the stresses involved in raising special needs children. These groups may be organized at the national, state, provincial, and local levels. If there is no local chapter in your area, you can contact the organization through its national, state, or provincial office (see Appendix 2 for a directory of these organizations).

Local Chapters

If you can contact a local chapter of a support group, you will find a wealth of information, support, and understanding. These groups are arenas for people with similar concerns who are familiar with most, if not all, of the difficulties that you might encounter. Fellow members will provide you with relevant facts about medical personnel, treatments, and community resources. In an environment of people sharing similar experiences, you can vent your frustrations, fears, and hopes, and work together to identify and fulfill mutual needs. Some groups, for example, will provide fellow members with used equipment such as crutches, wheelchairs, and car seats. (This equipment usually has to be replaced as children grow.) Other groups have members who can construct specialized equipment at substantially lower rates than what is commercially available.

Service Clubs

Service clubs are local, national, or international organizations whose main objectives are to improve the quality of life for citizens in their respective communities. Even though some of them may represent specific ethnic, cultural, or religious groups, they usually offer their broad range of services to all members of the community. In addition to financial assistance, many service clubs will be able to provide you with volunteers and equipment to ease the responsibilities of caring for your child. The Rotary, Shriners, Elks, Kinsmen, B'Nai Brith, and Kiwanis organizations, as well as many other groups have provided services to children and the parents of children with disabilities. These services range from providing equipment to arranging for hospitalization and care.

Community Volunteers

Once you have established your child's needs, it is helpful to find volunteers who can assist you in performing a number of roles central to your child's rehabilitation. These volunteers may be high school, college, or university students who are required to complete volunteer work as part of their degree programs. You may also be able to obtain the support of retired nurses, therapists, and teachers who can provide invaluable help in areas such as home therapy and education.

In addition, try to locate baby-sitters, who will give you much-needed break times away from your kids. You may have to provide them with special training so that they will be able to deal with any situation that might arise in your absence. Sometimes it is also worthwhile to have children who do not have disabilities play with your child on a regular basis. This can be very helpful in building your child's self-esteem and self-confidence.

The Government

Many people who care for children with special needs rely on the government for support. They believe that the government should provide the personal and financial aid required to help maintain the child in a home environment. This perspective has been enhanced by legislation mandating the integration of disabled children in all segments of society. The social movement of deinstitutionalization has further motivated the belief that government ought to support, at least in part, the home care of children with special needs.

The reality is that most government financial support is not sufficient to meet the costs of raising a child with serious disabilities. At present we are in a period of increasing government debt loads, growing conservatism, and cutbacks, which have had a disproportionate impact on people with disabilities and their families. Unfortunately, thousands of individuals spend untold hours in what turn out to be fruitless attempts to obtain adequate government support. Try to access whatever government support is available, but it is counterproductive to expend all of your energy attempting to obtain funds from politicians and bureaucrats who may have other priorities. This is where an advocacy group might be most effective.

Family and Friends
Family and friends make up another important segment of your support network. They can often be relied upon to provide constant social and physical support, and it is comforting to know that they can almost always be relied upon in emergencies.

HOW DO I SET UP A SUPPORT NETWORK?

It can be a long and difficult process to establish a committed care team to provide for your child's special needs. First of all, establish your own needs. How much time do you feel you need for yourself? How can you arrange to spend more quality time with your spouse, other children, and family members? How do you find time for recreation, physical fitness, or fun in your life? Then write down the needs of your child. Is your child enjoying the friendship and support of peers? Is your child participating in social and recreational activities that are fun for him? Is your child receiving the best treatment available? Is your child encouraged to be as independent and self-reliant as possible? Talk to his doctor and/or case manager to make sure you have covered the basics.

Once you have identified these needs, list the personnel and information required to meet them. Next, contact your child's specific disability organization. Its staff members will provide the information that you require to get started, including background information on your child's disability, the most current research on patterns of treatment, and the names of the specialized personnel available in your community. Many of these organizations, especially in larger communities, have established a network that you will be able to plug into in order to arrange the support you require.

If these organizations do not exist in your area, contact the nearest disability group specific to your concern and ask them how they have established support groups in their areas. It will then be up to you to plan a support network. This will require much time and effort, but the net result will be worthwhile.

Becoming an Organizer

Caring for a child with a disability may require regular or constant supervision and therapy. For children with multiple disabilities, establishing a support network involving a large number of people on a weekly or daily basis can be very effective. A schedule allows you to feel secure that your child's needs are being met. If you have all of your child's activities and appointments planned and written down, and you have arranged for caregivers and other providers of respite care weeks in advance, then you will be able to lower your anxiety level and function at a higher level.

Contact the individuals and groups who can provide the services that you need. For each individual and organization list the types of support that you require, and provide them with a schedule so that you can establish a permanent routine. Initially, this can be a time-consuming activity, as you may have to write or phone many different organizations and groups in order to build an effective support network.

Transportation, home care, therapy, and child care supports must include backup arrangements, because some volunteers, for many reasons, are unable to follow through on their commitments. Give all the volunteers precise information on what activities and aid they can provide, along with phone numbers where you and your spouse can be contacted in case of emergency. Have your caregivers note any unusual symptoms or reactions that your child may exhibit while in their care; this can provide you with a valuable early warning system that can allow you to avert crises before they arise.

A PARENT'S SUCCESS STORY

"We live in a large city and we never had trouble having our son looked after. The schools were accessible, support personnel was available, transportation was arranged, and the entire system worked very well for us, except for the fact that our son always sat home on weekends. This was very difficult for him. He was sometimes invited to parties, but when kids went to the movies or went to play baseball or whatever kids do on weekends, they usually didn't bother with him. In 1992 there were a lot of things going on with regards to Olympics for people with disabilities. Basketball, tennis, and various forms of ball games in the gym seemed to give kids with disabilities the opportunity to have fun. I was able to contact the local cub leader, who was very helpful. We set up basketball games for kids with problems that forced them to use a wheelchair. Some of these kids were not confined to a wheelchair, as they used crutches or braces, but they learned to play wheelchair basketball anyway.

"After wheelchair basketball, all sorts of things took off. We arranged wheelchair croquet, wheelchair soccer, and we worked on wheelchair hockey, which was one sport that just wasn't successful. One of the coaches, who was highly motivated, had kids who couldn't walk dress up in pads and a mask and full equipment, and they played goalie. They had lots of fun. It is amazing what can be done, and there are all sorts of activities that are now available. In our community we have golf for kids with neurological problems such as cerebral palsy, for kids who have artificial limbs, and so on. I have become very involved over the years, and so has my family. My son maintains now that we have made the kids too busy, but that's a big improvement over the way it was before."

ORGANIZING RESPITE CARE

You must also organize respite care so that you and your other family members can enjoy time away from the demands of your special needs child. In a best case scenario, you will have family or friends who can take care of your child for several days or even weeks. If that option is unavailable, it may be appropriate to find an overnight camp that can meet your child's needs, or even have your child placed with a foster family or in an institutional environment for a few days or weeks. You may also be able to arrange for attendant care in your home. It is important to organize this team of volunteers so you can avoid the consequences of burnout (see Chapter 6).

As I've mentioned, my parents had a large support network in their family. One aunt and uncle had a rustic cottage on Gull Lake in Alberta, and with the support of other relatives, this family frequently took me for a two-week vacation. These summer holidays were very important as I learned that it was often necessary to ask strangers for help in activities that most people take for granted, such as cutting up food (I required help in feeding until I was eight years old) and doing exercises. And they allowed my parents to have valuable respite time. On some of these occasions they remained at home, and at other times they would take a short vacation on their own or with my younger brother and sister. They knew it was important to spend time with all of their children, and they went out of their way to make sure that no one felt left out.

Support groups will make your life much easier. Their information, expertise, and respite care will reduce the stress that you feel, as well as educate you to become a more knowledgeable and effective parent. They will also grant you easy access to the newest innovations in your area of concern. Support groups allow you to share your hopes and worries with other parents who have the same concerns and can lend a sympathetic ear. Once you have gained some experience and confidence, support groups can provide you with an opportunity to help out other parents of children with disabilities.

Chapter

9

Choosing the Caregivers

All of the people who participate in your child's care will be instrumental in her physical rehabilitation, and they will also have a significant impact on her self-esteem, motivation, adjustment, and integration. All of these factors make the proper selection and continuing supervision of personnel so important.

Always apply the principles of advocacy to the selection of personnel who care for your child. Compare the services and treatments being offered to your child very *carefully* and make informed decisions based on thoughtful consideration. This attention to detail will give your child the best possible chance to receive the proper diagnosis and treatment. If unqualified or inferior personnel attend to your child, she may not receive the proper care, and inappropriate treatment can have exceptionally negative effects. It's important to keep an open mind, however, as there may be a variety of treatments that can benefit your child. Alternative medical treatments such as those applied in homeopathy (in which practitioners administer small doses of medicine that in a healthy person would bring on symptoms similar to those of the disease), naturopathy (in which practitioners advise patients to avoid anything artificial or unnatural in the diet or in the environment), or chiropractic (in which chiropractors attempt to restore or maintain health by manipulation, primarily of the spinal column and pelvis) may each be effective in your child's rehabilitation.

CRITERIA FOR SELECTING APPROPRIATE PERSONNEL

You can evaluate personnel through personal interviews, discussions with other parents, and suggestions from your family doctor and other professionals whom you trust. Making a checklist and rating each of the candidates on the basis of your criteria is a good way to compare their relative merits and flaws (e.g., Excellent, Satisfactory, Average, Fair, Poor). It will take time before you are able to evaluate personnel properly, but you should always be aware of how effectively they work with your child. Use the following standards for your evaluation.

- **Ethical Values:** There are a number of ethical principles you should use to evaluate personnel. Everyone dealing with you and your child should observe proper levels of conduct. All caregivers must be prepared to promote your child's welfare and to respect your freedom of choice in selecting your child's medical or rehabilitative program. Caregivers must *always* be committed to providing the most appropriate and compassionate care for your child.

- **Openness About Treatment:** Your specialists should always provide you with specific information about the details of the care that they will provide for your child, as well as the estimated cost of the care that they recommend. Professionals should also tell you the merits and shortcomings of any programs they suggest. When appropriate, they should inform you of any available alternatives, as your child's care may involve a number of viable options.

As parents of a child with special needs, you should always have real choices. Some professionals believe that they can automatically assume power over your child and prescribe the directives that you must follow. Parents of children with disabilities, and adults with disabilities, are often treated as clients whose future rests entirely in the hands of professionals instead of as rational, intelligent people who have minds of their own. Professionals may have the skills and ability to prescribe strategies, but the treatment that they propose for you and your child sometimes may not be appropriate (e.g., a new drug to which your child may be allergic).

In 1995, a physician at Toronto's Sick Children's Hospital recommended an experimental drug therapy to the parents of a teenager with a potentially fatal liver disease. After the teen was given this drug, her condition improved significantly. Preliminary tests have shown that the drug has a 90 percent effectiveness rate in controlling this condition. It is very difficult to allow your child to take an experimental drug, but in some cases the risk can pay off. Getting a second opinion on alternative treatments and consulting with other parents who face the same choices as you do can help you decide.

Physicians who recommend innovative treatments are usually well informed about the nature of the disease or disability and the associated risks involved. Even if your specialist does not want to proceed with experimental therapy, it is important that they are at least aware of its existence. Alert your child's doctors to any new procedures you hear about. Qualified physicians evaluate all new treatments, and will usually recommend adopting these procedures if other therapies have not been beneficial. Keep in mind that many doctors tend to be conservative, as they do not want to risk a patient's well-being as a consequence of unproven medical experimentation.

- **Personal Compatibility:** Some professionals are perceived by parents as dictatorial, abrupt, or even rude. While doctors do work under heavy pressure and on tight schedules, as parents you have the right to be treated in a fair and courteous manner. If this does not happen, then you should voice your dissatisfaction to your caregiver. If you are not satisfied by the response that you receive, you may wish to consider alternative care. If you do not take any steps to address your problems, this conflict can become a continuing burden. Realistically, however, on some occasions you may have to tolerate an impersonal or rude professional to receive the expertise your child requires.

If you think that it would be more productive to work with different personnel, consult other parents and advocates in order to locate more personable caregivers. Changing doctors, however, is not a decision to be taken lightly. If it is at all possible, try to work out your differences with your original doctor. Changing personnel because of a personality conflict should only be done as a last resort.

- **Respect:** Caregivers should respect, understand, and appreciate your values and opinions before approving the measures that will be taken in your child's habilitation or rehabilitation. If your child's professional caregivers are unable or unwilling to grant you the consideration you deserve, it may be appropriate to select alternative personnel.

- **Flexibility:** The willingness of a doctor to try something new or unique may make the difference in your child's care. However, be wary of the possibility that your child may be subject to experimental treatment that may be potentially harmful. Try to strike a balance between traditional and innovative therapies.

- **Time:** An important consideration in dealing with professionals is scheduling and time management. Try to assess how busy your child's caregiver is. It is very difficult to sit with children for hours awaiting an appointment in an office. To avoid long delays and unnecessary time spent waiting in a doctor's office you should always call ahead for an appointment. Several days later you should confirm the appointment, and on the day of the appointment you should call before leaving home to see if the doctor will be able to see you at the scheduled time. Professionals sometimes overbook appointments and will occasionally be forced to respond to emergencies which can delay your appointment. If you are very worried about being made to wait, you should attempt to schedule your appointment as the first one of the day.

Some experts may be too involved with other considerations to be able to meet your needs. Their patient loads may be too great or they may merely consider your child as part of a research project. In such a situation, you and your child may not receive the time and treatment necessary to obtain the best results.

PROBLEMS THAT CAREGIVERS ENCOUNTER

On the other side of the coin, caregivers sometimes face parents who are not always informed, or who are not ready or willing to make the decisions that are in their child's best interests. In these cases professionals must act using their own best judgment, and sometimes overrule a parent's wishes. A surgeon related the story of a child who needed surgery for a faulty heart valve. The child's parents insisted that their son not receive a blood transfusion as this intervention was against their religious beliefs. The surgeon decided to proceed with the surgery and also decided that a blood transfusion would be given if needed. It was his conviction that the child's life was more important than his parent's beliefs. In other cases, professionals can work to accommodate the parents' concerns. One set of parents were very reluctant to have their child receive a blood transfusion because they feared the possible transmission of the AIDS virus. The doctor obtained the compatible blood of one parent and a sibling in order to overcome the parents' fears and proceeded with the operation. The doctor's open-mindedness enabled him to avert a potentially tragic situation.

Another problem both caregivers and parents face is that not all patients with the same condition react to treatment in the same way. For example, the physician, therapist, and clergyman of a ten-year-old child who was required to use a wheelchair found a summer camp for him, where children with similar physical difficulties were accommodated in a warm, caring atmosphere. This child would not eat or participate in any of the camp programs, and after a week the senior camp staff informed the parents that they had to take him home, as the staff was worried about his emotional and physical well-being. In this case, the family physician, therapist, clergyman, and camp staff had done their utmost to ensure that the child would have a positive summer experience, but in spite of their best efforts, he did not. No one was negligent in this situation, but the child's failure to enjoy the camp illustrates that even the best conceived strategies designed by the most competent personnel may not always be effective.

HOW TO EVALUATE PERSONNEL AND THERAPIES

Always evaluate the qualifications and reputations of the personnel who treat and care for your child. Confirm their area or areas of specialty, their training, their membership in professional organizations, and their position in a clinic or other treatment center. Support groups and other parents may provide help in developing an assessment.

It is your job to find the best match for you and your child. Sometimes this decision will be based on your "gut" instinct, but there are several criteria that you ought to consider when selecting professionals and others who will be involved with you and your child.

- honesty
- integrity
- reputation
- compassion
- competency
- openness
- innovation
- references
- publications in appropriate journals
- seminar participation
- membership in professional organizations
- accreditation
- education
- experience

Occasionally, people will promise miraculous cures and therapies that may not be effective. For example, many people, including the parents of children with disabilities, have been attracted to the use of laetrile clinics. (Laetrile is manufactured from apricot pits and some people claim that it is effective in curing cancer.) Although these clinics give parents and patients examples of miraculous recoveries, no legitimate physician, university, or medical journal has validated laetrile-related cures. Look carefully at the viability of such promised "miracles" so that you or your child do not suffer any financial or physical harm.

However, it can be very difficult to evaluate rehabilitative therapies. In some instances, different therapies may be coordinated in an unconventional manner. In order to properly judge your child's programs of therapy you must read extensively, consult physicians, caregivers, your support group, other parents, and experts so that you become an informed and competent consumer of services. Use the Internet, libraries, and support group information to access the most current information.

MEDICAL AND PARAMEDICAL PERSONNEL

The following is a list of some of the personnel that you may consult and use in the care of your child.

Physicians
general practitioners
family doctors
specialists
psychologists
Dentists
Nurses
nurse's aides
Therapists
physical

occupational
speech
audiologists
personal attendants
Social Workers
Intervenors
Educational Specialists
    teachers' aides
    consultants
    school board members
    home and school associations
    universities and colleges
Government
    local, state, provincial, or federal legislators
Appeal Boards
"Private" Resources
    private organizations and foundations
    service clubs
    community groups
    advocacy groups
    support groups
    organizations representing specific interests of
    people with disabilities

These experts and specialists represent the wide body of resources that may be used productively in your child's treatment and rehabilitation. Identify your child's needs and then focus on the particular specialists and agencies who are qualified to provide the services that you require.

FINDING APPROPRIATE MEDICAL CARE

Many women who become pregnant are content to remain with the family physician who has previously treated them. Other women opt to be treated by an obstetrician and may later find a pediatrician to treat their child. Select a medical practitioner with whom you feel comfortable and confident.

Most physicians readily consult one another in situations where making a diagnosis is difficult or where programs of therapy are not readily available. In many situations open communication between family physicians and specialists is routine. Sometimes, however, physicians are reluctant to consult other experts because they believe that this may reflect badly upon their lack of knowledge or expertise. It is your responsibility as a parent to locate doctors who will meet your needs. In many cases, family practitioners will direct you to doctors or clinics that have recognized expertise. In other instances, support groups may suggest appropriate medical authorities.

You must be satisfied that the physician you choose has a competent background and the sufficient experience and professional integrity to be aware of the most recent innovations in treatment that are available. To stay informed physicians should read their professional journals and participate in seminars related to their field. Ask them what journals they read and how often they participate in seminars. Competent specialists can be found within directories, by referral from your family physician, by consultation with your local medical academy, or by the recommendations of other parents and support groups.

During or after each appointment, take notes and keep a regular diary of the medical care, therapy, drugs, and all other interventions on your child's behalf. Chart this information in an organized manner so that you, your spouse, and other caregivers will be able to evaluate the medical care your child is receiving on an ongoing basis. This is particularly important if you are required to relocate or change therapists.

PHYSICAL CARE

It is usually recommended that more than one physician be consulted in order to confirm the soundness of your child's treatment, and you should maintain a list of all of the attempted treatments to evaluate the success of each one. It is also important to maintain an up-to-date list of all of your child's medication, as some drugs react negatively when used in combination with one another. Chart your child's short- and long-term reactions to specific medications and diets. Be prepared for the possibility of allergic reactions. Try to use the same pharmacist who can keep track of all prescribed medications.

If your child exhibits noticeable problems after eating specific foods or ingesting certain drugs, it is imperative that the child receive medical attention, as reactions that seem minor may subsequently become more severe. Try to find out if your family has a history of allergies, and write down all the allergies you are aware of.

In some cases, your child may show fatigue or other common reactions to certain medications. At other times, your child may initially tolerate a prescription and then develop a negative reaction to the substance over a period of time. Keep your physician and pharmacist informed!

Sample Drug Chart

Name of Drug:	_____
Directions:	Note the dosage, frequency, and any special instructions.
Reactions Noted:	Keep track of all reactions, both positive and negative.
Possible Side Effects/Precautions:	Report any side effects to the doctor immediately; for example, drowsiness, nausea, headache, dizziness, bruising, bleeding, rash, sleeping difficulties, mental changes, weakness, hyperactivity, allergic reaction.
Drug Interactions:	Ask your pharmacist and physician as some medications must never be taken with others.
Missed Dose or Overdose:	Be aware of what to do and emergency procedures.
Storage:	Avoid moisture and sunlight. Watch expiry dates.

REHABILITATION COUNSELORS

When they experience a disability, many adults engage the services of rehabilitation counselors. These counselors are acquainted with most disabling conditions and the available medical resources and therapeutic procedures. Similarly, in many communities, individual counselors are available to provide services to parents in order to obtain the best desired results for their children. These individuals can be contacted through your local hospital, social service agencies, medical clinics, specialized treatment facilities, parent support groups, advocacy groups, and occasionally, through your local clergy. These people, who have specialized in obtaining the resources necessary to care for children with disabilities, may be able to overcome many of the roadblocks experienced by parents caring for their children. Unless these counselors come from local social service agencies, there is usually a cost attached to their services. Sometimes, medical insurance will cover their fee.

You may wish to consider employing such personnel as not only are they acquainted with the medical resources in your community, but they can also organize the support services that will allow you to cope more easily with the needs of your child. In relying on the services of outsiders, however, you may be relinquishing some control over your child's care. In the final analysis, your judgment is the most important and, therefore, I would carefully weigh the advisability of obtaining the services of these personnel before taking them on. If you do not have the time, or if you believe that you do not have the skills demanded by your responsibilities, it is appropriate to engage these specialists. They are particularly skilled in providing information and support during periods of crisis. These counselors are especially helpful for parents from abroad who come to the United States, Canada, or Britain to obtain treatment that is not available in their home countries. If these visiting families lack familiarity with the English language and with medical and support services, they might find a rehabilitation counselor or necessary resource.

OTHER SERVICE PROVIDERS

The same criteria of care that is applied to physicians should also be applied to the selection of other personnel involved in the care of your child. Social workers associated with local hospitals and clinics may direct you to the appropriate services as they are familiar with community resources. They may also be able to put you in contact with service clubs and similar organizations that might assist with financial and personal support. Some service clubs, such as Kiwanis, have programs catering to the needs of families and children with specific disabilities. Others provide hospital care and transportation to meet your needs. Some of these groups may also respond to unique requests. Home and school associations and church groups, for example, may furnish volunteers with physical and occupational programming training for your child, and provide respite care for you.

Professionally, social workers provide counseling for individuals and families to help them cope with the responsibilities of caring for a child with special needs, but occasionally, people who work with a social worker are dissatisfied with their therapist's approach. Remember that all personalities do not mix well, and do not dismiss professionals simply because of minor relationship problems. Parents should always be open and honest with all of their concerns. If difficulties are encountered in relationships with specific workers, it may be appropriate to engage other people with similar skills, but you should not make a change over one unfortunate incident. In difficult situations many attentive professionals will suggest to parents that it might be more productive to work with other people.

SPECIALIZED CLINICS

In many urban communities there exist specialized clinics such as rehabilitation centers that provide programs for the treatment of disabilities. These settings often provide staff who are specialists in the most progressive forms of treatment available. Such facilities are often regarded as being at the "leading edge" of innovation and research. Occasionally, there may be individuals in these facilities with whom you disagree over the treatment of your child. The facility usually expects that the parent will allow the organization to use its resources in whatever manner they see fit to maximize rehabilitation.

Some of these unique facilities will provide care that is subsidized, if not free. Unfortunately, they are few and far between, and most individuals who consider using these resources must either move on a temporary or permanent basis or consider having their child live in an institutionalized setting for an extended period of time.

In my own case, the experts at the Mayo Clinic in Rochester, Minnesota, encouraged my parents to have me reside at the clinic for three or four school years. They believed that they could teach me to write, and, through various types of occupational and physical therapy, create more opportunities for my integration. As previously mentioned, my parents declined this opportunity. The Mayo Clinic created an exercise program for me and demonstrated to my parents the types of equipment that might be useful for children with cerebral palsy. They had special shoes designed and braces that helped straighten my legs. The doctors and physiotherapists at the Mayo Clinic encouraged my parents to seek out supportive devices whenever required. They maintained that you have to be innovative on an individualized basis.

My parents used this information during my preteen years and had me follow a regimen of exercises. They also endeavored to locate physical and occupational therapists to provide assistance. My parents were firm in their conviction that our family should remain together, and were concerned that I might be treated like a "guinea pig."

I used to wonder whether attending the Mayo Clinic for a year or longer would have enabled me to learn to write effectively. But later on, I attended clinics and had treatment from occupational and physiotherapists, and I am now certain that the institutional program of the Mayo Clinic could not have accomplished anything that I did not achieve as a result of the therapy my parents obtained for me. A number of specialists at the Mayo Clinic provided my parents with schedules and outlines of specific therapies and my parents, relatives, and therapists applied these techniques. Even in the late 1940s, my therapists were very progressive — many of their treatments were presented to me in the form of games so that I would be more willing to participate.

The relationships that I developed and maintained at home were very important to me. I was six years old when I went to the Mayo Clinic for the second time, and I took part in the conversation in which some professionals attempted to influence my mother to leave me in Rochester for a year or two. I remember the fear that I might be left at the clinic. But my mother would have no part of this solution, and I became very secure in the knowledge that my parents would never send me away from home. Giving your children that same sense of security is one of the best things you can do.

If you contemplate using the facilities of a specialized clinic where institutionalization is required on a part-time basis, monitor your child's care closely. There are many advantages to be obtained from short-term, goal-directed institutional care. However, institutional care may not meet your child's social and psychological needs. Some children placed in these specialized clinics feel isolated and abandoned. This feeling is understandable as some children with disabilities can become totally reliant on their families for their social and physical needs. Institutional abuse, by neglect or by design, is not unheard of, and my current research in this field points toward some very frightening results. Many children do not receive their medication as prescribed by their physicians; some children are not as carefully bathed or kept as clean as necessary; and it is not uncommon for crying children to be ignored for long periods of time. It must be said that this type of neglect is usually due to understaffing. Understandably, these personnel, who are often overworked, can seldom establish or maintain emotional bonds with children in their care. People with disabilities who are in institutions lack power, and may only have limited, if any, contact outside the institution. The less power you have, the more vulnerable you become. People with disabilities, especially children, are the most vulnerable to psychological, social, physical, and sexual abuse.

If circumstances dictate that you have to place your child in an institution, contact a local support group or social work agency so that your child can be regularly visited and monitored. The majority of institutions are well run with excellent resources and personnel, but vigilance is still important and must be considered a parent's responsibility.

SPECIALIZED ATTENDANT CARE

Some families are in a financial position that allows them to provide specialized attendant care for their children. In some cases specialized attendants live with the child, and in other instances they are a part of the child's life for familial, educational, and recreational pursuits. A specialized attendant provides individual care and stimulation so that the child can maximize her potential. In many instances specialized attendants work with children only a few times a week because of financial constraints or other commitments. The criteria for selecting an attendant for your child is very similar to the criteria for selecting other health care personnel: They should be well-qualified, hard-working, and dedicated to your child. Because specialized attendants spend so much time with you and your child, it is also important that you have a good personal relationship with them. Over a prolonged period of time, a personality conflict at such close quarters could seriously hinder the quality of your child's care.

Perhaps the most famous example of successful specialized attendant care is the relationship between Anne Sullivan and Helen Keller. After Helen Keller became blind and deaf from an early childhood illness, her parents contacted Alexander Graham Bell, a leading authority on hearing disorders, who put them in touch with the most progressive clinic of the time, the Perkins Institution for the Blind in Boston, which referred Anne Sullivan to them. Anne had mastered the art of communicating to others by tapping fingers into a hand, the patterns of tapping standing for different letters (a hand version of the Morse Code). Anne came to the Keller home when Helen was six years old. Within a month of using this method of communication she opened the world of language and expression to Helen. Anne was a firm and demanding tutor and she remained Helen's devoted teacher and companion until she died in 1936.

INDIVIDUAL ATTENDANT CARE

In individual attendant care, there is one-on-one service provided for the child; whereas in specialized attendant care, the services are specific skills that may be provided by different caregivers. Although individual attendant care is expensive, it is usually a much more reasonable investment than placing a child in an institution. The individual care attendant functions to ensure that the child's developmental capacities are maximized. Government support for such personnel tends to be nonexistent, but in some cases, service clubs and philanthropic organizations will contribute part- or full-time attendant care. There are independent care personnel who have accompanied individuals with disabilities to high school, colleges, and universities. Some of the students have subsequently gained employment and become fully functioning adults. In many instances, their progress could not have taken place without the work of their attendants, who were able to provide physical and emotional support.

Individual attendants may include teachers, volunteers, baby-sitters, therapists, and friends and family. It is important that you, perhaps with the assistance of a physician or case manager, assemble and organize special needs caregivers to become an effective asset and regular part of your support team. These people should have an in-depth understanding of the nature of your child's disability and of the techniques that they can use to assist you. Although they may be volunteers, I recommend that you request references to ensure your child's well-being. There are some unscrupulous individuals who have been known to take advantage of parents in need, neglecting the children in their care or overcharging for their services.

One parent remembers the valuable attendant care for her child:

"Our son Michael was always a very active child. In the summer after grade ten Michael went out with seven of his friends to have a good time. They went swimming, and somehow Michael hit his head on the diving board. He was pulled out of the pool by his friends, but since that time has been "a paraplegic." It was really difficult for us to find someone to help us look after him. He was 180 pounds, and neither his father nor I could lift him. We needed people to help us out on a voluntary basis, as after the first seven months our insurance benefits ran out. We endeavored to find people who could lift Michael, but this was difficult because of his weight.

"We found, would you believe it, a part-time nurse who was only about 140 pounds herself, perhaps less. She had been laid off from work and was willing to work for us on a full-time basis, and, I might add, at substantially less money than she was getting as a nurse. She was aware of all the techniques that would allow Michael's life to be very comfortable. She has been not only a good nurse, but also a fabulous companion. She read to him and motivated him to get back to work, and he is now in a radio broadcasting school.

"Michael was, as you can understand, very depressed after his accident, because his entire life had changed. Soon after the accident he was giving up, and we were giving up as well. It was very depressing to all of a sudden have a child who has a disability, who had once been healthy, outgoing, not very bright as a student, but a first-rate athlete. May was a wonderful help. Mike now has a girlfriend, is doing fairly well at school, and maintains about a 68 percent average. He may not be on the honor roll, but when you consider all of his difficulties this is an extraordinary accomplishment. He could not have attained this level of success without May's help. She brings in cassettes, she takes him out for trips all over the city, and she does all sorts of things. This was especially true just after the injury. She has been with us ever since the injury and sometimes attends classes with Michael and takes notes. More than half her time is voluntary, as we really cannot afford all the cost, but she has been sensational. May has not only been a wonderful help to our family; she has become a family friend."

HOW TO PREPARE A TEMPORARY CAREGIVER

If you decide to leave your child with a caregiver, leave a list of the following information:

- the telephone number and address of where you can be reached;
- the telephone number of an alternative guardian;
- the local emergency numbers;
- the telephone number of your family practitioner or pediatrician;
- the telephone number of a neighbor;
- a list of indicators of distress to recognize and respond to;
- a list and location of medications with precise directions for administering them; and
- a list of alternative caregivers should the person responsible for care become indisposed.

What you are creating is an important back-up system. As discussed in Chapter 6, part-time care and respite care is important for you, your spouse, and other family members. This assistance allows you the time to "recharge your batteries" and contributes to the well-being of the entire family.

THE SUPPORT OF FAMILY AND FRIENDS

Family and friends may frequently provide back-up and support. Many parents with special needs children, however, discover that they cannot always rely on this group for comprehensive support. Some relatives may lack the sensitivity and commitment required to provide a positive atmosphere for your child. Others may be too busy to be relied upon. In one case I encountered, an insensitive grandmother kept referring to her grandchild who was affected by a growth disorder as "my poor little Albert." The child developed great sensitivity and embarrassment regarding his size, which was later accompanied by a severe stutter. The grandmother's remarks at times were not only heard by her family, but by her grandchild's playmates. Creating the most nurturing relationship for your child demands that you exercise extreme caution in the selection of those who will be involved in the treatment and care of your child.

OTHER SUPPORTS AND PROGRAM PROVIDERS

Groups for children, such as Scouts, Brownies, Girl Guides, religious youth groups, YMCAs, and YWCAs, often provide facilities for *all* children. When you can arrange for your child to join these groups, you will discover that mainstream opportunities can build her self-esteem. Your child may become comfortable and sometimes even fully integrated within a peer group. These opportunities for integration should be taken advantage of whenever possible. In many circumstances, even children with severe disabilities can become involved in social, educational, and recreational pursuits that may motivate them to become more active. The leaders of these extracurricular groups must be made aware of and sensitive to the needs of your child. This is important because it will allow them to support your child's effective integration into these activities.

Selecting the appropriate personnel is very important for you and your child, as it is important to have access to the people who are on the leading edge of their field to ensure that your child receives the most appropriate care. If you are well prepared and know what traits a good caregiver should have, then you will be able to choose wisely, and rest easy in the knowledge that your child will be taken care of by the best professionals and volunteers. If you make informed choices you can be confident that the people whom you select will be able to help her reach her maximum potential.

10

Housing and Long-Term Care

During the first five decades of the twentieth century, people with major disabilities, including children, were usually housed in institutions. The prevailing ideology of the times was "out of sight, out of mind." Parents were counseled to institutionalize their children, as people with severe disabilities were perceived to be a heavy and unnecessary burden on the family. In these sterile institutional surroundings, which tended to be underfinanced and understaffed, children with severe disabilities were seldom able to live fulfilling lives. Many residents of institutions were victims of active and passive abuse. The government would usually provide facilities for the care of these "unfortunates," but in this environment, the children were seldom able to develop, learn, and grow.

THE TREND TOWARD DEINSTITUTIONALIZATION

In the 1960s a new train of thought emerged, identifying people with disabilities as legitimate human beings who should be given the opportunity to maximize their potential and to enjoy life with their families with full rights as citizens. Proponents of these ideas maintained that all people with special needs should be given the opportunity to participate and to integrate into society; that they were, in fact, a legitimate minority group victimized by prejudice and discrimination.

When the trend toward deinstitutionalization began, the sterility of institutional life was exposed, and doctors, social workers, other professionals, and advocates began to move people who had disabilities into loving, productive, and stimulating family environments. Whenever possible, parents were encouraged to have their children with disabilities stay in the family home. Outside the home, particularly in larger urban areas, **specialized personnel and facilities** endeavored to create the conditions whereby people with the most severe disabilities could have access to a positive quality of life. Current policy tries to allow those with disabilities, no matter how severe, to reside in homelike settings.

RESIDENTIAL ALTERNATIVES FOR CHILDREN WITH DISABILITIES

There are at least eight alternatives for the accommodation of children and young adults with disabilities. The following is a survey of the range of options.

Home Care

Most experts agree that the best environment for any person who has a disability is the family home, and, indeed, that the family home provides the most supportive environment for all family members. Home care may, however, present the family with a number of social, psychological, and financial problems.

The Benefits of Home Care

- In the home the child is surrounded by family and friends who give him love, encouragement, self-esteem, and security.
- Children with disabilities can be constantly motivated in their rehabilitation and education, as their families are the people most concerned with their development. Families will also develop new opportunities and improve the existing opportunities for their child's independence, so that special needs children can enjoy activities with their peers and allow parents their own social and recreational time.
- There are more possibilities for the child to participate in activities and feel like a member of the family unit and extended family. This is difficult to develop if a child is away from home.
- There are more opportunities to develop and maintain friends.
- The cost of care, although expensive, is usually more reasonable than in an institution.
- Support and respite services are available from local volunteer, support, and advocacy groups to ease the problems of home care.

The Drawbacks to Home Care
- Parents cannot always provide the specialized care, therapy, or educational services and equipment that can be supplied in institutional environments.
- Home care is a lot of work. The tasks involved in caring for your special child can sometimes create physical and emotional problems for family members and other caregivers. If both parents hold jobs outside the home, providing the appropriate level of care for a child with severe disabilities is all but impossible without the aid of a full-time attendant.
- Because of financial burdens, it is difficult to provide and maintain all the specialized equipment that your child may need, ranging from ramps to respirators to computer technology.

Supports and Incentives to Home Care
In order to help alleviate these burdens, most governments are now providing incentives to encourage parents to keep children with special needs in the family home. These incentives include financial aid for physical alterations, such as ramps, widened doors, specialized washroom equipment, and prosthetics, that will allow children with disabilities to enjoy an easier time in the home. This support may be augmented by grants to allow for full-time or part-time support staff. Nurses, physiotherapists, and general caregivers may be paid for in part by assistance from civic, state, or provincial governments. In areas where this support is not available or is insufficient, many service groups, religious organizations, home and school organizations, and personnel from colleges and universities may provide excellent volunteer support. You can

access this support by contacting the actual institutions or your local support group, who should be aware of the available facilities.

Respite Care

All family members will require periods of freedom from caring for their child in order to reduce stress and successfully maintain their relationships. This relief may be provided by other family members or professional caregivers or volunteers, either in your home or at other residences.

The Benefits of Respite Care
- Respite care provides time out, relaxation, and support for parents involved in caring for their children.
- It also provides parents with time to recharge their batteries so that they can continue to provide quality of care.

The Drawbacks to Respite Care
- Respite care may not provide the same quality of care that parents give.
- Respite care personnel may not have the same commitment and skills that you have, but most of them, if properly trained and supervised, will be adequate for your purposes.

The Family Residence with In-Home Support

Many families are able to meet the requirements of raising a child with special needs with the help of a support attendant at home. This form of caregiving has many advantages as it allows for the child to benefit from a family setting even when he requires constant supervision or care. It's particularly beneficial for a child who is affected by a condition such as cystic fibrosis, which requires intermittent daily therapy, or a child with multiple disabilities who needs more intensive care. Keeping your child at home is advantageous for not only your family and the child himself, but also for the local government, as in-home care is usually a more cost-effective strategy. In some cases, members of your extended family and circle of friends may be able to provide the personnel and finances to support this pattern of care.

The Family Home with Part-Time Institutional Support

In this type of care, the child usually resides at home while an institution provides for his educational, recreational, medical, and rehabilitative needs. For many this pattern of care is the best choice because the child has access to specialized resources available to enhance his development in addition to having the benefits of their family environment.

Families in this situation frequently involve student volunteers in their child's education and rehabilitation programs. Students in training often have access to the most advanced techniques and technologies. In addition, they are closely supervised by teachers and other professionals who will ensure the quality of their care.

Part-Time Institutional Care

Part-time institutional care for children with special needs, where a child lives at home but goes to an institution full time for a short period of time, is available in most larger urban communities. These programs provide educational, rehabilitative, and recreational programs. They can be used on a short-term basis to allow a child to develop the special skills that are necessary for participating in a mainstream program. For example, some children who find writing difficult, if not impossible, are able to learn computer skills with the help of specially designed keyboards or voice activation, and can then join a mainstream classroom.

These programs are also an end in themselves. In them children develop self-esteem and may acquire a number of skills. Sometimes the best progress occurs as a result of children imitating the success of others. In an environment where they are surrounded by many of their peers, children can be pushed to higher levels by constantly viewing and trying to emulate the behavior of others. Even if a child never enters a regular school program, part-time institutional care can have some distinct benefits.

Full-Time Institutional Care

Full-time institutional care is usually chosen only as a last resort when parents find it extremely difficult to provide the necessary care for their child at home.

Although they are declining in number, there are two types of institutions that are still accessible for children with special needs. One, short-term institutions that provide specialized therapy for children with specific conditions (e.g., for the hearing and sight impaired); two, long-term care facilities for children who are extensively impaired. Multiply handicapped and severely developmentally impaired children often require more extensive care than can be given at home or on an outpatient basis. Occasionally children with Down syndrome or cerebral palsy are placed in this type of setting when, in fact, some might make better progress within a family environment. Because of increased public concern, these facilities have generally become much better supervised by local, provincial, and state agencies. However, governmental cutbacks in recent years are cause for concern.

Institutions provide the specialized care and equipment that allow people with severe disabilities to have access to adequate accommodation. The most effective institutional settings provide physical care for their residents as well as programs that are designed to stimulate and develop their abilities. These programs include physical and occupational therapy, games, and educational instruction through television and computers. Less effective institutions exhibit a tendency to "warehouse" residents. In these surroundings, the children's basic needs are usually met, but they seldom benefit from programs designed to maximize their quality of life.

The Benefits of Full-Time Institutional Care
- An institution offers specialized equipment; physical, occupational, and drug therapy; personnel; and programs that may not be available or cannot be operated in a home setting.
- They provide a place for the children of families who simply cannot afford or cope with home care.
- Most institutions are inspected on a regular basis by government personnel to maintain or improve the quality of care.

The Drawbacks to Institutional Care
- Institutions cannot duplicate the strong emotional ties that are developed in the family home.

- Most institutions are understaffed, leading to a weakening of the services provided.
- Some of the personnel may be underqualified or even completely unqualified for the job that they are performing. (In medical emergencies, for example, unqualified staff are unlikely to respond properly, and this can result in injury or the loss of life.)
- Institutions can be very expensive.
- Social, psychological, physical, and sexual abuse can occur.
- If the environment is not warm and supportive, the child may become withdrawn, unresponsive, or violent — and sometimes, as a result, he is restrained and drugged instead of being dealt with in a more constructive manner. In an extreme case, for example, a child who was autistic and acted out in emotional outbursts was restrained by the use of drugs and a straitjacket when he attempted to communicate the discomfort that he was suffering as a result of appendicitis. He subsequently died. If he had been in a home environment it is unlikely that this tragedy would have occurred.

Independent Living Centers

I feel strongly that whenever possible a child should enjoy the advantages of living with his family. However, children eventually grow up and their parents age. For parents, aging may make it difficult to physically care for their child with a disability. Beginning in their teenage years, young people often wish to live with their peers, wanting the advantages of more independent living. With this independence comes increased self-reliance and self-esteem, and it also allows individuals to make significant choices that may be at odds with the pattern of care provided by their parents.

Before the 1970s, there was no place for people with disabilities to move out to on their own; in the past three decades, however, independent living centers have filled this vacuum. Independent living centers provide residents with recreational, social, and educational programming to meet their needs. These apartment or home-style facilities are supervised so that the residents enjoy the advantages of independence, but are offered a protective environment at the same time. They are usually government subsidized, and may receive funding from service clubs and other specific organizations. Some residents are self-supporting and contribute to the cost of their own housing.

The Benefits of Independent Living Centers

- The supervision in these environments is provided by workers who are trained to meet the needs of the residents.
- Resident councils are often established so that the residents can determine the policies by which the centers are run. Through the councils the residents direct the workers into appropriate duties, which include supervising, providing care, and protecting, while at the same time maximizing residents' "safe independence."
- The concept of "safe independence" establishes the goal of giving each resident as much independence as possible without sacrificing his safety and security.
- Independent living centers usually cost less than a regular apartment of a similar size and location because the housing units are operated as nonprofit accommodations.

The Drawbacks to Independent Living Centers

- There may be problems with family acceptance. For example, some parents are reluctant to allow their children such a high level of independence, and fight their child's decision to move out. But most parents realize their children will outlive them, and therefore feel that it is important that their children be in a facility concerned with their care as well as their need for independence.

- In some cases children will be reluctant to leave the cozy environment of the family home. In other instances, children adapt very well to the independent living center, and become more and more reluctant to be involved in ongoing family matters.

The problems a family can have with independent living centers are illustrated in this story told by a nineteen-year-old young man who has cerebral palsy:

"I had always lived at home, and my parents took extra care of me from as far back as I can remember. In fact, I relied on them, probably too much. They took me to special schools, they took me to special recreational areas, and they were always with me. I appreciated my parents' efforts and I enjoyed their company. My father was always very tough on me in order to motivate me to do more things. I tried wheelchair racing and I can go a bit faster than other people, but I will never make the Olympics. I've tried other sports as well, including swimming. I can float, as long as they put me on a tarp.

"When I was about seventeen, however, I discovered that there was really one thing missing in my life, and that was friends. In the small town where I lived there was no community center or place where I could hang out and really enjoy things. Ottawa was a long way away, forty-five minutes by car. I discovered that there was an independent living center there, where people with disabling conditions could live independently. The living centers have a lot of volunteers and paid staff and they provide a lot of support. It sounded very appealing. But when I mentioned it to my mother, she became particularly upset. She did not think that I could be properly looked after, as I have to be fed and need assistance for the washroom.

"In any case, I made the phone call to the independent living center, and the people there seemed to think that they could look after me very well. They also told me that there were many people there with similar conditions and that I might enjoy living there. When I mentioned this to my parents, they were very upset. They told me that I wasn't grateful to them for looking after me, and that I would not be well looked after. They said that I would regret it and that basically I was selfish. I think that they felt that they were looking after my best interests. In addition, I think that I had become very important company for them too. For my entire life I had been the central focus of their lives. They spent most evenings and most holidays at home with me. I finally convinced them to let me try the group home for a week. It was fabulous. There were people around all the time. I really enjoyed myself and I am enjoying myself now. My parents were really upset when I moved out, but living independently is the only way for me."

Self-Contained Living Space

Self-contained living spaces — apartments, condominiums, or special suites — are particularly inviting alternatives in communities that do not have independent living centers. Independent living centers offer advantages to residents with special needs that cannot be obtained by the resident of a self-contained unit, such as being surrounded by peers and having staff around to provide "safe independence," but some people prefer the quiet of the independent living space to the group atmosphere of the living center. Many also find that the independent living space is less organized and restrictive and that they can have the support of a full- or part-time caregiver. The decision to enter a living center or independent space is largely dependent on personal tastes and choices, as some people enjoy the wide sphere of activities provided by the living center, while others prefer the independence and solitude of a self-contained space.

Some governments have recently established grants so that families can build "granny suites" attached to their homes. These allow family members to live independently from their families, but to remain in close proximity. Some areas, such as the province of Ontario, now permit the construction of similar facilities for young adults with disabilities. Often the local authorities refrain from reassessing property values following the construction of these suites to encourage families to maintain their "care system." It might be worthwhile to contact your municipal government to find out if you are eligible for this benefit.

HOUSING AND THE LAW

Prior to the 1980s, most landlords were reluctant to rent property to people with disabilities, and in many cases their rental accommodations did not meet the requirements of those with special needs. In the last fifteen years, laws have been enacted preventing landlords from discriminating against people with disabilities. With the establishment of the Americans with Disabilities Act, the Canadian Charter of Rights and Freedoms and Human Rights Act, and numerous civic ordinances, landlords are now often required to rent apartments to members of the community of people with disabilities. Now some landlords even seek out disabled people as tenants. These landlords have come to realize that their rent is almost guaranteed (because local, municipal, provincial, or state governments often pay the landlord directly) and that the anticipated problems of having a tenant with a disability seldom arise. Also, some landlords are entitled to special allowances and tax breaks if they redesign their rental space to meet the needs of members of the disabled community. Although much progress has been made in recent years, if your child faces discrimination on the basis of their disability they now have the legal protection to ensure that they will be treated fairly.

In addition to the options outlined in this chapter, adoption and foster care, which are outlined in more detail in chapter 4, are also viable choices. These types of placements can be arranged through approved community agencies. No matter what option you choose for your child, try to create an environment that will protect your child and allow him to experience both freedom and security.

Chapter

11

Finances

As a result of your child's condition, there are two types of financial responsibilities you will have to undertake: (1) the direct and immediate costs that you will incur; and (2) matters of long-term financial need. These costs may at first appear to be astronomical, but with the proper planning and advice your anticipated expenses can be drastically reduced.

IMMEDIATE COSTS

You can determine a large number of your immediate expenses once you have an accurate diagnosis of your child's condition. Your costs can be divided into three main groups — equipment, medical bills, and support staff.

Equipment
>Lifting Devices
>Breathing Apparatus
>Wheelchairs
>Walkers
>Exercise Equipment
>Braces
>Ramps
>Alterations to the Home
>Lighting Devices
>Special Doorbells or Fire Alarms or Carbon Monoxide Detectors
>Prostheses
>Computers/Printers/Word Processors
>Specialized Reading/Hearing Devices
>Specialized Rental Equipment (sometimes tax deductible if disability related)
>Other

Medical Bills
>Prescription Drugs and Other Medications
>Insurance
>Counseling
>Other Expenses
>Travel
>User Fees and Assessment Fees
>Hospital Charges
>Medical Procedures

Support Staff
>Case Managers

Physiotherapists and Occupational Therapists
Nurses
Attendant Care
Tutors
Medical Social Workers
Counselors
Other Staff

Some Common Problems and How to Solve Them

1. **The Equipment Is Unavailable:** Your child may need a wide variety of special devices in order to contend with his disability. Although the array of equipment to ease the lives of people with disabilities is expanding at an unprecedented rate, the equipment that your child needs may not be readily available. In some cases you and your therapist may be required to design and build this equipment. Local engineers, computer scientists, and carpenters can be asked to design and build custom equipment for your child. You may find that many of these people will even donate their services. You can find these people through your local support groups, through other parents of children with the same needs, or through medical personnel.

2. **The Equipment Is Too Expensive:** You may find that the equipment you need is extraordinarily expensive. You can purchase used equipment, which can be found through newspaper advertisements, or through the services of support and advocacy groups. Sometimes these groups will have collections of used devices they can give to you free of charge.

3. **We Purchased Expensive Equipment That Is Not Necessary:** The best way to avoid this problem is by knowing exactly what your child needs, and by refusing to be persuaded into buying anything else. For example, many parents are inclined to buy a top-of-the-line computer for their child when a less powerful computer will do the job. If you are not familiar with computers, it is a good idea to go to a computer store with someone who knows the available technology, as well as your child's needs. (Keep in mind that when businesses, government departments, and other groups upgrade to new technology, they may be willing to donate old equipment. It is important to canvass sources through the mail, telephone calls, and personal contact. Members of your support group will usually be familiar with the best resources.)

Sources of Support

Help in defraying the costs of your child's care can come from several sources — family, friends, government agencies, private foundations, charities, service clubs, and specific fundraising events.

Family and Friends

It is sometimes difficult to ask family members and friends for financial support. Some people are very lucky and don't have to worry about it — their families are very close-knit and can always be relied upon. I recently learned of a family whose fourteen-year-old son was injured in a biking accident and who received money and other support before they had even thought of asking for help. As one of the relatives said, "We are family, and if the need is there, we will help. Isn't that what families are for?"

Other families may be equally close, yet may not have the available financial resources to give. Help can be given in other ways: equipment can be built, baby-sitting and other needed attendant care can be performed at little or no charge, and emotional support can be given. This help is equally, if not more important, than straightforward gifts of money. Every hour that a niece or nephew baby-sits for you is one less hour that you have to pay a stranger.

Some parents are reluctant or embarrassed to ask for help. If you feel this way, remember this: no parent or set of parents can do everything alone; all of your friends and family are resources that can and should be used to help your child. **Most of the people you know will want to help you out,** but they may feel like they are interfering if they offer help without your asking first. You can alleviate this concern by taking the initiative. The worst thing that can happen is that they will say no.

Government Agencies

Social services agencies and health departments often have funds available for what you need. It is not unusual for these resources to go untapped, as people are often unaware of their existence. Use the information compiled by your support groups and the techniques of advocacy to access this financial aid.

On occasion government bureaucracies may claim that as a matter of policy they never provide certain types of aid. Through the exertion of influence on politicians and bureaucrats, however, advocacy groups may be able to motivate governments to respond favorably to your requests.

Private Foundations, Service Clubs, and Charities
Many of these groups can support your requests. Organizations such as the Shriners support hospitals and provide funds to meet the needs of children with disabilities.

Telephone to identify the presidents and treasurers of the local charities, and contact these people directly by letter. Your support groups will often encourage and direct you as to the best approaches and personnel available to make these requests. If possible, send copies of these letters to other people in the respective organizations. In your letters, always outline the exact nature of the problem, the precise equipment or program needed, and the costs involved that you are able to determine. Your potential benefactors should have no doubt about the need and legitimacy of your request.

If you don't feel confident enough to ask for yourself, often someone in your support group or a friend will make the request on your behalf. (See the final letter in Appendix 1.)

Other Organizations
A number of special organizations may be prepared to undertake specific fund-raising on your child's behalf. For example, across Canada and the United States, there are many children who need bone marrow transplants. This requires a careful matching of donor and recipient, which is difficult and expensive. The mass media, service clubs, and the government have often cooperated to motivate individuals to donate blood, tissue, and organs to meet the needs of transplant recipients.

LONG-TERM CONSIDERATIONS

The second major set of financial concerns you will face involves long-term planning. Parents usually want to provide for the future needs of their children; the importance of a solid financial base for your child after she has moved out on her own, or after you are no longer there to provide for her, cannot be underestimated. It's a good idea to consult a financial planner to deal with your long-term considerations. But no matter what your child's specific situation, there are a couple of concerns that you should keep in mind.

The Cost of Care Liability

People with disabilities who are taken care of by the government are often required to give up whatever financial resources they have in order to pay the costs of the care that they receive. This is what is known as the cost of care liability. The cost of care liability allows the government to access the funds of people with disabilities in return for the provision of residential and support services.

There are some problems with the cost of care liability, as an individual's contributions to it may not result in her receiving any benefits. The money obtained from people with disabilities goes into a pool used to pay for all government services provided to those with disabilities. Parents who are in a position to pass on the benefits of their estate to their children who need long-term care should carefully consider the implications of the strategy that they choose to adopt. Encourage grandparents and other family members who wish to make estate provisions for special needs children to examine the best strategies available.

The Special Needs Child As a Beneficiary

You must have a will. If you don't have one, in most jurisdictions, the government will distribute your assets equally among your survivors. In this case, your child who has a disability will receive her share, which may be subsequently obtained by the state as a "cost of care liability." The most viable strategy in drawing up a will is not to have the person with the disability inherit the benefit.

You might want to consider, for purposes of the estate, that you disinherit your child and contribute her share to another surviving relative who will guarantee that the funds will be used for the best interests of your child. In this way you can avoid the possibility that the government will take your funds. However, you do run the risk that the person whom you place in charge of the inheritance may not direct the funds as you intended for the welfare of your child.

Occasionally, parents design a will that leaves their assets to the surviving spouse. This strategy is not recommended because of the possibility of both spouses dying at the same time, or a situation in which the surviving spouse suffers a disability that prevents him or her from administering the funds as intended. This situation can cause hardship for the entire family and lead to a situation where assets are used for legal costs instead of support measures.

Elements of an Effective Will

Suggest to your estate planner or lawyer that the following provisions be considered in your will.

- You should have a reliable, trustworthy executor to distribute the proceeds of your will.
- The executor should generally not be your spouse, in

case your spouse becomes incapacitated or dies at the same time that you do.

- Your special needs child should not directly receive the benefits of your estate as she may be required to relinquish her financial holdings to the government or institution that assumes responsibility for the cost of her care.

- The executor must agree to oversee your child's care on a regular basis in order to guarantee that she receives the best care possible.

- The trustee should be empowered to select alternative plans of care if the existing one is no longer satisfactory.

- When the child or adult dies, provisions should be made to have the residuals of the will distributed to designated siblings, institutions, or charities.

In many families, the parents' assets pass between spouses outside of the will by way of joint ownership of the family home, joint ownership of investments, joint bank accounts, designated beneficiaries of life insurance, and RRSPs. If this situation exists, a will can be designed so that on the death of the first spouse all assets pass to the surviving spouse to conform with the joint ownership arrangements. Subsequently, the will can make provisions for the needs of the child with a disability by way of a special discretionary trust, which gives the trustee or trustees the authority to administer the funds in such a manner that the child is provided for without losing any of the benefits she may receive from any other source. This also protects the capital for any other beneficiaries, including other children.

A Sample Will

This is an excerpt from an actual will prepared to meet the needs of a child with disabilities. It is written in precise legal language, and is thus very difficult to understand, but it contains the key elements necessary to provide for the needs of a special child. When you draft your own will you can give this to your lawyer or estate planner as a guide, or use the ideas that the example contains to provide your own suggestions.

   iv) To keep invested during the lifetime of my daughter one (1) of such equal shares of the residue of my estate and to pay any amount or amounts or the whole of the capital thereof to or for the benefit of my said daughter as my Trustee shall, in the exercise of an absolute and unfettered discretion, consider advisable from time to time. Any income not so paid in any year shall, until the date twenty-one (21) years after the date of my death, be accumulated by my Trustee and added to the capital of such share, provided, however, that after the date twenty-one (21) years after the date of my death, then the said income not so paid in any year to or for the benefit of my said daughter shall be paid to my sons, **************** and ************* who are alive at the end of such year in equal shares per capita. I declare that the equal share of the residue of my estate and the income therefrom shall not vest in my said daughter and the only interest she shall have therein shall be the payments actually made to her or for her benefit therefrom. Without in any way binding the discretion of my Trustee I further declare that it is my wish that in exercising its discretion in accordance with the provisions of this paragraph, my Trustee take such steps as will maximize the benefits which my said daughter will receive from other sources if payments from the income and the capital of the equal share of the residue of my estate were not paid to her, or if such payments were limited as to amount or time. In order to maximize such benefits, I specifically authorize my Trustee to make payments varying in amount and at such time or times as my Trustee in the exercise of an absolute discretion considers advisable keeping in mind that the comfort and welfare of said daughter is my first consideration. I expressly declare that my Trustee shall not be required to maintain an even hand between the income beneficiary and the remainder beneficiaries, when investing and administering this fund but may in its absolute discretion, favor one class of beneficiary over another. Upon the death of the survivor of my said daughter and me, my Trustee shall pay out of the equal share of my estate the funeral expenses of my said daughter and, subject thereto, the equal share of the residue of my estate or the amount thereof then remaining shall be paid or transferred to my said daughter's children then alive in equal shares per capita. Provided that if any of my said daughter's children are born or become mentally or physically handicapped in any way, then the aforesaid trust in favor of my daughter, is to continue to be administered in favor of said children. Provided further that if there are no children born of my daughter and survive her, then the equal share of the residue of my estate is to be divided upon my said daughter's death as follows:

(A) One half (1/2) of the remainder of such equal share shall be divided equally between my son ************** and my son ************* or pay all to the survivor of them if only one of them is living at the time of the distribution of the said equal share.

(B) One half (1/2) of the remainder of such equal share shall be paid or transferred to ************** to be used by the Building Fund to provide additional space.

Guardianship and Trust Funds

It may be appropriate to appoint a guardian or to create a discretionary trust for your child. Where they are valid, these trusts add to, rather than replace, state benefits. The trustee has the obligation to use the trust funds to benefit the child to whom it is directed. You must be careful to specify that you are creating a discretionary trust as opposed to a support trust, as in many jurisdictions, support trusts may be used by the government as a "cost of care."

Each local jurisdiction has its own requirements. In seeking financial advice, try to avoid all unnecessary costs as they subtract from your benefits. Bank managers and other financial advisors may not only provide free advice, but they may also direct you toward financial plans that do not have loading and unloading costs. Loading and unloading costs are compulsory fees that are charged when you buy or sell company stocks or other funds.

Insurance

Another financial vehicle often used by parents to provide support is insurance. It is generally suggested that you talk to an expert in insurance who is not going to sell you an insurance policy, as insurance agents may influence you to buy the policy that is in their best interest. An unbiased expert will show you what package best meets your needs.

Some parents have insured the lives of their children who have disabilities, but this is not always a wise financial strategy. The purpose of life insurance is to protect survivors and to protect the insured individuals when they are no longer able to provide for their families. The money would be better spent on insuring both parents. Nowadays, both parents can be providers or caregivers. Both parents, therefore, should be adequately insured so that the financial needs and care requirements of the child can be taken care of in the event of the death of one or both parents. Most analysts suggest that you and your survivors will be better off if you have the protection of term insurance. Life insurance provides the benefit of savings to your estate but many financial experts believe that you may do better investing your funds regularly in a private portfolio. However, this advice may not be the best strategy for individuals who cannot save on a regular basis.

Registered Retirement Savings Plans (RRSPs)

It is possible for many employees to defer income taxes and to build retirement benefits by contributing to RRSPs. This can be an excellent financial strategy as it avoids many of the costs associated with other types of investments, and very often the contributions are supplemented by an employer. Again, you should consider avoiding the designation of your special child as a beneficiary in the event of your death to avoid the costs associated with cost of care liability provisions.

Educational Plans

You may also have access to an educational plan for your special needs child. If you are able to establish during your child's early years that she is capable of obtaining an advanced education, you might consider putting aside a portion of your taxable income into an educational support program. Before adopting this strategy, investigate the available plans, required contributions, allowable deductions, and the amount of contributions that are returned to you in the event that your child does not pursue higher education. Be aware of the payout should your child attend an alternative postsecondary educational program; some of these educational funds will not support nontraditional programs or part-time courses of study. You should know if your principal and accumulated interest (or a portion thereof) will be returned to you in the event your child does not attend a facility approved by the plan. This is important to consider as many students with disabilities are able to benefit from part-time postsecondary education, but may not be able to enroll in a full-time program due to limitations related to their disability. Many experts believe that a sound financial investment program is a much better strategy in generating financial protection for a child.

Government Benefits

There are a variety of government benefits available. It is vital to contact your support group, caseworker, lawyer, and financial planner to understand and obtain access to these entitlements. Government agencies may provide education, transportation, and grants designed to integrate children with disabilities into various pursuits. This aid can range from very little funding to covering the full cost of your child's care. These benefits are usually available while children are at home, but in other instances, specific supports are only available when parents or caregivers die or become unable to continue care.

There will usually be standard procedures that you must follow in order to reach these government funds. If you run into problems when applying to the government for funds, consult with your local advocacy and support groups, and perhaps a lawyer. Your initial request should be well documented, because once these documents have been reviewed by the proper authorities it is usually difficult to have them reviewed again successfully. Try to do everything right the first time.

Support from the Private Sector

Not all parents have the financial resources to meet the long-term needs of their children. If this is your case, try to access whatever help is available. Your support groups should be familiar with alternatives. Design an appeal that is well written, describing the needs of your child. Send this request for support to religious organizations, service clubs, foundations, and, if appropriate, private businesses that occasionally make donations to be helpful and to create goodwill in the community. Even if specialized support is not a regular part of their policies, many organizations and foundations will make special provisions to support bona fide needs. This may take hours of telephone consultation with many community representatives, but persistence will be necessary as these efforts do require enormous amounts of time and commitment.

Many private organizations provide financial and volunteer services to those in need. Remember that groups and people will not always respond to your first request. Be persistent. If you keep at it you will find that sources that may have been initially reluctant may eventually help you out.

Specialized Hospitals and Medical Clinics
Throughout the United States and Canada, there are hospitals, clinics, and specialized schools that have discretionary funds available to support children in need. For example, the Shriners Hospitals and Toronto Sick Children's Hospital may be accessed on the recommendation of your doctor, support group, case manager, or organizations such as the Shriners. These groups have adopted a goal of providing aid to children with disabilities.

Assuming the responsibilities of parenthood is a difficult but rewarding process. Having a thorough knowledge of the legal system and of the benefits that you are entitled to, as well as the process required to obtain them will enhance your child's opportunities. In some instances resources for special needs have not been traditionally provided, but through legitimate requests and advocacy efforts you may find support.

In Closing

By reading this book you have already shown that you are a motivated and caring parent who wants to achieve the best for your child. You have made yourself aware of the best strategies to confront the problems that you and your child face, and you are now prepared to begin facing a significant challenge. Even though the road may seem hard and long, always believe that you can do it! You can do it for your child who has a disability, you can do it for your family, and you can do it for yourself.

Whenever you start to worry about whether the pressures and burdens you face will be too great, think of all the parents of children with disabilities who have succeeded in the past, of all the resources that are now available to help you, and of all the wonderful support that your friends and family can provide. You must have the confidence that you can succeed, and you can instill this confidence in your child.

My parents taught me to have courage, self-confidence, and perseverance, and whenever I had any doubts as to whether I would succeed they told me, "Yes, you can!" I hope that you can pass this message on to your children, and that they will reward you and make you proud of their triumphs. I have every faith that you can meet this challenge.

If you have any observations or suggestions, please address them to me at:

> Mark Nagler
> 94 Oak Knoll Drive
> Hamilton, Ontario
> Canada
> L8S 4C5

> e-mail: nagler@interlynx. net

Appendix 1

Sample Letters

The following sample letters may be helpful in allowing you to gather your allies and to obtain the best opportunities and resources for your child. To accomplish your goals you should send copies of your letters to *all* of the relevant people involved. These might be school superintendents, principals, teachers, recreational specialists, editors of local newspapers, or representatives of groups who may be able to assist you in gaining the rights and benefits to which you are entitled.

By writing a letter, you are doing the following things: (1) you are selecting a course of action or suggesting a policy that may help you, your child, and other children who have the same needs; (2) you are trying to develop a partnership that will allow you to work with professionals or other concerned citizens to meet your goals.

These sample letters will provide you with a framework for your own letters. Feel free to use them exactly, substituting the specifics of your situation for the example in the letter, or only use the letters as a rough guide for what you want to say. Mixing and matching sections from different letters may also be helpful. No matter what the situation, your letters should always be courteous and to the point. Haranguing someone through the mail will not solve any problems. Always include your name, address, and phone number in the return address at the top right corner of the page. The sample letters contain the standard greeting, "Dear Sir or Madam," but wherever possible, try to find out the name of the person you are addressing the letter to.

Sample letter #1

This letter requests accommodation for your child from a new school board. This letter should be sent to the superintendent of the school board with copies forwarded to the principal of your local school and perhaps your child's future teacher.

Dear Sir or Madam:

We have just moved to your community from San Francisco. My child uses a wheelchair, and she was accommodated in a regular school which was accessible by ramp.

We were very surprised to learn that the local junior high school does not have ramp access for students in wheelchairs. We hope that you and the Board will install an appropriate ramp in the George Washington School before school commences in late August. We would also urge you to have the school program slightly modified so that teachers will move from classroom to classroom rather than having the students move, at least for the classes in which our daughter is enrolled. We realize that the George Washington School was built in the mid-1940s in a time when access issues were not relevant. We also realize that it would be prohibitively expensive to have an elevator installed at the school.

Our child is bright and has completed her first eight years of school in the prescribed time. In the past, she has taken advantage of all the activities that occur for students within the school. We truly believe that she benefits from being integrated into the public school system.

We hope that you will arrange to have a ramp installed and to have classes coordinated so that our daughter can continue to enjoy all of the benefits of a public education.

If we can help in any way, please contact us at the above address. Our home phone number is ***-**** and during the day, my husband can be reached at work at ***-****.

Thanking you in advance for your concern and cooperation.

Sincerely,

Sample letter #2
This letter requests action from the entire school board to allow children with mobility impairments proper access to public schools in their district. Copies of this letter should be sent to your local newspapers and the school board.

Dear Sir or Madam:

I represent the local branch of the National Association of Children with Cerebral Palsy. It has been brought to our attention that there are a large number of students who have difficulty in gaining access to many of our local schools. Some of these students use wheelchairs, while others use crutches or walkers. These students generally have average, if not above average, abilities.

However, many of these children are being denied an education because it is difficult for them to gain access to local schools or to obtain transportation, as they are unable to ride most of the buses in the school transportation system.

We are therefore asking you to address these access problems as soon as possible, as it is important to guarantee these children a public education. Our group is ready to cooperate with you in any way in order to provide the facilities necessary to make our school system accessible.

Thanking you for your time and cooperation.

Sincerely,

Sample letter #3
This letter requests a meeting for an IEP. It should be sent to the principal of your local school with copies forwarded to your child's teacher and the school superintendent.

Dear Sir or Madam:

Our daughter has been diagnosed as a child with several learning disabilities. She has the ability to do well in biology, mathematics, chemistry, and physics. It is, however, extremely difficult for her to complete courses in English, history, geography, and social studies. Her difficulties involve language comprehension and expression.

We moved from Boston, and in that city we were successful in having an educational program designed to meet Gail's needs. As you are aware, progressive educational policy now makes provisions for students like our daughter who have average or above average potential in some academic fields but who are unable to perform satisfactorily in other areas.

We would like to meet with you at your earliest possible convenience. We have copies of previous IEPs that were successful when we were living in Boston. We hope that you will utilize this information and design a course of study for her that will allow her to graduate from the high school system. We would like to share these with you and provide you with whatever other assistance is appropriate.

Thank you for your time and consideration.

Sincerely,

Sample letter #4
This letter gives instructions about a child's medication. It explains how and when to administer the necessary doses to the child, and what effects the medication has. It provides a number where the parents can be reached during the day, and shares basic information about the child's disability. This letter

should be mailed to the principal of the child's school, with copies forwarded to the appropriate teachers and the chairperson of the local school board.

Dear Sir or Madam:

My son has been diagnosed with problems related to Attention Deficit Disorder. The precise nature of these difficulties is only now being diagnosed, but it is our physician's belief that our son has adequate academic potential.

He is currently on Ritalin and two other drugs, which are administered every four hours. We have found that treating him with this medication alleviates and in most instances eliminates most of his inappropriate behavior.

He receives his first tablets at 6:30 in the morning and subsequently at four-hour intervals. We would therefore be most appreciative if you could administer his prescriptions at 10:30 a.m. and at 2:30 p.m. each day.

Drug therapy usually produces the anticipated results. If, however, Fred acts in an inappropriate manner, please contact us immediately. Up to this point he has never experienced any negative reactions, but drug therapy should always be monitored.

As far as we know, he has no food allergies or other difficulties. I also have a number of books and pamphlets that describe our son's disability and I would be happy to share this information with you. If there are any other concerns, please contact me.

Sincerely,

P.S. My husband and I will be willing to sign a legal waiver stating that you will not be legally responsible for any problems that may occur. We appreciate and are thankful for your cooperation.

Sample letter #5
This is an example of a letter written to a medical clinic requesting an examination for a child. It provides a brief outline of the child's difficulties, and explains the parent's financial needs.

Dear Sir or Madam:

Our child has been diagnosed with multiple disabilities which may include Attention Deficit Disorder, Tourette's syndrome, and characteristics associated with autism.

We enrolled him at the local school, and the principal and teachers have informed us that it is impossible for them to accommodate our child in the public school system. Our local pediatrician and other specialists with whom we have consulted have not effectively been able to diagnose and treat the disabilities that our child experiences on a daily basis.

Enclosed are the diagnoses, medical histories, and programs of treatment that have been recommended without much success.

We would be most appreciative if you or members of your clinic would examine our child, as it is our understanding that the best medical advice available is from the specialists in your center.

Unfortunately for us, financial considerations are a major concern. We would appreciate whatever help you can offer.

Sincerely,

Sample letter #6
This is an example of a letter written to the chairperson of the Department of Physical and Occupational Therapy at a university, requesting the assistance of volunteers.

Dear Sir or Madam:

We have a three-year-old child who has cerebral palsy. Warren is very bright, but at this stage he is only beginning to crawl. His coordination skills are very poor, but his speech development is more than satisfactory.

We have been directed by our family pediatrician, Doctor X, to ask if you could be of assistance to our family. Our child requires expensive and regular occupational and physiotherapy. We know that your Department at the University of X has an excellent reputation in the training of specialists in this field. Would it be possible for your students to work with our child on a regular basis as part of their training? We know that our child would receive excellent care, and we understand that this training is a part of the program used to educate students in occupational and physical therapy at your school.

Our phone number is ***-****. If there is no one

home, please leave a message on our answering machine and we will return your call as soon as possible. Although it may be possible to arrange transportation of our son to the university, it would be much more convenient if your volunteers could work with Warren at our home, which is only a fifteen-minute walk from the university.

Thanking you for your time and consideration.

Sincerely,

Sample letter #7
This is an example of a letter that explains a child's condition and how to deal with it. It should be sent to the child's teacher as well as the school principal.

Dear Sir or Madam:

Our daughter has a severe case of asthma, which can be triggered by overexertion as well as some foods, pollens, and other airborne pollutants.

When the condition is triggered it leads to severe coughing and sneezing, and if it is not treated immediately Sarah may pass out — a situation that has not yet occurred. When our daughter begins to wheeze, please give her the inhaler, which should immediately alleviate all of her symptoms. If the symptoms persist, please have someone call 911 and have her sent to Holy Cross Hospital. At the same time, please call Dr. Hanson at ***-**** and he will assure that our daughter receives the proper treatment. Again, such a serious situation has never occurred, but we are concerned with providing the necessary protection for our child.

We want our daughter to enjoy the benefits of a public education. She is a bright child who does not usually experience difficulties related to her disability. We realize that we are asking you to assume a significant responsibility, and we will gladly sign a waiver which absolves you of any responsibility. We appreciate everything that you can do to help us deal with Sarah's condition.

Thank you for your time and consideration.

Sincerely,

Sample letter #8
This is an example of a letter explaining a child's need for a classroom assistant. It also explains what functions the classroom assistant will provide. It ensures that the teacher will not be surprised by the assistant's presence in the classroom and provides an opportunity for the teacher to put forward his or her own ideas about the child's treatment. A copy of this letter should be sent to the child's classroom teacher, with copies forwarded to the school's principal.

Dear Sir or Madam:

Our son Albert suffers from paraplegia as a result of a traffic accident that occurred last summer. He now uses a wheelchair, and it is very difficult for him to write at the present time. He is currently on a program of occupational and physiotherapy and these programs will continue for a two-hour period every day after school.

As a result of this accident, our son will require a full-time educational assistant, at least for the next academic school year. Mr. Smith will bring Albert to class and take notes for him and assume all of the other physical responsibilities associated with our son's care.

The accident, as far as we can determine, has had no effect on our son's intelligence. However, he will require oral exams or placement in an enclosed environment where he can dictate his assignments to Mr. Smith. Mr. Smith is a very involved individual who has worked extensively with children who have disabilities. He will also be more than willing to help Albert's classroom teachers develop and administer classroom projects and programs.

If there is any other information I can provide, please contact me at the following numbers. Also, if you have any suggestions that may be helpful in Albert's rehabilitation, my wife and I would be very appreciative.

Sincerely,

Sample letter #9
This is an example of a letter written to a service club requesting financial support.

Dear Sir or Madam:

Our son is fifteen years old and has been diagnosed with muscular dystrophy. He is currently enrolled in grade ten and is maintaining an excellent academic record in spite of the difficulties he is encountering.

My husband and I have been informed by the local Muscular Dystrophy Association that your service group has had an outstanding record of providing the financial resources and/or equipment necessary to maintain a child in his home.

We have enclosed a number of films, booklets, and pamphlets that describe all of the needs and requirements our son will encounter in the next few years. As my husband and I do not have the financial resources to meet all of Robert's needs, we would appreciate any help your organization could provide.

Sincerely,

Sample letter #10
This is an example of a letter requesting information about the patterns of treatment for a child's condition. This letter should be sent to major universities and other research centers. This letter can also be adapted to request basic information from national agencies, hospitals, and health clinics.

Dear Sir or Madam:

Our child has been diagnosed with a serious liver

ailment. Three local pediatricians have informed us that the prognosis is not positive.

We have been led to believe that the research currently being conducted at your center is the state of the art. Although we do not expect miracles, we would be very grateful if you could inform us of any patterns of treatment that may be successful in treating this liver disease.

As our child is very lethargic and is having related difficulties, we would appreciate this information as soon as possible. If you believe that it would be helpful for us to visit your facilities, we would be glad to come as soon as an appointment can be arranged.

I am certain that you understand the concern we are experiencing. Thanking you for your time and consideration.

Sincerely,

Sample letter #11
This is an example of a letter written to the director of a regional summer camp explaining the extent and effects of a child's disability. You may also wish to include any measures that could be taken in order to alleviate the effects of your child's disability. This type of letter helps to eliminate apprehension and will make sure that everyone has an easier time adapting.

Dear Sir or Madam:

We have a ten-year-old son who is just completing his

fifth year of school and we are proud to say that he has done very well in spite of the fact that he has a severe hearing impairment. He is very adept at lip-reading and has managed to enjoy a regular life in spite of his disability.

We would be very grateful if you would consider having Jacob enrolled for a three-week period in your summer camp. He has normal strength, he is an excellent swimmer, and he enjoys participating in activities with other children. I am certain he would not constitute a burden for any counselor, but as you can understand, he should have supervision by a conscientious counselor.

We would be very appreciative if you could have our son enrolled in any of your three-week camping sessions during this coming summer. He is looking forward to a camping experience, especially in view of the fact that some of his friends have attended your camp in the past and are intending to do so this summer.

If there is any other information that you require, please contact me at the above address.

Sincerely,

Sample letter #12
This is an example of a letter explaining what measures can be taken in order to ease a child's transition to a mainstream classroom. The letter should be sent to the child's teacher and the school principal.

Dear Sir or Madam:

Our daughter has a severe hearing disability. She is now seven years old and for the first two years of school, she has attended a special school for the hearing impaired. We are very pleased with her progress, and as she has mastered the art of lip-reading, we now believe that she is ready to attend a regular school program.

There are just a few minor provisions that must be made. Paula should always be seated in the first row and her teacher must always face her when teaching. As you are aware, many teachers have the habit of writing notes on the board and speaking at the same time. In this type of situation, Paula would be in an unstimulating environment of silence. In terms of her accommodation, these two provisions — sitting in the front row and always facing the teacher — are our daughter's only requirements.

As I am sure you recognize, an integrated education is in the best interest of children with disabilities. We hope you will be able to facilitate our request. If there is any other information we can provide, please contact us at the above address.

Sincerely,

Sample Letter #13
This is an example of a letter that is sent to the parents of children who have disabilities and attend a local public school. It encourages these parents to form an advocacy group so that their children will have full access to educational, recreational,

and social programs. It can be modified to invite parents to form a group that is pursuing a variety of goals or services.

Dear Parent:

As you may know, we are the parents of a child who uses a walker. Our child is encountering a number of barriers at George Washington Public School. We have been informed that your child also has a disability that may limit some of his (or her) own educational activities.

We are writing you and all parents of children with disabilities at this school so that we can meet and organize a parent support group to work together to identify and then alleviate or eliminate the problems that our children are encountering at the school. Hopefully we will be able to form a committee of interested parents to help solve these difficulties.

It has been suggested to us that problems are occurring in three main areas: access, education, and recreation. If we all act together we should be able to influence the school board, the principal, and the teachers into responding positively to our children's needs.

The meeting will be held at _____ on Tuesday the __ of September, 199_.

If you are aware of any other parents who may be interested, or other people who have skills that can address our concerns, then please invite them to the meeting.

If transportation or baby-sitting is a problem, please contact us by September __ and we will do our best to make arrangements for your attendance.

This will be an organizational and brainstorming meeting. We want and need your ideas. We look forward to meeting you and sharing our experiences and goals.

Sincerely,

Sample letter #14
This is an example of a letter written to a service organization, requesting financial assistance. The letter is addressed to the president of the service organization, and is specific as to costs and details of the disability.

Dear Sir or Madam:

Our son Anthony was seriously injured in an automobile accident several months ago. He no longer has the use of his legs and we do not yet know if he will ever be able to walk again.

Anthony is sixteen years old and a Grade 11 student at Madison High School. He wishes to return to school as soon as possible, but he needs an electric wheelchair in order to have any mobility. The school is completely accessible and the principal has assured us that Anthony would be more than welcome. The estimated cost of such a chair is $2,700 and, unfortunately, our family does not have the resources to buy this equipment.

We would be very appreciative if your organization

would consider contributing toward the cost of a chair for our son.

If Anthony should regain the use of his legs, we would be happy to return the chair to you so that someone else might benefit from its use.

Thank you for your consideration.

Sincerely,

Appendix 2

Directory of Disability-Related Organizations

This appendix is designed to provide a resource base of disability-related organizations. Before contacting any of these support groups, it would be best to get in touch with your local Easter Seals Association, who provide a variety of services and equipment.

Most of these organizations will have lists of specialists and support groups in your area and will be able to supply you with literature relevant to your child's disability. The organizations listed are mainly national offices or central offices representing specific conditions. Before contacting the national or central office, it may be advantageous to contact the head office in your state or provincial capital. If you reside in a larger urban area, you may find a chapter of the group in your locale. The directory also includes service organizations, charitable organizations, advocacy groups, and legal aid organizations. There are many wonderful and important disability-related organizations that could not be included in this chapter because of space limitations, but this alphabetical list should be able to provide you with the key addresses of the organizations, support groups, and foundations that can meet your needs. Please note: these are the most up-to-date addresses at the time of going to press, but they may change.

Representative Organizations
Serving Persons with Disabilities
(Canada)

Abilities Foundation of Nova Scotia
3670 Kempt Road
Halifax, NS B3K 4X8
(902) 429–3420
fax: (902) 454–6121

AboutFace (for Facial Disfigurement)
99 Crown's Lane, 3rd Floor
Toronto, ON M5R 3P4
Toll-Free: (800) 665-3223
fax: (416) 944–2488

Aboutface — Anorexia and Bulimia Outreach Facilities
1393 Avenue Road
Toronto, ON M5N 2H3

Accessible Housing Society
#103, 2003 – 14 Street NW
Calgary, AB T2M 3N4
(403) 282–1872
fax: (403) 284–0304
Housing Registry: (403) 282–3373

Acoustic Neuroma Association of Canada (ANAC)
PO Box 369
Edmonton, AB T5J 2J6
(403) 428–3384
Toll-Free: (800) 561–2622

Action League for Physically Handicapped Adults
#8, 1940 Oxford Street East
London, ON N5V 2Z8
(519) 433–7221
fax: (519) 457–3069

Active Living Alliance for Canadians With A Disability
#707A, 1600 James Naismith Drive
Gloucester, ON K1B 5N4
(613) 748–5747
fax: (613) 748–5782

Advocacy Resource Centre for the Handicapped (ARCH)
40 Orchard View Boulevard
Toronto, ON M4R 1B9
(416) 482–8255
fax: (416) 482–2981
TDD: (416) 482–1254

Allergy and Asthma Information Association
30 Eglinton Avenue West
Suite 750
Mississauga, ON L5R 3E7
(905) 712–2242
fax: (905) 712–2245

Alternative Computer Training for the Disabled
#300, 562 Eglinton Avenue East
Toronto, ON M4P 1B9
(416) 488–4076
fax: (416) 488–5079

Alva Foundation
175 Cumberland Street
Suite 1003
Toronto, ON M5R 3M9

Association for the Neurologically
Disabled of Canada
59 Clement Road
Etobicoke, ON M9R 1Y5
(416) 244-1992
fax: (416) 244-4099
Toll-Free: (800) 561-1497

Association for the Rehabilitation
of the Brain Injured
3412 Spruce Drive SW
Calgary, AB T3C 3A4
(403) 242-7116

Association for Vaccine Damaged
Children
56 Brisco Street
Brampton, ON L6V 1W8
(905) 454-2237

Asthma Society of Canada
#425, 130 Bridgeland Avenue
Toronto, ON M6A 1Z4
(416) 787-4050
fax: (416) 787-5807
Toll-Free: (800) 787-3880

Autism Society Canada
#202, 129 Yorkville Avenue
Toronto, ON M5R 1C4
(416) 922-0302
fax: (416) 922-1032

Autism Society Ontario
#302, 300 Sheppard Avenue West
North York, ON M2N 1N5
(416) 512-9880
fax: (416) 512-8026

Autism Treatment Services of
Canada
404-94 Avenue SE
Calgary, AB T2J 0E8
(403) 253-6961
fax: (403) 253-6974

Big Brothers of Canada
5230 South Service Road
Burlington, ON L7L 5K2
(905) 639-0461
fax: (905) 639-0124
Toll-Free: (800) 263-9133

Big Brothers of Ontario
5230 South Service Road
Burlington, ON L7L 5K2
(905) 639-0461
fax: (905) 639-0124

Bridge Research Foundation —
Optimal Life for the Handicapped
5 Ashford Drive
Nepean, ON K2H 6V4
(613) 828-9032 and
(613) 596-9189

Burn Survivors Association
c/o Ross Tilley Burn Centre
Wellesley Hospital
160 Wellesley Street East
Toronto, ON M4Y 1J3
(416) 791-0545
Info Line: (416) 926-7021

Calgary Society for Effective
Education of Learning Disabled
#315, 86 Avenue SE
Calgary, AB T2S 2Y1
(403) 290-0446
fax: (403) 232-6422

Canadian AIDS Society
#400, 100 Sparks Street
Ottawa, ON K1P 5B7
(613) 230-3580
fax: (613) 563-4998
Toll-Free: (800) 499-1986

Canadian Association for
Community Care
#701 Rideau Street
Ottawa, ON K1N 5W8
(613) 241–7510
fax: (613) 241–5923
Toll-Free: (800) 391-6033

Canadian Association for
Community Living
4700 Keele Street
North York, ON M3J 1P3
(416) 661–9611
fax: (416) 661–5701
Toll-Free: (800) 856-2207

Canadian Association of the Deaf
#205, 2435 Holly Lane
Ottawa, ON K1V 7P2
(613) 526–4785
fax: (613) 526–4718

Canadian Association for Disabled
Skiing
PO Box 307, 2860 Rotary Drive
Kimberley, BC V1A 1E9
(604) 427–7712
fax: (604) 427–7715

Canadian Association of Speech-
Language Pathologists and
Audiologists
#2006, 130 Albert Street
Ottawa, ON K1P 5G4
(613) 567–9968
fax: (613) 567–2859

Canadian Association for
Williams Syndrome
PO Box 2115
Vancouver, BC V6B 3T5

Canadian Blind Sports Association
1600 James Naismith Drive
Place R. Tait McKenzie #606A
Gloucester, ON K1B 5N4
(613) 748–5609
fax: (613) 748–5899

Canadian Cancer Society
#200, 10 Alcorn Avenue
Toronto, ON M4V 3B1
(416) 961–7223
fax: (416) 961–4189
Toll-Free: (888) 939-3333
(ON): (800) 263-6750

Canadian Cardiovascular Society
#401, 360, avenue Victoria
Westmount, QC H3Z 2N4
(514) 482–3407
fax: (514) 482–6574

Canadian Celiac Association
65198 Mississauga Road
Missisauga, ON L5N 1A6
(905) 567–7195
fax: (800) 363-7296
Toll-Free: (800) 363–7296

Canadian Centre for Philanthropy,
a.k.a. Imagine
1329 Bay Street, 2nd Floor
Toronto, ON M5R 2C4
(416) 515–0764
fax: (416) 515–0773
Toll-Free: (800) 263-1178

Canadian Cerebral Palsy Sports
Association
Place R. Tait McKenzie
#606A, 1600 James Naismith Drive
Gloucester, ON K1B 5N4
(613) 748–5725
fax: (613) 748–5899

The Canadian Council of the Blind
#405, 396 Cooper Street
Ottawa, ON K2P 2H7
(613) 567–0311
fax: (613) 567–2728

The Canadian Council on
Rehabilitation and Work
20 King Street West, 9th Floor
Toronto, ON M5H 1C4
(416) 974-5575
fax: (416) 974-5577

Canadian Cystic Fibrosis Foundation
2221 Yonge Street
Toronto, ON M4S 2B4
(416) 485-9149
fax: (416) 485–0960
Toll-Free: (800) 378-2233

Canadian Deaf, Blind and Rubella
Association
350 Brant Avenue
Brantford, ON N3T 3J9
(519) 759-0520
fax: (519) 754-0397

Canadian Deaf Sports Association
#218, 1367 West Broadway
Vancouver, BC V6H 4A9
(604) 737–3041
fax: (604) 738–7175

Canadian Deafness Research and
Training Institute
2300 boulevard René Lévesque ouest
Quebec City, PQ H3H 2R5

Canadian Diabetes Association
National Office:
#800, 15 Toronto Street
Toronto, ON M5C 2E3
(416) 363–3373
fax: (416) 363–3393
Toll-Free: (800) 226-8464
(ON): (800) 361-1306

Canadian Disability Rights Council
#208, 428 Portage Avenue
Winnipeg, MB R3C 0E2
(204) 943–4787
fax: (204) 949–1223

Canadian Down Syndrome Society
#206, 12837–76 Avenue
Surrey, BC V3W 2V3
(604) 599–6009
fax: (604) 599–6165

Canadian Dyslexia Association
25, rue St. Médard
Aylmer, QC J9H 1Z4
(514) 684–9040
fax: (514) 684–6157

The Canadian Education Charity
for Children
236 Berkley Street
Toronto, ON M5A 2X4

Canadian Federation of Sport
Organizations for the Disabled
1600 Naismith Place
Ottawa, ON K1B 5N8
(613) 748–5630

Canadian Foundation for Physically
Disabled Persons
731 Runnymede Road
Toronto, ON M6N 3V7
(416) 760–7351
fax: (416) 760–9405

Canadian Foundation for Ileitis and
Colitis (Crohn's Disease)
12 Parkmount Crescent
Nepean, ON K2M 5T4
(613) 596–9635

Canadian Foundation for Physically
Disabled Persons
731 Runnymede Road
Toronto, ON M6N 3V7
(416) 760–7351
fax: (416) 760–9405

Canadian Foundation for
Poliomyelitis and Rehabilitation
2020, 15th Street NW
Calgary, AB T2M 3N8
(403) 284–1161
fax: (403) 284–9899

Canadian Genetic Diseases
Network
University of British Columbia
#348, 2125 East Mall
Vancouver, BC V6T 1Z4
(604) 822–7189
fax: (604) 822–7945

Canadian Guide Dogs for the Blind
(CGDB)
4120 Rideau Valley Drive North
PO Box 280
Manotick, ON K4M 1A3
(613) 692–7777
fax: (613) 692–0650

Canadian Hard of Hearing
Association
#205, 2435 Holly Lane
Ottawa, ON K1V 7P2
(613) 526–1584
fax: (613) 526–4718

Canadian Hearing Society (CHS)
271 Spadina Road
Toronto, ON M5R 2V3
(416) 964–9595
fax: (416) 964–2066
Toll-Free: (800) 465–4327

Canadian Hemochromatosis Society
#272, 7000 Minoru Boulevard
Richmond, BC V6Y 3Z5
(604) 279–7135
fax: (604) 279–7138

Canadian Hemophilia Society
#1210, 625 rue President Kennedy
Montreal, QC H3A 1K2
(514) 848–0503
fax: (514) 848–9661

Canadian Home Care Association
#1005, 350 Sparks Street
Ottawa, ON K1R 7F8
(613) 569–1585
fax: (613) 569–1604

Canadian Infectious Disease Society
(CIDS)
CTTC Suite 3400
1125 Colonel By Drive
Ottawa, ON K1S 5R1
Toll-Free: (800) 668-3740 ext. 251
fax: (613) 523-2552

Canadian Institute for Barrier-
Free Design
Faculty of Architecture,
University of Manitoba
Winnipeg, MB R3T 2N2
(204) 474–8588
fax: (204) 474–6450

Canadian Institute of Health Care
1851 Eglinton Avenue West
Toronto, ON M6E 2J6
(416) 785–5572

Canadian League Against Epilepsy
c/o Division of Neurology
Hospital for Sick Children
555 University Avenue
Toronto, ON M5G 1X8

Canadian Liver Foundation
#200, 365 Bloor Street East
Toronto, ON M4W 3L4
(416) 964–1953
fax: (416) 964–0024
Toll-Free: (800) 563–5483

Canadian Lung Association
#508, 1900 City Park Drive
Gloucester, ON K1J 1A3
(613) 747–6776
fax: (613) 747–7430

**Canadian Mental Health
Association**
2160 Yonge Street
Toronto, ON M4S 2Z3
(416) 484–7750
fax: (416) 484–4617

**Canadian National Institute for the
Blind**
1931 Bayview Avenue
Toronto, ON M4G 4C8
(416) 480–7580
fax: (416) 480–7677

**Canadian Occupational Therapy
Foundation**
#308, 55 Eglinton Avenue East
Toronto, ON M4P 1G3
(416) 487–5404

**Canadian Osteogenesis Imperfecta
Society**
128 Thornhill Crescent
Chatham, ON N7L 4L4

Canadian Paraplegic Association
#320, 401 Prince of Wales Drive
Ottawa, ON K2C 3W7
(613) 723–1033
fax: (613) 723–1060

Canadian Pediatric Foundation
2204 Walkley Road,
Suite 100
Ottawa, ON K1G 4G8
Toll-Free: (800) 580–0940

**Canadian Physiotherapy
Association**
890 Yonge Street
Toronto, ON M4W 3P4
(416) 924–5312
fax: (416) 924–7335
Toll-Free: (800) 387–8679

Canadian Psychiatric Association
#200, 237 Argyle Drive
Ottawa, ON K2P 1B8
(613) 234–2815
fax: (613) 234–9857
Toll-Free: (800) 267–1555 ext. 26

Canadian Red Cross Society
1800 Alta Vista Drive
Ottawa, ON K1G 4J5
(613) 739-3000
fax: (613) 731–1411

**Canadian Rehabilitation Council
for the Disabled**
#511, 90 Eglinton Avenue East
Toronto, ON M4P 2Y3
(416) 932-8382
fax: (416) 932-9844
TDD: (416) 250–7490

**Canadian Rett Syndrome
Association**
#301, 555 Fairway Road
Kitchener, ON N2C 1X4
(519) 494–1954
fax: (519) 893–1169

Canadian Sickle Cell Society
#33, 6999 Cote des Neiges
Montreal, QC H3S 2B8
(514) 735–5109
fax: (514) 735-5100

Canadian Special Olympics
#209, 40 St. Clair Avenue West
Toronto, ON M4V 1M2
(416) 927–9050
fax: (416) 927–8475

Canadian Spinal Research Organization
#32, 120 Newkirk Road
Richmond Hill, ON L4C 9S7
(905) 508–4000
fax: (905) 508–4002
Toll-Free: (800) 361–4004

Canadian Thoracic Society
c/o Canadian Lung Association
#508, 1900 City Park Drive
Gloucester, ON K1J 1A3
(613) 747–6776

Canadian Transplantation Society
c/o Toronto General Hospital
200 Elizabeth Street, Room NU 10–152
Toronto, ON M5G 2C4
(416) 340–4252
fax: (416) 340–3492

Canadian Wheelchair Sports Association
#212A, 1600 James Naismith Drive
Gloucester, ON K1B 5N4
(613) 748–5685
fax: (613) 748–5722

Candlelighters Childhood Cancer Foundation
55 Eglinton Avenue East
Toronto, ON M4P 1G8
(416) 489-6440
fax: (416) 489-9812

Children North Early Childhood Intervention Program Inc.
PO Box 925
La Ronge, SK S0J 1L0
(306) 425–3777
fax: (306) 425–5310

Children's Heart Association for Support and Education
c/o Cardiac Clinic, Division of Cardiology
Hospital for Sick Children
555 University Avenue
Toronto, ON M5G 1X8
(416) 410-2427

Children's International Hope Fund
#605, 1825 Bayview Avenue
Thornhill, ON L3T 7N2

Children's Oncology Care of Ontario Inc. (a.k.a. Ronald McDonald House)
26 Gerrard Street East
Toronto, ON M5B 1G3
(416) 977–0458
fax: (416) 977–8807

Children's Psychiatric Research Institute
600 Sanitorium Road
London, ON N6H 3W7
(519) 471–2540
fax: (519) 641-1922

Children's Rehabilitation and Cerebral Palsy Association
The Neurological Centre, 2805 Kingsway
Vancouver, BC V5R 5H9
(604) 451–5511
fax: (604) 451–5651

The Children's Wish Foundation of Canada
#8C, 1735 Bayly Street
Pickering, ON L1W 3G7
(905) 420–4055
fax: (905) 831–9733
Toll-Free: (800) 267–9474
Info Line: (905) 831–9610

Council of Canadians with Disabilities
#926, 294 Portage Avenue
Winnipeg, MB R3C 0B9
(204) 947–0303
fax: (204) 942–4625

Counselling Foundation of Canada
#410, 1 Toronto Street
Toronto, ON M5C 2W3

Crohn's and Colitis Foundation of Canada
#301, 21 St. Clair Avenue East
Toronto, ON M4T 1L9
(416) 920–5035
fax: (416) 929–0364
Toll-Free: (800) 387-1479

Deaf Youth Canada
c/o Alberta School for the Deaf
6240, 113th Street
Edmonton, AB T6H 3L2
(403) 422–0244

Disabled People's International
#101, 7 Evergreen Place
Winnipeg, MB R6L 2Z3
(204) 957–1784

Dysautonomia Association
#1103, 343 Clark Avenue West
Thornhill, ON L4J 7K5
(905) 882-7725
fax: (905) 764-7752

Easter Seals Society/Easter Seals Research Institute
250 Ferrand Drive
Toronto, ON M3C 3P2
(416) 421–8377
fax: (416) 696–1035
Toll-Free: (888) 377-5437

Epilepsy Canada
#745, 1470, rue Peel
Montreal, QC H3A 1T1
(514) 845–7855
fax: (514) 845–7866
Toll-Free: (800) 860-5499

Ethnic Organization for the Handicapped
#5, 3585 Keele Street
Downsview, ON M3J 3H5
(416) 631–6540
fax: (416) 631–6461

Family Services Canada
#600, 220 Laurier Avenue West
Ottawa, ON K1P 5Z9
(613) 230–9960
fax: (613) 230–5884

Freedom in Travelling
65 Tromley Drive
Etobicoke, ON M9B 5X7
(416) 234–8511

Goodwill Industries — Toronto
234 Adelaide Street East
Toronto, ON M5A 1M9
(416) 362–4711
fax: (416) 362–0720

Huntington Society of Canada
13 Water Street North, PO Box 1267
Cambridge, ON N1R 7G6
(519) 622–1002
fax: (519) 622–7370

International Association for Education of the Deaf-Blind
20 Scotia Avenue
Brantford, ON N3R 5R1

International Council of AIDS Service Organizations
Central Secretariat
#400, 100 Sparks Street
Ottawa, ON K1P 5B7
(613) 230–3580
fax: (613) 563–4998

International Society for Augmentative and Alternative Communication
PO Box 1762, Station R
Toronto, ON M4G 4A3
(416) 737–9308

International Society for Pediatric Neuro-Surgery
Hospital for Sick Children
#1504, 555 University Avenue
Toronto, ON M5J 1X8
(416) 813–6427

Interstitial Cystitis Association of Canada
PO Box 5814, Station A
Toronto, ON M5W 1P2
(905) 723–9368
fax: (905) 432–3847

John Milton Society for the Blind in Canada
#202, 40 St. Clair Avenue East
Toronto, ON M4T 1M9
(416) 960–3953

Juvenile Diabetes Foundation of Canada
89 Granton Drive
Richmond Hill, ON L4B 2N5
(905) 889–4171
fax: (905) 889–4209

The Kidney Foundation of Canada
#300, 5165 Sherbrooke Street West
Montreal, QC H4A 1T6
(514) 369–4806
fax: (514) 369–2472
Toll-Free: (800) 361–7494

Lamplighters: Children's Leukemia Cancer Association
PO Box 1285, Station H
Montreal, QC H36 2N2
(514) 933–5384

Learning Disabilities Association of Canada
#200, 323 Chapel Street
Ottawa, ON K1N 7Z2
(613) 238–5721
fax: (613) 235–5391

Leukemia Research Fund (LRF)
#220, 1110 Finch Avenue West
Toronto, ON M3J 2T2
(416) 661–9541
fax: (416) 661–7799
Toll-Free: (800) 268–2144

Lions of Canada Foundation
PO Box 907
Oakville, ON L6J 5E8
(905) 842–2891
fax: (905) 842-3373

Lupus Canada
#040, 635–6 Avenue
Calgary, AB T2P 0T5
(403) 274–5599
fax: (403) 274–5599
Toll-Free: (800) 661–1468

M.E. Association of Canada
#400, 246 Queen Street
Ottawa, ON K1P 5E4
(613) 563–1565
fax: (613) 567–0614
Info Line: (613) 563–1565

Multiple Sclerosis Society of Canada
#1000, 250 Bloor Street East
Toronto, ON M4W 3P9
(416) 922–6065
fax: (416) 922–7538
Toll-Free: (800) 268–7582

Muscular Dystrophy Association of Canada
#900, 2345 Yonge Street
Toronto, ON M4P 2E5
(416) 488–0030
fax: (416) 488–7523
Toll-Free: (800) 567–2873

National Cancer Institute of Canada
#200, 10 Alcorn Drive
Toronto, ON M4V 3B1
(416) 961–7223
fax: (416) 961–4189

National Capital Sports Council of the Disabled, Inc.
#505, 885 Meadowlands Drive
Ottawa, ON K2C 1N6
(613) 228–8132
fax: (613) 228–9511

National Eating Disorders Information Centre (NEDIC)
Women's College Hospital
College Wing 1–304
200 Elizabeth Street
Toronto, ON M5G 2C4
(416) 340–4156
fax: (416) 340–3430

National Education Association of Disabled Students (NEADS)
4th Level Unicentre
Carleton University
1125 Colonel By Drive
Ottawa, ON K1S 5B6
(613) 526-8008
TDD: (613) 526-8008

National Tay-Sachs and Allied Diseases of Canada
c/o 512 Wicklow Road
Burlington, ON L7L 2H8
(905) 634-4101

North American Chronic Pain Society of Canada
#105, 150 Central Park Drive
Brampton, ON L6T 2T9
(905) 793–5230
fax: (905) 793–8781
Toll-Free: (800) 616–7246

Ontario March of Dimes
10 Overlea Boulevard
Toronto, ON M4H 1A4
(416) 425–3463
fax: (416) 425–1920
Toll-Free: (800) 263–3463

The Order of United Commercial Travellers of America
901 Centre Street North, Rm. 300
Calgary, AB T2E 2P6
(403) 277–0745
fax: (403) 277–6662

Parents of Asthmatic Children
c/o 170 Huntington Park Drive
Thornhill, ON M2M 3K1
(905) 881–8416

People First of Canada
#308, 489 College Street
Toronto, ON M6G 1A5
(416) 920–9530
fax: (416) 920–9503

Physically Challenged Outdoors
Association
#202, 26 Gignac Street
PO Box 1777
Penetanguishene, ON L0K 1P0

Premier's Council on the Status of
Persons with Disabilities
#250, 11044–82 Avenue
Edmonton, AB T6G 0T2
(403) 422–1095
fax: (403) 422–9691

Reena Foundation
#200, 75 Dufflaw Road
Toronto, ON M6A 2W4
(416) 787–0131
fax: (416) 787–8052

Retinol Blastoma Family
Association
14 Annette Gate
Richmond Hill, ON L4C 5P3

Reye's Syndrome Foundation of
Canada
Children's Hospital of
SouthWestern Ontario
PO Box 5375
London, ON N6A 4G5

Robin Hood Association for the
Handicapped
3 Spruce Avenue
Sherwood Park, AB T8A 2B6
(403) 467–7140
fax: (403) 449–2027

The Roeher Institute
Kinsmen Building, York University,
4700 Keele Street
North York, ON M3J 1P3
(416) 661–9611
fax: (416) 661–5701
Toll-Free: (800) 856–2207

Ronald McDonald Children's
Charities of Canada
McDonald's Restaurants of
Canada, McDonald's Place
Toronto, ON M3C 3L4
(416) 443–1000
fax: (416) 446–3588
Toll-Free: (800) 387-8808

RP Research Foundation
#704, 366 Adelaide Street West
Toronto, ON M5V 1R9
(416) 598–4951
fax: (416) 598–9763
Toll-Free: (800) 461–3331

Schizophrenia Society of Canada
#814, 75 The Donway West
North York, ON M3C 2E9
(416) 445–8204
fax: (416) 445–2270
Toll-Free: (800) 809-HOPE

Scleroderma International Center
P.O. Box 640C4
5512 4th St. NW
Calgary, AB T2K 6J1

The Seizure Disorder Foundation of
Canada
303 York Street
PO Box 335, Station B
Sudbury, ON P3E 4N2

Seva Service Society
#104, 1926 Broadway Avenue West
Vancouver, BC V6J 1Z2
(604) 733–4284
fax: (604) 733–4292

Society for Technology and
Rehabilitation
#200, 1201–5 Street SW
Calgary, AB T2R 0Y6
(403) 262–9445
fax: (403) 262–4539

Spina Bifida Association of Canada
#220, 388 Donald Street
Winnipeg, MB R3B 2J4
(204) 957–1784
fax: (204) 957–1794
Toll-Free: (800) 565–9488

Sunrise Equestrian & Recreation
Centre for the Disabled
PO Box 133
Guelph, ON N1H 6J6
(519) 837–0558

Support Group for Trisomy Canada
#420, 769 Brant Street
Burlington, ON L7R 4B8
(905) 632–7755
Toll-Free: (800) 668–0696

Thyroid Foundation of Canada
1040 Gardiners Road
Kingston, ON K7P 1R7
(613) 634–3420
fax: (613) 634–3483

Tourette Syndrome Foundation of
Canada
#203, 3675 Keele Street
North York, ON M3J 1M6
(416) 636–2800
fax: (416) 636-1688
Toll-Free: (800) 361-3120

Tuberous Sclerosis Canada Sclérose
Tubéreuse
2443 New Wood Drive
Oakville, ON L6H 5Y3
(905) 257–1997
Toll-Free: (800) 347–0252

Turner's Syndrome Society
7777 Keele Street, 2nd Floor
Concord, ON L4K 1Y7
(905) 660–7766
fax: (905) 660–7450
Toll-Free: (800) 465–6744

Vocational and Rehabilitation
Research Institute
3304–33 Street SW
Calgary, AB T2L 2A6
(403) 284–1121
fax: (403) 289–6427

Voice for Hearing Impaired
Children
#420, 124 Eglinton Avenue West
Toronto, ON M4R 2G8
(416) 487–7719
fax: (416) 487–7423

The War Amputations of Canada
2827 Riverside Drive
Ottawa, ON K1V 0C4
(613) 731–3821
fax: (613) 731–3234
Toll-Free: (800) 267-4023

A World of Dreams Foundation —
Canada
#708, 465, rue St. Jean
Montreal, PQ H2Y 2R6
(514) 843–7254
fax: (514) 843–3822
Toll-Free: (800) 567–7254

Representative Organizations
Serving Persons With Disabilities
(U.S.)

A Special Wish Foundation
c/o Ramona Fickle
2244 S. Hamilton Road, Suite 202
Columbus, OH 43232
(614) 575–9474
fax: (614) 575–1866
Toll-Free: (800) 486–9474

A Wish with Wings
PO Box 3479
Arlington, TX 76007
(817) 469–9474
fax: (817) 275–6005

**Accreditation Council on Services
for People with Disabilities**
100 West Road, Suite 406
Towson, MD 21204
(410) 583–0060
fax: (410) 583–0063

**Adventures in Movement for the
Handicapped**
945 Danbury Road
Dayton, OH 45420
(513) 294–4611
fax: (513) 294–3783
Toll-Free: (800) 332–8210

Advocacy Institute
1707 L Street NW, Suite 400
Washington, DC 20036
(202) 659–8475
fax: (202) 659–8484

**Advocates for Communication
Technology for Deaf/Blind People**
1498M Reisters Town Road,
Suite 289
Baltimore, MD 21208
Toll-Free: (800) 290-9092

**Alexander Graham Bell Association
for the Deaf**
3417 Volta Place, NW
Washington, DC 20007-2778
(202) 337–5220

The Allan Guttmacher Institute
120 Wall Street, 21st Floor
New York, NY 10005
(212) 248–1111
fax: (212) 248–1951

**Allergy and Asthma
Network/Mothers of Asthmatics**
3554 Chain Bridge Road, Suite 200
Fairfax, VA 22030–2709
(703) 385–4403
fax: (703) 352–4354
Toll-Free: (800) 878–4403

AMBUCS (Volunteer Service)
PO Box 5127
High Point, NC 27262
(910) 869–2166
fax: (910) 887–8451

**American Academy for Cerebral
Palsy and Developmental Medicine**
2315 Westwood Avenue, Box 11083
Richmond, VA 23230
(804) 282–0036

American Alliance for Health,
Physical Education, Recreation,
and Dance
Program for the Handicapped
1900 Association Drive
Reston, VA 20191
(703) 476–3400
fax: (703) 476–9527
Toll-Free: (800) 213-7193

American Amputee Foundation
Box 250218 Hillcrest Sta.
Little Rock, AR 72225
(501) 666–2523
 fax: (501) 666–8367

American Anorexia/Bulimia
Association
293 Central Park West, Suite 1R
New York, NY 10024
(212) 501–8351
fax: (212) 501–0342
Toll-Free: (800) 924–2643

American Association of the Blind
and the Retarded
164–09 Hillside Avenue
Jamaica, NY 11432
(718) 523–2222
fax: (718) 739–4750

American Association of Kidney
Patients
100 S. Ashley Drive, Suite 280
Tampa, FL 33602–5346
(813) 223-7099

American Association on Mental
Retardation
444 N. Capitol Street NW, Suite 846
Washington, DC 20001–1512
(202) 387–1968
fax: (202) 387-2193
Toll-Free: (800) 424–3688

American Cancer Society
1599 Clifton Road, NE
Atlanta, GA 30329
(404) 320–3333 or (404) 329–7648
Toll-Free: (800) ACS-2345
fax: (404) 325–0230

American Civil Liberties Union
132 W. 43rd Street
New York, NY 10036
(212) 944–9800
fax: (212) 354–5290
Toll-Free: (800) 775-ACLU

American Cleft Palate-Cranio-
Facial Association
1218 Grandview Avenue
Pittsburgh, PA 15211
(412) 481–1376
fax: (412) 481–0847
Toll-Free: (800) 24-CLEFT

American Council for the Blind
1155 15th Street NW, Suite 720
Washington, DC 20005
(202) 467–5081
fax: (202) 467–5085
Toll-Free: (800) 424–8666

American Counseling Association
5999 Stevenson Avenue
Alexandria, VA 22304–3300
(703) 823–9800
fax: (703) 823–0252
Toll-Free: (800) 347–6647

American Diabetes Association
PO Box 25757
National Center, 1660 Duke Street
Alexandria VA 22314
(703) 549–1500
fax: (703) 836–7439
Toll-Free: (800) ADA-DISC

American Digestive Disease
Education and Information
Clearinghouse
1555 Wilson Boulevard, Suite 600
Rosslyn, VA 22209

Americans with Disabilities Act
10765 SW 104 Street
Miami, FL 33176
(305) 271–0012 or (305) 271–0011
fax: (305) 273–1221

American Disability Association
2121 8th Avenue North,
Suite 1623
Birmingham, AL 35203
(205) 323–3030
fax: (205) 251–7417

American Foundation for the Blind
(AFB)
11 Penn Plaza, Suite 300
New York, NY 10001
(212) 502–7600
fax: (212) 502–7777
Toll-Free: (800) AFB-LINE

American Genetic Association
PO Box 257
Buckeystown, MD 21717–0257
(301) 695–9292
fax: (301) 695–9292

American Heart Association
7272 Greenville Avenue
Dallas, TX 75231–4596
(214) 369-3685
fax: (214) 369–3685
Toll-Free: (800) 242–8721

American Juvenile Arthritis
Organization
1330 West Peachtree Street
Atlanta, GA 30309
(404) 872–7100
fax: (404) 872–0457

American Kidney Fund
6110 Executive Boulevard, Suite 1010
Rockville, MD 20852
(301) 881–3052
fax: (301) 881–0898
Toll-Free: (800) 638–8299

American Liver Foundation
1425 Pompton Avenue
Cedar Grove, NJ 07009
(201) 256–2550
fax: (201) 256–3214
Toll-Free: (800) 223–0179

American Lung Association
1740 Broadway
New York, NY 10019
(212) 315–8700
fax: (212) 315-8872

American Mental Health
Foundation
1049 5th Avenue
New York, NY
10028–0505
(212) 737–9027

American Network of Community
Options and Resources
4200 Evergreen Ln., Suite 315
Annandale, VA 22003
(703) 642–6614
fax: (703) 642-0497

American Occupational Therapy
Association (AOTA)
4720 Montgomery Ln.
PO Box 31220
Bethesda, MD 20824–1220
(301) 652–2682
 fax: (301) 652–7711

American Pain Society
4700 W. Lake Avenue
Glenview, IL 60025
(847) 375–4715
fax: (847) 375-4777

American Paralysis Association
500 Morris Avenue
Springfield, NJ 07081
(201) 379–2690
fax: (201) 912–9433
Toll-Free: (800) 225–0292

American Pseudo-Obstruction and
Hirschsprung-Disease Society
158 Pleasant Street
No. Andover, MA 01845-2797
(508) 685-4477
fax: (508) 685-4488
Toll-Free: (800) 394-2747

American Physical Therapy
Association
111 N. Fairfax Street
Alexandria, VA 22314
(703) 684–4782

American Printing House for the
Blind
1839 Frankfort Avenue
PO Box 6085
Louisville, KY 40206
(502) 895–2405
fax: (502) 899–2274
Toll-Free: (800) 223–1839

American Rehabilitation
Association
1910 Association Drive, Suite 200
Reston, VA 20191-1502
(703) 648–9300
fax: (703) 648–0346
Toll-Free: (800) 368-3513

American Rehabilitation
Counseling Association (ARCA)
5999 Stevenson Avenue
Alexandria, VA 22304
(703) 823–9800
fax: (703) 823-0252

American Social Health Association
PO Box 13827
Research Triangle Park, NC 27709
(919) 361–8400
fax: (919) 361–8425

American Speech, Language, and
Hearing Association
10801 Rockville Pike
Rockville, MD 20852
(301) 397-8682
Toll-Free: (800) 638–8255

American Therapeutic Recreation
Association
PO Box 15215
Hattiesburg, MS 39404
(601) 264–3413
fax: (601) 264–3337
Toll-Free: (800) 553–0304

Assistance Dogs of America
8806 State Route 64
Swanton, OH 43558
(419) 825–3622

Assisted Living Facilities
Association of America
9411 Lee Highway, Suite J
Fairfax, VA 22030
(703) 691–8100
fax: (703) 691–8106

Association of Birth Defect Children
400-10300 Eaton Place
Orlando, FL 32803
(407) 245–7035
Toll-Free: (800) 313-ABCD

Association for Children with
Down Syndrome
2616 Martin Avenue
Bellmore, NY 11710
(516) 221–4700
fax: (516) 221–4700

Association for Children with
Learning Disabilities
4156 Library Road
Pittsburgh, PA 15234
(412) 341–1515 or (412) 341–8077
fax: (412) 344–0224

The Association for the Education
and Rehabilitation of the Blind and
Visually Impaired
#430, 4600 Duke Street
Alexandria, VA 22304
(703) 823-9690
fax: (703) 823-9695

The Association of Glycogen-
Storage Disease
Box 896
Durant, IA 52747
(319) 785–6038
fax: (319) 785–6038

Association on Higher Education
and Disability
PO Box 21192
Columbus, OH 43221–0192
(614) 488–4972
fax: (614) 488–1174

Association for Research of
Childhood Cancer
PO Box 251
Buffalo, NY 14225–0251
(716) 681–4433

The ARC: Association for Retarded
Citizens of the United States
500 E. Border Street, Suite 300
Arlington, TX 76010
(817) 261–6003
fax: (817) 277–3491
TDD: (817) 277–0553

Association for Voluntary Safe
Contraception
79 Madison Avenue, 7th Floor
New York, NY 10016–7802
(212) 561–8000
fax: (212) 779–9439

Asthma and Allergy Foundation of
America
1125 15th Street NW, Suite 502
Washington, DC 20005
(202) 466–7643
fax: (202) 466–8940
Toll-Free: (800) 7-ASTHMA

Autism Society of America
7910 Woodmont Avenue, Suite 650
Bethesda, MD 20814
(301) 657–0881
fax: (301) 657–0869
Toll-Free: (800) 3-AUTISM

Beach Center on Families and
Disability
University of Kansas
3111 Haworth Hall
Lawrence, KS 66045
(913) 864-7600
fax: (913) 864-7605

Blind Children's Fund
211, 2875 Northwind Drive
East Lansing, MI 48823
(517) 333–1725
fax: (517) 333–1730

Brain Injury Association
1776 Massachussetts Avenue NW,
Suite 100
Washington, DC 20036–1904
(202) 296–6443
fax: (202) 296–8850
Toll-Free: (800) 444–6443

**Candlelighters Childhood Cancer
Foundation**
7910 Woodmont Avenue, Suite 460
Bethesda, MD 20814–3015
(301) 657–8401
fax: (301) 718–2686
Toll-Free: (800) 366–2223

**Canine Companions for
Independence**
PO Box 446
Santa Rosa, CA 95402
(707) 528–0830
fax: (707) 577-1711
Toll-Free: (800) 572-2275

CDC National AIDS Clearinghouse
PO Box 6003
Rockville, MD 20849–6003
Toll-Free: (800) 458–5231
fax: (301) 738–6616

Center on Human Policy
805 S. Crouse Avenue
Syracuse, NY 13244–2280
(315) 443–3851
fax: (315) 443–4338
Toll-Free: (800) 894-0826

Child Neurology Society
3900 Northwoods Drive, Suite 175
St. Paul, MN 55112–6966
(612) 486–9447
fax: (612) 486–9436

**Childhood Life-Threatening
Illnesses**
The Candlelighters Foundation
7910 Woodmont Avenue, Suite 460
Bethesda, MD 20814–3015
(301) 657–8401
fax: (301) 718–2686
Toll-Free: (800) 366–2223

**Children and Adults with Attention
Deficit Disorder**
499 NW 70th Avenue, Suite 101
Plantation, FL 33317
(954) 587-3700
fax: (954) 587–4599
Toll-Free: (800) 233-4050

**Children in Hospitals
(Support Group)**
300 Longwood Avenue
Boston, MA 02115
(617) 355–6000
fax: (617) 355–7429

Children Inc.
PO Box 5381
1000 Westover Road
Richmond, VA 23220
(804) 359–4562
fax: (804) 353–7541
Toll-Free: (800) 538–5381

Children NOW
1212 Broadway, Suite 530
Oakland, CA 94612
(510) 763–2444
fax: (510) 763–1974
Toll-Free: (800) CHILD-44

Children's Blood Foundation
333 E. 38th Street, Suite 830
New York, NY 10016
(212) 297–4336
fax: (212) 297–4340

Children's Defense Fund
25 E. Street NW
Washington, DC 20001
(202) 628–8787
fax: (202) 662–3530

Children's Heartlink
5075 Arcadia Avenue
Minneapolis, MN 55436–2306
(612) 928–4860
fax: (612) 928–4859

**Children's Wish Foundation
International**
8615 Roswell Road
Atlanta, GA 30350
(770) 393–9474
fax: (770) 393-0683
Toll-Free: (800) 323-WISH

**Clearinghouse on Disability
Information**
United States Department of
Education
Office of Special Education and
Rehabilitative Services
Switzer Building, Room 3132
Washington, DC 20202–2524
(202) 205–8241

**Coalition on Sexuality and
Disability**
122 East 23rd Street
New York, NY 10010
(212) 242–3900
fax: (516) 737–5547

**Committee for the Promotion of
Camping for the Handicapped**
PO Box 973
Traverse City, MI 49685

Compassion International
3955 Cragwood Drive, PO Box 7000
Colorado Springs, CO 80933
(719) 594–9900
fax: (719) 594–6271
Toll-Free: (800) 336–7676

**Congress of Organizations of the
Physically Handicapped**
16630 Beverly
Tinley Park, IL 60477–1904
(708) 532–3566

Cooley's Anemia Foundation
129–09 26th Avenue
Flushing, NY 11354
(718) 321–2873
fax: (718) 321–3340
Toll-Free: (800) 522–7222

Council for Exceptional Children
1920 Association Drive
Reston, VA 20191-1589
(703) 620–3660
fax: (703) 264–9494
Toll-Free: (800) 845–6232

**Council of Families with Visual
Impairment**
26616 Rouge River Drive
Dearborn Heights, MI 48127
Toll-Free: (800) 424–8666

**Council of State Administrators of
Vocational Rehabilitation**
PO Box 3776
Washington, DC 20007
(202) 638–4634

**Crohn's and Colitis Foundation of
America**
386 Park Avenue South
New York, NY 10016–7374
(212) 685–3440
fax: (212) 779–4098
Toll-Free: (800) 932–2423

APPENDIX 2

Cystic Fibrosis Foundation
6931 Arlington Road, No. 200
Bethesda, MD 20814
(301) 951-4422
Fax: (301) 951-6378
Toll-Free: (800) 344-4823

Deaf Pride
Chapel Hall
800 Florida Avenue NE
Washington, DC 20002
(202) 675–6700
fax: (202) 547–0547

Deafness Research Foundation
15 West 39th Street
New York, NY 10018
(212) 768-1181
fax: (212) 768-1782
Toll-Free: (800) 535–3323

Disability Rights Education and Defense Fund
2212 6th Street
Berkeley, CA 94710
(510) 644–2555
fax: (510) 841–8645
TDD: (800) 466-4232
ADA Hotline: (510) 644–2626

Disabled and Alone
c/o Leslie D. Park
352 Park Avenue South, Suite 703
New York, NY 10010
(212) 532–6740
fax: (212) 532–6740
Toll-Free: (800) 995–0066

Disabled Business Persons Association
9625 Black Mountain Road, Suite 207
San Diego, CA 92126–4564
(619) 594-8805
fax: (619) 578–0637

Division of Mental Retardation and Developmental Disabilities of the Council for Exceptional Children
Arkansas University Affiliated Faculty
1120 Marshall Street, Suite 120
Little Rock, AR 72202

Dogs for the Deaf
10175 Wheeler Road
Central Point, OR 97502
Voice/TTD: (541) 826–9220
fax: (541) 826–6696

Down Syndrome Congress
1605 Chantilly Drive, Suite 250
Atlanta, GA 30324
(404) 633–1555
fax: (404) 633–2817
Toll-Free: (800) 232-NDSC

Dream Factory
315 Guthrie Green
Louisville, KY 40202
(502) 584–3928
Toll-Free: (800) 456–7556

Dysautonomia Foundation, Inc.
20 E. 46th Street, 3rd Floor
New York, NY 10017
(212) 949–6644
fax: (212) 682–7625

Dystonia Medical Research Foundation
1 E. Wacker Drive, Suite 2430
Chicago, IL 60601–2001
(312) 755–0198
fax: (312) 803–0138

Epilepsy Foundation of America
4351 Garden City Drive, Suite 500
Landover, MD 20785
(301) 459–3700
fax: (301) 577–2684
Toll-Free: (800) 332-4050

Extensions for Independence
555 Saturn Boulevard, B-368
San Diego, CA 92154
(619) 423–7709

Family Resource Center on
Disabilities
20 E. Jackson Road, Room 900
Chicago, IL 60604
(312) 939–3513
Toll-Free: (800) 922–4199

Family Service America
11700 W. Lake Park Drive
Milwaukee, WI 53224
(414) 359–1040
fax: (414) 359–1074
Toll-Free: (800) 221–3726

Federal Employment and Guidance
Service
114 5th Avenue, 11th Floor
New York, NY 10011
(212) 266–8400 or (516) 496–7550
fax: (212) 366–8490

Flying Wheels Travel
143 West Bridge
PO Box 382
Owatonna, MN 55060
Toll-Free: (800) 535-6790

Foundation for Exceptional
Children
1920 Association Drive
Reston, VA 20191
(703) 620–1054
fax: (703) 264-9494

Gazette International Networking
Institute
4207 Lindell Boulevard, No. 110
St. Louis, MO 63108–2915
(314) 534–0475
fax: (314) 534–5070

Goodwill Industries of America
9200 Wisconsin Avenue
Bethesda, MD 20814
(301) 530–6500
fax: (301) 530–1516
TDD: (301) 530–9579

Grant a Wish Foundation
PO Box 21211
Baltimore, MD 21228
(410) 242–1549
fax: (410) 242–8818
Toll-Free: (800) 933–5470

Guide Dogs of America
13445 Glenoaks Boulevard
Sylmar, CA 91342
(818) 362–5834
fax: (818) 362–6870

Guide Dogs for the Blind
PO Box 151200
San Rafael, CA 94915–1200
(415) 499–4000
fax: (415) 499–4035
Toll-Free: (800) 295-4050

Guiding Eyes for the Blind
611 Granite Springs Road
Yorktown Heights, NY 10598
(914) 245–4024
fax: (914) 245–1609
Toll-Free: (800) 942–0149

Head Injury Hotline
PO Box 84151
Seattle, WA 98124
(206) 329–1371
fax: (206) 623–4251

Health Services and Mental Health
Administration
Maternal and Child Health Services
Suite 739, Parklawn Building
5600 Fisher's Lane
Rockville, MD 20852

Hear Now
9745 E. Hampden Avenue, No. 300
Denver, CO 80231
(303) 695–7797
fax: (303) 695–7789
TDD/Toll-Free: (800) 648-HEAR

Helen Keller International
90 Washington Street, 15th Floor
New York, NY 10006
(212) 943–0890
fax: (212) 943–1220

Human Growth Foundation
7777 Leesburg Pike
Falls Church, VA 22043
(703) 883–1773
fax: (703) 883–1776
Toll-Free: (800) 451–6434

Human Resources Development
Institute
815 16th Street NW
Washington, DC 20006
(202) 638–3912
fax: (202) 783–6536

Huntington's Disease Society of
America, Inc.
140 West 22nd Street, 6th Floor
New York, NY 10011
(212) 242–1968
fax: (212) 243–2443
Toll-Free: (800) 345–4372

Independent Educational
Consultants Association
4085 Chain Bridge Road, Suite 401
Fairfax, VA 22030–4106
(703) 591–4850
fax: (703) 591–4860
Toll-Free: (800) 808-IECA

Indoor Sports Club
1145 Highland Street
Napoleon, OH 43545
(419) 592–5756

International Association of
Official Human Rights Advocates
444 N. Capitol Street, Suite 408
Washington, DC 20001
(202) 624–5410
fax: (202) 624-8185
TDD: (202) 624-4792

International Hearing Society
20361 Middlebelt Road
Livonia, MI 48152
(810) 478–2610
fax: (810) 478–4520
Toll-Free: (800) 521–5247

International Rett Syndrome
Association
9121 Piscataway Road, No. 2B
Clinton, MD 20735
(301) 856–3334
fax: (301) 856–3336
Toll-Free: (800) 818-RETT

John Tracy Clinic (for deafness,
hearing impairments, deaf-blind)
806 West Adams Boulevard
Los Angeles, CA 90007

Joubert Syndrome Parents in Touch
Network
12348 Summer Meadow Road
Rock, MI 49880
(410) 992-9184

The Juvenile Diabetes Foundation
International
120 Wall Street, 19th Floor
New York, NY 10005
(212) 889–7575
fax: (212) 785-9595
Toll-Free: (800) JDF-CURE

Kiwanis International
3636 Woodview Trace
Indianapolis, IN 46268–3196
(317) 875–8755
fax: (317) 879–0204
Toll-Free: (800) 549–2647

Learning Disabilities Association of America
4156 Library Road
Pittsburgh, PA 15234
(412) 341–1515 or (412) 341–8077
fax: (412) 344–0224

Learning How
PO Box 35481
Charlotte, NC 28235
(704) 376–4735
fax: (704) 376–4738

Leukemia Society of America
800 Second Avenue
New York, NY 10017
(212) 573–8484
fax: (212) 856–9686
Toll-Free: (800) 955–4LSA

Lions Clubs International
300 22nd Street
Oak Brook, IL 60521
(630) 571–5466
fax: (630) 571–8890

Little People of America
7238 Piedmont Drive
Dallas, TX 75227–9324
(214) 388–9576

Lowe's Syndrome Association
222 Lincoln Street
West Lafayette, IN 47906
(317) 743–3634

Magic Foundation for Children's Growth
1327 North Harlem Avenue
Oak Park, IL 60302
(708) 383–0808
fax: (708) 383–0899
Toll-Free: (800) 3MA-GIC3

Mainstream
3 Bethesda Metro Center, Suite 830
Bethesda, MD 20814
(301) 654–2400
fax: (301) 654–2403
TDD: (202) 654–2400

Make a Wish Foundation of America
100 West Clarendon Avenue,
Suite 2200
Phoenix, AZ 85013–3518
(602) 279–9474
fax: (602) 279–0855
Toll-Free: (800) 722-WISH

March of Dimes
1275 Mamaroneck Avenue
White Plains, NY 10605
(914) 428–7100
fax: (914) 428-8203
Toll-Free: (888) MODIMES

Medic Alert Foundation International
8201 Greensboro Drive, Suite 300
McLean, VA 22102
(703) 610-9011
fax: (703) 610-9005

Mental Retardation Association of America
211 East 300 South, Suite 212
Salt Lake City, UT 84111
(801) 328–1575

Mobility International USA
PO Box 10767
Eugene, OR 97440
(541) 343–1284
fax: (541) 343–6812

Mothers United for Moral Support
150 Custer Court
Green Bay, WI 54301
(414) 336–5333
fax: (414) 339–0995

Muscular Dystrophy Association of America
3300 E. Sunrise Drive
Tucson, AZ 85718
(520) 529–2000
fax: (520) 529–5300

Music Services Unit
National Library Service for the
Blind and Physically Handicapped
1291 Taylor Street NW
Washington, DC 20542
(202) 707-5100
fax: (202) 707-0712
Toll-Free: (800) 424-8567

National Adrenal Diseases Foundation
505 Northern Boulevard, Suite 200
Great Neck, NY 11021
(516) 487–4992

National AIDS Hotline
215 Park Avenue South, Suite 714
New York, NY 10003
(800) 342-AIDS

National Amputation Foundation
38–40 Church Street
Malverne, NY 11565
(516) 887–3600
fax: (516) 887–3667

National Association for Adults with Special Learning Needs
PO Box 716
Bryn Mawr, PA 19010
(610) 446-6126
fax: (610) 446-6129
Toll Free: (800) 869-8336

National Association of Anorexia Nervosa and Associated Disorders
Box 7
Highland Park, IL 60035
(847) 831–3438
fax: (847) 433–4632

National Association of the Deaf
814 Thayer Avenue
Silver Spring, MD 20910
(301) 587–1788
fax: (301) 587–1791

National Association of Developmental Disabilities Councils
1234 Massachusetts Avenue NW, Suite 103
Washington, DC 20005
(202) 347–1234
fax: (202) 347–4023

National Association of Disability Evaluating Professionals (Resource Center)
PO Box 35407
Richmond, VA 23235–0407
(804) 378–8809

National Association for Down Syndrome
PO Box 4542
Oak Brook, IL 60522–4542
(630) 325–9112

National Association for Hearing
and Speech Action
10801 Rockville Pike
Rockville, MD 20852
(301) 897–5700
fax: (301) 571–0457
Hearing and Speech HELPLINE:
(800) 628–8255

The National Association for
Home Care
228 7th Street SE
Washington, DC 20003
(202) 547–7424
fax: (202) 547–3540

National Association of Insurance
Commissioners
120 West 12th Street, Suite 1100
Kansas City, MO 64105
(816) 842–3600
fax: (816) 471–7004

National Association for Parents of
the Visually Impaired
PO Box 317
Watertown, MA 02272
(617) 972–7441
fax: (617) 972–7444
Toll-Free: (800) 562–6265

National Association of the
Physically Handicapped Inc.
Bethesda Scarlet Oaks, No. 6A4
440 Lafayette Avenue
Cincinnati, OH 45220–1000
(513) 961–8040 or (517) 799–3060

National Association of Private
Schools for Exceptional Children
1522 K Street NW, Suite 1032
Washington, DC 20005
(202) 408–3338
fax: (202) 408–3340

National Association of Protection
and Advocacy Systems
900 2nd Street NE, Suite 211
Washington, DC 20002
(202) 408–9514
fax: (202) 408–9520

National Ataxia Foundation
15500 Wayzata Boulevard,
Suite 750
Wayzata, MN 55391
(612) 473–7666
fax: (612) 473–9289
Toll-Free: (800) 854-7240

National Benevolent Association of
the Christian Church
11780 Borman Drive, Suite 200
St. Louis, MO 63146–4157
(314) 993–9000
fax: (314) 993–9018

National Center for Disability
Studies
201 I.U. Willets Road
Albertson, NY 11507-1599
(516) 747–5400
fax: (516) 747–5378

National Center for Learning
Disabilities
381 Park Avenue South, Suite 1420
New York, NY 10016
(212) 545–7510
fax: (212) 545–9665

National Center for Youth with
Disabilities
University of Minnesota, Box 721
420 Delaware Street SE
Minneapolis, MN 55455-0392
(612) 626–2825
fax: (612) 626–2134

APPENDIX 2

National Charities Information Bureau
19 Union Square West
New York, NY 10003
(212) 929-6300

National Clearinghouse for Human Genetic Diseases
805 15th Street, Suite 500
Washington, DC 20005
(202) 842–7617

National Consortium for Child Mental Health Services
601 13th Street NW, Suite 400
North Washington, DC 20005
(202) 347–8600
fax: (202) 393–6137
Toll-Free: (800) 336-5475

National Council of Guilds for Infant Survival
8178 Nadine River Circle, Suite 440
Fountain Valley, CA 92708
Toll-Free: (800) 336–4363

National Council on Independent Living
2111 Wilson Boulevard, Suite 405
Arlington, VA 22201
(703) 525–3406
fax: (703) 525-3409
TDD: (703) 525-3407

National Down Syndrome Congress
1605 Chantilly Drive, Suite 250
Atlanta, GA 30324
(404) 633–1555
fax: (404) 633–2817
Toll-Free: (800) 232-NDSC

National Down Syndrome Society
666 Broadway
New York, NY 10012
(212) 460–9330
fax: (212) 979–2873
Toll-Free: (800) 221–4602

National Easter Seal Society
230 W. Monroe
Chicago, IL 60606
(312) 726–6200
fax: (312) 726–1494
Toll-Free: (800) 221–6827

National Federation of the Blind
1800 Johnson Street
Baltimore, MD 21230
(410) 659–9314
fax: (410) 685–5653

National Foundation of Dentistry for the Handicapped
1800 Glenarm Place, Suite 500
Denver, CO 80202
(303) 298–9650
fax: (303) 298-9649
Toll-Free: (800) 298-6334

National Foundation for Facial Reconstruction
317 East 34th Street, Suite 901
New York, NY 10016
(212) 263–6656
fax: (212) 263–7534

National Handicapped Sports
451 Hungerford, Suite 100
Rockville, MD 20850
(301) 217–0960
fax: (301) 217–0968

National Hearing Dog Project
American Humane Association
63 Inverness Drive East
Englewood, CO 80112-5117
(303) 792–9900
fax: (303) 792–5333
Toll-Free: (800) 227-4645

National Hemophilia Foundation
110 Greene Street, Suite 303
New York, NY 10012
(212) 219–8180
fax: (212) 431–0906
Toll-Free: (888) INFO NHF

National Information Center for Children and Youth with Disabilities
University of South Carolina
Center for Developmental Disabilities
Benson Building, 1st Floor
Columbia, SC 29208
(803) 777–4435
fax: (803) 777–6058
Toll-Free: (800) 922–9234

National Institute for Rehabilitation Engineering
PO Box T
Hewitt, NJ 07421
(201) 853–6585
fax: (800) 736–2216

NISH (Employment Service)
2235 Cedar Lane
Vienna, VA 22182–5200
(703) 560–6800
fax: (703) 849–8916

National Kidney Foundation, Inc.
30 East 33rd Street, Suite 1100
New York, NY 10016
(212) 889–2210
fax: (212) 689–9261
Toll-Free: (800) 622–9010

National Marfan Foundation
382 Main Street
Port Washington, NY 11050
(516) 883–8712
fax: (516) 883–8040
Toll-Free: (800) 862–7326

National Maternal and Child Health Clearinghouse
2070 Chain Bridge Road, Suite 450
Vienna, VA 22182–2536
(703) 821–8955
fax: (703) 821–2098

The National Mental Health Association
1021 Prince Street
Alexandria, VA 22314–2971
(703) 684–7722
fax: (702) 684–5968
Toll-Free: (800) 969-NMHA

The National Multiple Sclerosis Society
733 3rd Avenue
New York, NY 10017
(212) 986–3240
fax: (212) 986–7981
Toll-Free: (800) FIGHT-MS

National Neurofibramatosis Foundation
95 Pine Street, 16th Floor
New York, NY 10005
(212) 344-6633
fax: (212) 747-0004
Toll-Free: (800) 323–7938

National Organization on Disability
910 16th Street NW, Suite 600
Washington, DC 20006
(202) 293–5960
fax: (202) 293–7999

National Organization for Rare Disorders
PO Box 8923
New Fairfield, CT 06812–8923
(203) 746–6518
fax: (203) 746–6481

National Perinatal Information Center
1 State Street, Suite 102
Providence, RI 02908

National Rehabilitation Association
633 South Washington Street
Alexandria, VA 22314
(703) 836–0850
fax: (703) 836–0848

National Rehabilitation Counseling Association
8807 Sudley Road, Suite 102
Manassas, VA 20110-4719
(703) 361–2077
fax: (703) 361–2489

National Scoliosis Foundation
5 Cabot Place
Stoughton, MA 02072
(617) 341-6333
fax: (617) 341-8333
Toll-Free: (800) 673-6922

National Self-Help Clearinghouse
25 West 43rd Street, Room 620
New York, NY 10036–7406
(212) 354–8525
fax: (212) 642–1956

National Sickle Cell Disease Program
National Heart, Lung and Blood Institute
Room 504, Federal Building
7550 Wisconsin Avenue
Bethedsa, MD 20892
(301) 496–4236

National SIDS Resource Center
8201 Greensboro Drive, Suite 600
McLean, VA 22102
(703) 821–8955
fax: (703) 821–2098

National Spinal Cord Injury Foundation
545 Concord Avenue No. 29
Cambridge, MA 02138–1122
(617) 441–8500
fax: (617) 441–3449
Toll-Free: (800) 962–9629

National Support Group for Arthrogryposis (Multiplex Congenita)
PO Box 5192
Sonora, CA 95370
(209) 928–3688

National Tay-Sachs and Allied Disease Association
2001 Beacon Street
Brookline, MA 02146
(617) 277–4463
fax: (617) 277–0134
Toll-Free: (800) 906–8723

North American Riding for the Handicapped Association
PO Box 33150
Denver, CO 80233
(303) 452–1212
fax: (303) 252–4610
Toll-Free: (800) 369–7433

Organ Transplant Fund
1102 Brookfield, Suite 202
Memphis, TN 38119
Toll-Free: (800) 489–3863
fax: (901) 684-1697

Orton Dyslexia Society
Chester Building, Suite 382
8600 LaSalle Road
Baltimore, MD 21286–2044
(410) 296–0232
fax: (410) 321–5069
Toll-Free: (800) ABCD-123

Paralyzed Veterans of America
801 18th Street NW
Washington, DC 20006
(202) USA-1300
fax: (202) 785–4452
Toll-Free: (800) 424-8200

Parents Helping Parents
3041 Olcott Street
Santa Clara, CA 95054–3222
(408) 727–5775
fax: (408) 727–0181

Parents' Educational Resource
Center
1660 South Amphlett Boulevard,
Suite 200
San Mateo, CA 94402–2508
(415) 655–2410
fax: (415) 655–2411

The Parkinson's Disease
Foundation
Neurological Institute
710 West 168th Street
New York, NY 10032
(212) 923–4700
fax: (212) 923–4778
Toll-Free: (800) 457–6676

Parents Without Partners Inc.
401 North Michigan Avenue
Chicago, IL 60611–4267
(312) 644–6610
fax: (312) 321-5144
Toll-Free: (800) 637-7974

Partners of the Americas
Rehabilitation Education Program
1424 K Street NW, Suite 700
Washington, DC 20005
(202) 628–3300
fax: (202) 628–3306

Paws with a Cause
1235 100th Street SE
Byron Center, MI 49315
(616) 698–0688
fax: (616) 698–2788
Toll-Free: (800) 253-PAWS
TDD: (616) 698–0688

People-to-People Committee on
Disability
PO Box 18131
Washington, DC 20036
(301) 774–7446

Planned Parenthood Federation of
America
810 Seventh Avenue
New York, NY 10019
(212) 541–7800
fax: (212) 245–1845
Toll-Free: (800) 230-PLAN

Population Council, Inc.
One Dag Hammarskjöld Plaza
New York, NY 10017
(212) 339–0500
fax: (212) 755–6052

Prader-Willi Syndrome Association
2510 South Brentwood Boulevard,
Suite 220
St. Louis, MO 63144
(314) 962–7644
fax: (314) 962-7869
Toll-Free: (800) 926–4797

PRIDE Foundation: Promote Real
Independence for the Disabled and
Elderly
Box 1293
391 Long Hill Road
Groton, CT 06340
(860) 445–8320
fax: (860) 445–1448

Project HEATH
1 Dupont Circle NW, Suite 800
Washington, DC 20036–1193
(202) 939–9320
fax: (202) 833–4760
Toll-Free: (800) 544–3284

Rehabilitation Engineering and
Assistive Technology Society of
North America
1700 North Moore Street, Suite 1540
Arlington, VA 22209–1903
(703) 524–6686
fax: (703) 524–6630

Rehabilitation International
The International Society for
Rehabilitation of the Disabled
25 East 21st Street
New York, NY 10010
(212) 420–1500
fax: (212) 505–0871

Scleroderma International
Foundation
704 Gardiner Center Road
New Castle, PA
(412) 652–3109

Scoliosis Association
PO Box 811705
Boca Raton, FL 33481–1705
(407) 994–4435
fax: (407) 368–8518

Scoliosis Research Society
6300 North River Road, Suite 727
Rosemont, IL 60018–4226
(847) 698–1627
fax: (847) 823–0536

Self Help for Hard of Hearing
People
7910 Woodmont Avenue,
Suite 1200
Bethesda, MD 20814
(301) 657–2248
fax: (301) 913–9413

Sex Information and Educational
Council for the United States
130 West 42nd Street, Suite 350
New York, NY 10036
(212) 819–9770
fax: (212) 819–9776

Shriners Hospital for Crippled
Children
2900 Rocky Point Drive
Tampa, FL 33607
(813) 281–0300
fax: (813) 281–8146
Toll-Free: (800) 237–5055

Sibling Information Network
c/o University of Connecticut
Box U-64, 249 Glenbrook Road
Storrs, CT 06269–2064
(860) 486–4985 or (860) 486–5035
fax: (860) 486–5037

Sickle Cell Disease Association of
America
200 Corporate Pointe, Suite 495
Culver City, CA 90230–7633
(310) 216–6363
fax: (310) 215–3722
Toll-Free: (800) 421–8453

SIDS Alliance
1314 Bedford Avenue, Suite 210
Baltimore, MD 21208
(410) 653–8226
fax: (410) 653–8709
Toll-Free: (800) 221-SIDS

Sister Kenny Institute
800 East 28th Street at Chicago
Avenue
Minneapolis, MN 55407
(612) 863–4457

**Society for the Advancement of
Travel for the Handicapped**
347 5th Avenue, Suite 610
New York, NY 10016
(212) 447–7284
fax: (212) 725–8253

Special Olympics International
1325 G Street NW, Suite 500
Washington, DC 20005
(202) 628–3630
fax: (202) 824-0200

Special Recreation, Inc.
362 Koser Avenue
Iowa City, IA 52246
(319) 337–7578

Spina Bifida Association of America
4590 MacArthur Boulevard NW,
Suite 250
Washington, DC 20007–4226
(202) 944–3285
fax: (202) 944-3295
Toll-Free: (800) 621–3141

Spinal Cord Society
Wendell Road
Fergus Falls, MN 56537
(218) 739–5252
fax: (218) 739–5262

Starlight Foundation
12424 Wilshire Boulevard,
Suite 1050
Los Angeles, CA 90025–1044
(310) 207–5558
fax: (310) 207–2554
Toll-Free: (800) 274–7827

STD National Hotline
(800) 227–8922

Sunshine Foundation
1001 Bridge Street
Philadelphia, PA 20001
(215) 535–1413
fax: (215) 535–8397
Toll-Free: (800) 767–1976

**Symbral Foundation (Financial
Assistance)**
7826 Eastern Avenue NW,
Suite 18A, LL18
Washington, DC 20012
(202) 726–1444
fax: (202) 726–1448

TASH (Support Group)
29 West Susquehanna Avenue,
Suite 210
Baltimore, MD 21204–5201
(410) 828-8274
fax: (410) 828-6706
TDD: (410) 828-1306

Telecommunications for the Deaf
8719 Colesville Road, Suite 300
Silver Spring, MD 20910
(301) 589–3786
TDD: (301) 589-3006
fax: (301) 589–3797

Thyroid Foundation of America
Ruth Sleeper Hall, RSL 350
40 Parkman Street
Boston, MA 02114–2698
(617) 726–8500
fax: (617) 726–4136
Toll-Free: (800) 832–8321

Tourette Syndrome Association
42–40 Bell Boulevard
Bayside, NY 11361
(718) 224–2999
fax: (718) 279–9596
Toll-Free: (800) 237–0717

Tuberous Sclerosis Association of
America
8181 Professional Place, Suite 110
Landover, MD 20785
(301) 459–9888
fax: (301) 459–0394
Toll-Free: (800) 225–6872

Transplant Recipients International
Organization
1735 I Street NW, Suite 917
Washington, DC 20006
(202) 293–0980
fax: (202) 293–0973
Toll-Free: (800) TRID-386

Turner Syndrome Society of the
United States
1313 SE 5th Street, Suite 327
Minneapolis, MN 55414
(612) 379-3607
fax: (612) 379-3619
Toll-Free: (800) 365–9944

United Cerebral Palsy Association/
Research and Educational
Foundation
1660 L Street NW, Suite 700
Washington, DC 20036
(202) 776-0406
fax: (202) 776–0414
Toll-Free: (800) USA-5UCP

United Ostomy Association
36 Executive Park, Suite 120
Irvine, CA 92614
(714) 660–8624
fax: (714) 660–9262
Toll-Free: (800) 826–0826

United States Association for Blind
Athletes
33 N. Institute Street
Colorado Springs, CO 80903
(719) 630–0422
fax: (719) 630–0616

United States Cerebral Palsy
Athletic Association
200 Harrison Avenue
Newport, RI 02840
(401) 848-2460
fax: (401) 848-5280

United States Organization for
Disabled Athletes
143 California Avenue
Uniondale, NY 11553-1131
(516) 485-3701
fax: (516) 485-3707
Toll-Free: (800) 25 US ODA

Very Special Arts
1300 Connecticut Avenue NW,
Suite 700
Washington, DC 20036
(202) 628–2800
fax: (202) 737–0725
Toll-Free: (800) 933-USA1
TDD: (202) 737-0645

Voice of the Retarded
5005 Newport Drive, Suite 108
Rolling Meadows, IL 60008
(847) 253–6020
fax: (847) 253–6054

Volunteers of America
110 South Union Street, 2nd Floor
Alexandria, VA 22314
(703) 548-2288
fax: (703) 684-1972

Wheelchair Sports, USA
3595 East Fountain Boulevard,
Suite L-1
Colorado Springs, CO 80910
(719) 574–1150
fax: (719) 574–9840

World Institute on Disability
510 16th Street, Suite 100
Oakland, CA 94612
(510) 763–4100
fax: (510) 763–4109

World Rehabilitation Fund
386 Park Avenue South, Suite 500
New York, NY 10016
(212) 725–7875
fax: (212) 725–8402

Young Adult Institute and Workshop
460 West 34th Street
New York, NY 10001
(212) 563-7474
fax: (212) 268–1083

Bibliography

Adams, Francis V., M.D. *The Asthma Sourcebook*. Los Angeles: RGA Publishing Group, 1995.

Albrecht, Donna G. *Raising a Child Who Has a Physical Disability*. New York: John Wiley & Sons Inc., 1995.

Allentuck, Andrew. *The Crisis in Canadian Health Care: Who Speaks for the Patient?* Don Mills, ON: Burns & MachEachern, 1978.

Backstrom, Gayle. *The Resource Guide for the Disabled*. Dallas: Taylor Publishing Co., 1994.

Baron Cohen, Dr. Simon, and Dr. Patrick Bolton. *Autism: The Facts — A Guide for Parents*. Oxford: Oxford University Press, 1993.

Bateson-Koch, Carole, M.D. *Allergies: Disease in Disguise*. Burnaby, BC: Alive Books, 1994.

Batshaw, Mark L., M.D. *Your Child Has a Disability: A Complete Sourcebook of Daily and Medical Care*. Boston: Little, Brown and Company, 1991.

Betschert, Jean, MN, RN, CDE. *It's Time to Learn About Diabetes — A Workbook on Diabetes for Children*. Minneapolis: Chronimed Publishers, 1995.

Bombeck, Erma. *I Want to Grow Hair, I Want to Grow Up, I Want to Go to Boise (Children Surviving Cancer)*. New York: HarperPaperbacks, 1989.

Bruch, Hilde, M.D. *The Golden Cage: The Enigma of Anorexia Nervosa*. New York: Vintage Books (Random House), 1979.

Byrne, Katherine. *A Parent's Guide to Anorexia and Bulimia*. Markham, ON: Fitzhenry and Whiteside, Ltd., 1987.

Cantor, Robert Chernin. *And a Time to Live: Toward Emotional Well-Being During the Crisis of Cancer*. New York: Harper Colophon Books, 1978.

Capossela, Cappy, and Sheila Warrock. *Share the Care: How to Organize a Group for Someone Who Is Seriously Ill*. New York: Simon and Schuster, 1995.

Carlisle, Jock A. *Tangled Tongue: Living with a Stutter.* Toronto: University of Toronto Press, 1985.

Crohn's and Colitis Foundation of America. *The Crohn's Disease and Ulcerative Colitis Fact Book.* New York: MacMillan General.

Davis, Ronald D. *The Gift of Dyslexia: Why Some of the Smartest People Can't Read and How They Can Learn.* Burlingame, CA: Ability Workshop Press, 1994.

Dickman, Irving, with Dr. Sol Gordon. *One Miracle at a Time: Getting Help for a Child with a Disability.* New York: Simon & Schuster, 1993.

Douglas, Paul Harding, and Laura Pinsky. *The Essential AIDS Fact Book.* New York: Pocket Books, 1996.

Follman, John M., M.D., Eileen Virion, P.G., M.D., and Diana J. Pillas. *Seizures and Epilepsy in Childhood - A Guide For Parents.* Baltimore, MD: Johns Hopkins Press, 1990.

Fraiberg, Selma. *Insights from the Blind: Comparative Studies of Blind and Sighted Infants.* New York: New American Library, Meridian, 1977.

Frith, Uta, ed. *Autism and Asperger Syndrome.* Cambridge: Cambridge University Press, 1991.

Fuller, Dawn Winkelman. *The Heart of Joshua: A Story of Hope for All Parents of Children with Chronic Illnesses.* Toronto: University of Toronto Press, 1987.

Gino, Carol. *Rusty's Story: The Dramatic True Story of One Woman's Triumphant Fight Against Illness.* Toronto: Bantam Books, 1986.

Goble, John L. *Visual Disorders in the Handicapped Child.* New York: Marcel Dekker, Inc., 1984.

Goldfarb, Lori A., et al. *Meeting the Challenge of Disability or Chronic Illness: A Family Guide.* Baltimore: Paul H. Brookes Publishing Co., 1986.

Hanson, Peter G., M.D. *The Joy of Stress: How to Make Stress Work for You.* Islington, ON: Hanson Stress Management Organization, 1985.

Hart, Charles A. *A Parent's Guide to Autism: Answers to the Most Common Questions.* New York: Pocket Books, 1993.

Hillson, Dr. Dowan. *Diabetes: The Complete Guide.* London: Vermillion, 1992.

Horne, Jo. *When Caring Becomes Caring For: A Survival Guide for Family Caregivers: Strength, Support, and Sources of Help for All Those Caring for Aging or Impaired Family Members.* Minneapolis: CompCare Publishers, 1991.

Jarvis, Terry, and Tannis Jarvis. *You Are Not Alone: A Parent to Parent Handbook Dealing with the Realities of Life with a Child Recently Diagnosed as Having a Handicap.* London, ON: Terry P. Jarvis, 1985.

Kelley, Jerry D., Ph.D., and Lex Frieden, eds. *Go For It! A Book on Sport and Recreation for Persons with Disabilities.* Orlando: Harcourt Brace Jovanovich Publisher, 1989.

Kent, Ann. *Family Health Guide: Asthma and Allergies.* London: Wardlock, 1995.

Kreinberg, Nancy, and Stanley H. L. Chow, eds. *Configurations of Change: The Integration of Mildly Handicapped Children into the Regular Classroom.* San Francisco, CA: Far West Laboratory for Educational Research and Development, 1973.

Lam, Susan S., and Richard B. Patt, M.D. *You Don't Have to Suffer: A Complete Guide to Relieving Inner Pain For Patients and Their Families.* New York: Oxford University Press, 1994.

Levert, Suzanne. *When Someone You Love Has Cancer.* New York: Dell Publishing, 1995.

Lewis, Jenny, with the British Migraine Association. *The Migraine Handbook.* London: Vermillion, 1993.

Lilleman, John S. *Childhood Leukaemia: The Facts.* New York: Oxford University Press, 1994.

Marinelli, Robert P., and Arthur E. Dell Orto, eds. *The Psychological and Social Impact of Disability.* 3rd ed. New York: Springer Publishing Company, 1991.

Moss, Robert A., M.D., with Helen Huff Dunlap. *A Groundbreaking Guide for Parents and Teachers: Why Johnny Can't Concentrate — Coping with Attention Deficit Problems.* New York: Bantam Books, 1990.

Mulliken, Ruth K., and John J. Buckley. *Assessment of Multihandicapped and Developmentally Disabled Children.* Rockville, MD: Aspen Publication, 1983.

Neuwirth, Michael, M.D., and Kevin Osborn. *The Scoliosis Handbook.* New York: Holt and Company, 1996.

Poneroy, Dana Rue. *When Someone You Love Has Cancer.* New York: Berkeley Books, 1996.

Reisner, Helen, ed. *Children with Epilepsy: A Parent's Guide.* Bethesda, MD: Woodbine House, 1988.

Schaefer, Nicola. *Does She Know She's There?* Toronto: Fitzhenry & Whiteside, 1978.

Severo, Richard. *Lisa H.: The True Story of an Extraordinary and Courageous Woman.* New York: Harper & Row Publishers, 1985.

Stritch, Elaine. *Living with Diabetes, and, Dammit, Having Fun! Am I Blue?* New York: M. Evans and Company, Inc., 1984.

Welsh, Dr. Linda, and Marian Betancourt. *Chronic Illness and the Family: A Guide for Every Day Living.* Holbrook, MA: Adams Media Corporation, 1996.

Williams, Donna. *Somebody, Somewhere: Breaking Free from the World of Autism.* Toronto: Doubleday Canada, 1994.

Williams, Dr. Deryk, Anna Williams, and Lauran Croker. *Asthma: The*

Complete Guide for Sufferers and Carers. London: Piatkus Publishers, 1996.

Windell, Ellen, Ph.D. *Coping With Limb Loss.* Garden City Park, NY: Area Publishing Group, 1995.

Zellerbach, Merla. *The Allergy Sourcebook.* Los Angeles: Lovell Books, 1996.

Zimmerman, Barry, M.D., et al. *The Canadian Allergy and Asthma Handbook.* Mississauga, ON: Random House, 1996.

Index

cancer, children with, 27, 101, 117
cardiopulmonary resuscitation
(CPR), 108
caregivers. *See also* health care
professionals
problems encountered by, 184–85
relationship between parents
and, 119, 182–83
selection of, 179–84, 185–87, 202
temporary, 200–201
case manager, 49–51, 155
relationship between parents
and, 118–19
causes of disability, 29–30
alcohol, drugs, and smoking, 32
congenital factors, 30–31
environmental factors, 31–32
maternal injury or illness, 31
trauma during birth, 33
cerebral palsy, children with, 4–5,
27, 28, 52, 127, 138, 144–45,
153, 194, 209, 213–14
charities, 222
Charter of Rights and
Freedoms, 55, 170, 216
Children's Aid Society (CAS), 88
children with disabilities. *See also*
names of specific disabilities
dependence on parents by, 35
exclusion from activities, 34, 85,
103, 137
and fear of failure, 37, 105–6
insensitive reactions of people to,
36, 84–85, 104
as self-advocates, 47–48
chiropractic, 180
civil rights movement, 169
cleft palates, children with, 26, 33
clinics
legal, 51–52, 56, 138, 160
specialized, 193–96, 232
computers, 220
control, importance of parents
taking, 7, 10, 29
coping, negatively. *See* negative coping
cost of care liability, 223

counseling, 77, 78–79, 123–25
crises, preparing for and handling,
109–10, 128, 176, 192
cystic fibrosis, children with, 94, 208

death, premature, 7–8
coping with, 78–79, 117
decision-making, stress of, 120
deinstitutionalization, trend toward,
204
denial, of negative diagnosis, 76
depression
of child, 85
of parent, 80
diabetes, children with, 109
diagnosis, 9
accurate, importance of, 28–29
parental reaction to initial,
15–18, 22–23, 28, 74–78,
80–82, 115, 116
diets, specialized, 95–96
disability
adapting to. *See* adapting to
disability, stages of
causes of. *See* causes of
disability
definition of, 23
invisible, 24
organizations, 171–72
Phase I, 26
Phase II, 26–27
Phase III, 27–28, 37
spectrum of, 25–26
visible, 24
discipline, 98–100
discrimination, 55, 134, 170, 216
Down syndrome, children with, 10,
125, 209
drug chart, 191
drug therapy, 86–87, 181–82, 190

education, 134–35. *See also*
educational options; Individualized Education Plan
classroom environment
necessary for, 161–63

benefits of, 212
drawbacks to, 213
individual care attendant, 198–200
Individualized Education Plan (IEP),
  136, 138–39, 154–55
  importance of, 153
  problems with, 158–61
  strategies for an effective, 155–58
infant, bonding with, 74–75
institution(s), 28
  alternatives to, 41–42, 205–8
  benefits of, 209, 210
  drawbacks to, 8, 40, 140, 150,
    195–96, 210–11
  education in, 149–50
  history of, 203
  maintaining relationship with
    child in, 40
insurance, 228–29
integration, 35, 59, 170
  in daycare, 140
  in extracurricular children's
    groups, 201–2
  full, 137–38, 141–43, 153
  partial, 143
  "supported," 143–44
intervenors, 146–47
isolation
  of children with disabilities, 81,
    141, 148
  of parents, 82, 120–21

jealousy
  of parents, 20–21
  of siblings, 83
Joy of Stress, The, 113

Keller, Helen, 37–38, 197
labels, incorrect, 38
laetrile clinics, 186–87
landlords, and discrimination against
  people with disabilities, 216
laws regarding disability, 55,
  135–36, 215–16
lawyers, 51–52, 56
legal challenge, mounting a, 58–60

legal clinics, 51–52, 56, 138, 160
letters, writing, 67, 235–36
love, importance of unconditional,
  7, 105

Mahoney, Dr. William, 140
Make a Child Smile Foundation, 131
malignant hyperthermia, children
  with, 109–10
Mask, 25–26
Mayo Clinic, 2, 3, 5, 194, 195
medical care, finding appropriate,
  189–90
medical history, 68, 189–90
medical and paramedical personnel.
  See health care professionals
MedicAlert bracelet, 109–10
mobility impairments, children with,
  45–46, 96, 106, 164, 176–77
multiple disabilities, children with,
  146, 147–48, 175, 208, 209
muscular dystrophy, children with,
  51
My Left Foot, 27–28
Nagler, Ann, 1–4, 5–6, 10–11, 17, 38,
  95, 105, 167, 178, 194–95
Nagler, Leo, 1–4, 5–6, 10–11, 17,
  38, 95, 105, 167, 178,
  194–95
Nagler, Mark, 1–7, 8, 11, 38, 59,
  95, 105, 106, 108, 162–63,
  164, 194–95
naturopathy, 180
negative coping, 79
  for child with disabilities, 83–87
  for parents, 80–82
  for siblings, 83

outcomes, dealing with unknown
  long-term, 117
overanxiety, of parents, 80
overmedication, 87
overprotection, 36, 81, 105–7, 109

pain
  easing physical, 102–3, 117–18